Employee Engagement FOR DUMMIES
A Wiley Brand

by Bob Kelleher

Foreword by Wayne F. Cascio, PhD

Employee Engagement For Dummies®

Published by:
John Wiley & Sons, Inc.,
111 River Street,
Hoboken, NJ 07030-5774,
www.wiley.com

For general information on our other products and services, please contact our Customer Care Department within the U.S. at 877-762-2974, outside the U.S. at 317-572-3993, or fax 317-572-4002. For technical support, please visit www.wiley.com/techsupport.

Wiley publishes in a variety of print and electronic formats and by print-on-demand. Some material included with standard print versions of this book may not be included in e-books or in print-on-demand. If this book refers to media such as a CD or DVD that is not included in the version you purchased, you may download this material at http://booksupport.wiley.com. For more information about Wiley products, visit www.wiley.com.

Library of Congress Control Number: 2013952423

ISBN 978-1-118-72579-5 (pbk); ISBN 978-1-118-75606-5 (ebk); ISBN 978-1-118-75618-8 (ebk); ISBN 978-1-118-75626-3 (ebk)

Manufactured in the United States of America

10 9 8 7 6 5 4 3 2 1

Contents at a Glance

Table of Contents

Chapter 9: Go, Team! Driving Engagement through Team Development 139

Chapter 10: Brandy, You're a Fine Girl: Driving Engagement through Branding. 163

Chapter 11: Game On! Driving Engagement with Gamification 177

Foreword

*W*ouldn't you love to have a job where you woke up every morning with such a "fire in your belly" that you couldn't wait to get to work? Wouldn't you love it if you could be absolutely passionate about the work in which you're engaged, feeling a sense of deep purpose, meaning, and challenge in what you're doing? Finally, wouldn't it be great if you were so deeply engrossed in your work that you completely lost track of time? These three characteristics — vigor, dedication, and absorption — define a highly engaged employee. No wonder managers are striving to create conditions in which employees can experience high engagement. Those same managers see employee engagement as a sustainable source of competitive advantage that their competitors simply cannot copy. More specifically, they see high employee engagement as something that is valuable, rare, and difficult to imitate.

There is a well-defined logic that links employee engagement to bottom-line results, but several important preconditions, or characteristics of an organization's culture, need to be in place before employees can become highly engaged. These include features such as job challenge and a sense that employees are learning continuously; job autonomy, or the opportunity to work without close supervision; a supportive supervisor; an organizational climate of respect and trust; a work arrangement that matches each employee's desire for work–life fit; and economic security, the belief that your job is not at risk because your employer practices smart management to avoid downsizing. If those conditions are present, employees tend to be highly engaged and committed to their employers, and they intend to stay.

Employee engagement – at the individual, work team, and organizational levels is a topic of great practical importance to employees and to their managers, and there is a strong business case to encourage organizations of every stripe to take steps now to enhance employee engagement. Bob Kelleher's *Employee Engagement For Dummies* provides solid guidance about how to do just that, whether by promoting a sense of purpose and meaning in the work that an organization does, through leadership and coaching strategies, by harnessing generational values, by developing work teams that really work, by branding, or by gamification. The evidence to date suggests that high employee engagement levels are a win-win for all concerned, and that we all should strive to promote high levels of engagement. Yes, work can be fun!

Wayne F. Cascio, PhD
Denver, Colorado

Introduction

In recent years, the business world has reached a consensus: Employee engagement is good for the bottom line. It's a simple equation, really: If you can't satisfy the demands of your clients or customers, you're going to lose business. And the way to reach extraordinary levels of client and customer service is through engaged employees.

Employees' dedication speaks volumes to clients and customers. Not to be clichéd, but a company's employees truly are its greatest asset! Most leaders understand this connection on an intellectual level, but they often struggle with what to *do* to foster this type of dedication. Enter employee engagement . . . and this book!

Coming across such a universally agreed-upon "win-win" is rare, but employee engagement truly benefits everyone — including management. Why? Because it boosts discretionary effort, or employees who go above and beyond, which in turn drives superior business results. I would even go so far as to say that employee engagement is the foundation of a healthy organization.

And yet, many organizations haven't added employee engagement to their list of key objectives. According to a 2013 study by the human capital technology firm SilkRoad, less than 40 percent of companies focus on employee engagement at all. And those that do often view it as a "program." But the fact is, engaging employees requires a cultural shift — a change in how things are done and communicated from the top to the bottom of your organization.

Engaging your employees won't be easy, and it will take time. But when it occurs, the results will astonish you! How do I know? Because I've worked for and with large global companies to boost employee engagement and have experienced firsthand what happens when you capture your employees' discretionary effort. It's magic!

About This Book

Above all, *Employee Engagement For Dummies* is a reference tool. You don't have to read it from beginning to end. If you prefer, you can turn to any part of the book that gives you the information you need, when you need it.

In addition, you can keep coming back to the book over and over. If you prefer to read things in order, you'll find that the information is presented in a natural, logical progression.

Sometimes I have information that I want to share with you, but it relates only tangentially to the topic at hand. When that happens, I place that information in a *sidebar* (a shaded gray box). Even though it may not be mission critical, I think you'll find it worth knowing. But you don't have to read it if you don't want to.

Within this book, you may note that some web addresses break across two lines of text. If you're reading this book in print and want to visit one of these web pages, simply key in the web address exactly as it's noted in the text, pretending as though the line break doesn't exist. If you're reading this as an e-book, you've got it easy — just click the web address to be taken directly to the web page.

Foolish Assumptions

You don't need an MBA to understand the contents of this book. It's written in conversational, jargon-free prose. However, you'll note that much of the advice in this text is geared toward those in management. In other words, its focus is on engaging others more than on engaging oneself.

That said, the principles and best practices outlined in this book apply to everyone. So, even if you manage no one, you'll find loads of tips and ideas in this book that will help you boost your own personal engagement level. Who knows, after reading this book, your raised level of engagement may even be the boost you need to reach new career heights!

Icons Used in This Book

Icons are those little pictures you see in the margins throughout this book, and they're meant to draw your attention to key points that can help you along the way. Here's a list of the icons we use and what they signify:

When you see this icon in the margin, the paragraph next to it contains valuable information that will help make your life easier.

Some information is so important that it needs to be set apart for emphasis. This icon — like a string tied around your finger — is a friendly reminder of info that you'll want to commit to memory and use over the long haul.

This icon highlights common mistakes and pitfalls to avoid. An important part of achieving success is simply eliminating the mistakes; the information marked by this icon helps you do just that.

On occasion, I use real-world examples to illustrate the topic at hand. When I do, I mark them with this icon.

Beyond the Book

In addition to the material in the print or e-book you're reading right now, this product also comes with some access-anywhere goodies on the web. Check out the free Cheat Sheet at www.dummies.com/cheatsheet/employeeengagement for tips on conducting an employee engagement survey, suggestions for identifying your "engagement ambassadors," and tips on engaging employees by engaging their spouses. You'll also find links on each of the part intro pages for accessing additional content, including articles on establishing a corporate university, using social media in your recruitment efforts, establishing an employee engagement committee, and more.

Where to Go from Here

This book isn't linear. Although you certainly can read it from cover to cover, you don't have to. You can start anywhere!

Glance through the Table of Contents and find the part, chapter, or section that flips your switch. That's the best place to begin. If you're already sold on employee engagement and you want some ideas for launching your own program, turn straight to Part II. If you're keen to gauge the level of engagement at your own organization, start with Chapter 3. If you're in hiring mode, Chapter 12 — which discusses the traits and behaviors of engaged employees — is a great place to start. Or you might turn to Chapter 16 for info on revamping your performance appraisal process to boost engagement. Finally, the resources I list in Chapter 20 of this book can further enrich your understanding of employee engagement.

When you're finished reading this book, feel free to check out my company's website (www.employeeengagement.com). On the Resources page of the site, you'll find links to loads of engagement blogs, articles, case studies, resources, and suggested videos and readings, all free of charge.

Part I
Getting Started with Employee Engagement

In this part...

✔ Get clear on what employee engagement is and what it means for your organization.

✔ Gauge your organization's level of employee engagement.

✔ Understand what motivates people so you can better lead and engage them.

✔ Develop a communication strategy to build alignment, engagement, and transparency.

Chapter 1

Basic Training: Employee Engagement Basics

Something's not quite right at work. People talk about leaving as soon as the economy improves. They no longer speak well of the company to each other or to potential recruits. It's as though people are just getting through the day, the week, or the month — that they're only there for the paycheck. There's a growing sense among employees that they've become easily replaceable commodities — or, worse, that their positions could simply be eliminated to "save payroll." Or maybe things aren't so dire — people don't seem to be complaining, but your organization or department just lacks oomph. No one seems to be putting in the extra effort. Your colleagues seem to run out the door at quitting time.

Does any of this sound familiar? If so, what you're witnessing is a lack of engagement among employees. And you're not alone. In recent years, companies all over the world have seen employees tune out. Whether due to the changing global economy, job instability, changes in the world of work, changes in society as a whole, or any number of other reasons, this lack of employee engagement is a serious problem for businesses and workers alike!

Don't believe me? A 2013 report released by Gallup, titled "State of the American Workplace Report," concludes that only 30 percent of workers are engaged, 52 percent are disengaged, and 18 percent are actively disengaged. Author Mark Crowley of Fast Company likens the workforce to a crew team. On this team, three of the rowers are paddling like crazy, five are casually taking in the scenery, and two are actively trying to sink the boat. Obviously, this team will not win the regatta!

It's not just Americans whose boats are sinking, so to speak. A 2013 survey on engagement by Dale Carnegie Training found that, globally, 34 percent of workers are engaged, 48 percent are disengaged, and 18 percent are actively disengaged.

Fortunately, lack of engagement is a problem that you can solve. As you'll see in this book, you can take any number of steps to engage your employees. The first of those steps is simply to read on!

Say What? Defining Employee Engagement

So, what is employee engagement anyway? One common definition, which has become the gold standard, describes employee engagement as "the capture of discretionary effort." *Discretionary effort* refers to employees going above and beyond. This is in contrast to the ordinary effort required to simply get the job done without attracting negative attention.

Other definitions or descriptions you're likely to hear include the following:

- ✔ The capture of an employee's head and heart
- ✔ Employees who have their hearts and minds in the business
- ✔ Intellectual understanding and emotional commitment
- ✔ Employees who go the extra mile in loyalty and ambassadorship
- ✔ Employees who say, stay, and strive
- ✔ Employees who think and act as business people

My favorite definition, though, is my own:

> Employee engagement is the mutual commitment between an organization and an employee, in which the organization helps the employee meet his or her potential and the employee helps the organization meet its goals.

This mutual commitment is what truly defines employee engagement and results in discretionary effort. It's also what makes employee engagement a win-win for both the employer and the employee.

Although engagement is about capturing your employees' discretionary effort, it isn't based on workaholism!

Engagement is not a "program"

Engagement is more than a program; it entails a cultural shift — a change in how things are done and communicated from the top to the bottom of an organization. Engagement can't be shunted to the end of every meeting, where it will stand a higher chance of being given short shrift. It's no one person's job; it is an ongoing part of business. And after you embark on systemic employee engagement, there is no finish line — it's a journey without a destination.

Often, people confuse employee *engagement* with employee *satisfaction.* This is a mistake. You can always throw money around or offer perks to boost employee satisfaction. But *satisfied* and *engaged* are two very different things. Simply put, engagement boosts performance, while satisfaction does not. The last thing you as an employer want is a satisfied but underperforming employee — or worse, a whole cadre of satisfied employees in an underperforming business! Don't get me wrong: Having a bunch of happy and satisfied employees walking around is a-okay. Employee satisfaction very well may be an outcome of an excellent company culture. But unlike employee engagement, it shouldn't be your goal per se.

Engagement is not an end in and of itself. It's not about having *things* (for example, the best benefit program, the biggest workstations, or the highest bonus checks). It's not even about instituting a training program or a flexible workweek. Successful engagement is about acknowledging that a business is, in essence, like a society. When everyone pulls together with common purpose, both its citizens and its economy will thrive. Engagement is about people's heads as well as their hearts.

For engagement to exist, there must be mutual commitment between the employer and employee. The employer helps the employee reach his or her untapped potential, and the employee helps the employer meet and surpass its business goals.

To sum up, employee engagement *is* about

- ✔ Mutual commitment between the company and employee
- ✔ People
- ✔ Relationships
- ✔ Alignment

✔ Shared purpose for creating the future together

✔ Success of the business *and* its employee

✔ Work environment and culture

✔ Continuous communication

✔ Opportunities for performers (and consequences for non-performers)

✔ Staff development

Engagement is *not* about

✔ Things

✔ Having the best of every amenity

✔ Avoiding making tough decisions

✔ Pleasing all the people all the time

There is no "there": Engagement is a journey, not a destination

When my kids were young, my wife and I often took them for Sunday drives to look at the New England autumn foliage. We quickly discovered that children are not into scenery and suffered through their never-ending badgering: "Are we there yet?" I still remember my wife responding, "There is no *there*" (meaning there is no destination — we're taking a drive and then returning home). This was a concept our kids could never really understand.

Engagement is a little like that. Because the rewards of an engaged culture are numerous and enduring, many leaders reading this book may be tempted to make engagement an action item to get "there" right now. There's nothing wrong with that enthusiasm, but it needs to be tempered by the sober realization that any kind of cultural change is a multi-year process. I like to refer to engagement, in particular, as "a journey with no destination." In other words, there is no *there*. Your engagement journey will be ongoing. You'll never "arrive." The journey doesn't meander, however; it takes companies with purpose from point to point, creating a road map along the way. There is always a goal to be set, measured, and communicated, and — if your organization fosters innovation — always another stop along the road.

Think about your quality programs. Best-in-class companies are never really satisfied with the level of quality of their products or services, which is why initiatives such as total quality management (TQM) have become part of the fabric of so many businesses. The same needs to happen with your engagement efforts.

What has surprised me since I left corporate America to spread the employee engagement gospel is how often I'm asked to counsel companies who don't really need much help. Indeed, many of them have already won various "Best Place to Work" awards! These companies already have an engaged culture but hire me in to help them get even better. They understand that there is no destination in their engagement efforts, just as there is no destination in their quality efforts. No doubt, these companies will seek out this book for even more ideas. And for all the other companies, this book is for you!

Making It Happen: Driving Engagement

Chapter 2 makes the business case for employee engagement. In it, you'll find out why employee engagement is such a big deal, the dangers of disengagement, as well as employee engagement's effect on employee turnover, customer satisfaction, profitability, and innovation. When you finish reading that chapter, you'll be hungry to learn what, exactly, drives employee engagement.

To whet your appetite, here are a few key strategies:

- **Driving engagement with a sense of purpose:** Companies that know their own purpose, values, vision, and strategic plan, and that believe in corporate social responsibility, are better able to win over the hearts and minds of their employees. And not surprisingly, employees who are duly won over are significantly more likely to be engaged! (See Chapter 6 for more on driving engagement with a sense of purpose.)

- **Engaging employees through leadership:** A *manager* manages process, programs, and data. *Leaders,* on the other hand, guide people, build followers, and steer organizations to success. Leaders are the ones who define and uphold an organization's principles. And it's leaders who really drive engagement in an organization. (See Chapter 7 for more on engaging employees through leadership.)

- **Driving engagement across generations:** People of different generations (Baby Boomers, Generation Xers, and Millennials) have different motivational drivers — which means they become engaged in different ways. Smart managers drive engagement by adjusting their communication, leadership, oversight, recognition, and patience levels when leading a department populated by people of different generations. (See Chapter 8 for more on driving engagement across generations.)

- **Driving engagement through team development:** Working with great co-workers, helping each other out, and having great camaraderie, trust, and love for one another is engaging. In other words, a great team environment can engage a person as much as a great job! (See Chapter 9 for more on driving engagement through team development.)

✔ **Driving engagement through branding:** Many firms focus all their branding efforts on their product brand — "what they do." But they invest virtually no time communicating their employment brand — "who they are." Ideally, "what we do" and "who we are" will be like two sides of the same coin. Engagement is about capturing your employees' heads and hearts. Firms that spend all their time branding "what they do" most likely are making an intellectual connection with their employees. But *true* engagement occurs when you make an emotional connection. This occurs only when you can define "who you are" and even "why you exist." When that happens, engagement flourishes! (See Chapter 10 for more on driving engagement through branding.)

✔ **Engaging employees through gamification:** For years, neuroscientists have known that people whose lives involve fun and enjoyment are healthier. The same is true of employees. One way to introduce fun as an engagement driver is to embrace the growing trend toward *gamification* (using game mechanics and rewards in a non-game setting to increase user engagement and drive desired user behaviors). Good gamification programs reward people for behaviors they're already inclined to perform or required to perform, increasing their engagement and enjoyment. In other words, gamification makes the things you have to do more fun. And injecting fun in the workplace goes a long way toward increasing employee engagement. (See Chapter 11 for more on gamification.)

To drive engagement, you must also have a firm grasp on what motivates people (see Chapter 4 for details), and commit to effectively communicating your engagement objectives (see Chapter 5). Finally, recognition (discussed in Chapter 17) is an important ingredient in your engagement stew.

Before embarking on any effort to drive employee engagement at your organization, you need to accept that tangible results may not be immediately forthcoming. The investments you'll be making will take time to take root and grow. Many companies make the mistake of moving on to something else if they don't see immediate results. Accept from the outset that your initiatives may take up to two years to show their desired effects. It's a little like the grease pole at the county fair. Fairgoers eagerly climb the pole, but as they get closer to the top, they discover increasing amounts of grease. This results in a loss of grip and an embarrassing slide back down the pole. Well, your engagement efforts will likely be similar. If there is a business hiccup, a change in your market, a turnover of key staff, a change in leadership, or an economic downturn, your engagement efforts may slip down the grease pole. Don't get discouraged. Stay the course. *Remember:* Engagement is a marathon, not a sprint!

Also, accept that you'll never say, "Well, we're done with engagement. Now on to quality control, customer service, and so on." If you're hoping to check off a box marked "employee engagement" for Year X and then move on to the next important thing, not only will *you* be disappointed, but you'll engender cynicism about the entire process among your staff. And cynicism is corrosive to engagement.

Pick Me! Pick Me! Picking the Right People for Engagement

As you'll learn in Chapter 12, a big part of cultivating an engaged workforce is choosing the right people as employees. Often, when faced with selecting employees (in other words, hiring), employers focus on candidates' education and skills. And yes, those are important. After all, if you're looking to hire a rocket scientist, you should probably make sure any candidates you consider have the necessary schooling and abilities (think: knowledge of calculus and deftness with a pocket protector) to do the job. But really, it's a candidate's traits and behaviors that will be key to his or her success in an organization.

What kinds of traits and behaviors do engaged employees display? According to Gallup, engaged employees

- Show consistent levels of high performance
- Have a natural drive for innovation and efficiency
- Intentionally build supportive relationships
- Are clear about the desired outcomes of their roles
- Are emotionally committed to what they do
- Have high levels of energy and enthusiasm
- Never run out of things to do
- Create positive things on which to act
- Broaden what they do and build on it
- Are committed to their companies, work groups, and roles

The specific behaviors and traits that you're looking for may differ from firm to firm. You'll want to pinpoint just what traits and behaviors you seek (see Chapter 12).

Of course, sussing out whether someone possesses these qualities during the course of a few interviews is no easy feat. For advice on telling interview questions and other hiring best practices, see Chapter 13.

After you've landed the perfect candidate — one whose traits and behaviors mesh with your firm — you'll want to take care to ensure that he or she gets up to speed as quickly as possible. That means using onboarding techniques that foster engagement. For details, see Chapter 14.

Measure Twice, Cut Once: Measuring and Recognizing Engagement

If your goal is to improve employee engagement at your firm — and I hope that after you read this book, it will be — you first need to find out just how engaged your employees are now. In Chapter 3, you discover various ways to gauge employee engagement, both now and in the future. These include employee surveys, exit interviews, "stay" interviews, and other engagement barometers such as training investment and employee referrals.

A balanced scorecard, discussed in Chapter 15, is also helpful, not just in measuring employee engagement but also in assessing performance in general. This approach can be applied to organizations as a whole, to teams, and to individuals. Speaking of measuring individual performance, odds are, you'll want to retool the performance appraisal process at your firm to gain a more accurate read. Your new process should involve establishing goals for employees that are specific and achievable — an engagement driver in and of itself. The performance appraisal process should also help employees develop their own employee development plan — that is, their own sense of where they are in the company and where they're going. For more, see Chapter 16.

Employees who demonstrate high performance should be duly recognized and rewarded. Positive reinforcement is a key pillar of engagement. It's not enough to simply tell your employees that you want them to perform; you must also recognize that performance and perhaps even reward it. Chapter 16 discusses rewards (which usually have a cost associated with them) and recognition (which are typically free or of minimal cost), both essential components of an effective engagement strategy.

On the flip side, employees who fail to perform also need your attention. What can you do to help a struggling employee get back on track? First, you must identify the cause of the poor performance. (If you guessed "disengagement," you're right!) Then you can take steps to address the problem. Only in very rare circumstances should this involve firing the employee. As discussed in Chapter 18, typically only bad bosses or bosses who make poor hiring decisions routinely give employees the ax. Good bosses — bosses who are engaged — have an ongoing performance-related dialogue with their employees, giving their staff the chance to improve long before their performance becomes cause for termination.

Chapter 2

The Hard Sell: Making a Business Case for Employee Engagement

*N*o offense to employee engagement, but it's a bit "soft." That is, it has to do with people and their investment in their jobs and their companies. That may make it a bit of a hard sell for the powers that be — CEOs, CFOs, and others. These folks tend to be, well, a bit "harder." That is, they're about hard data — numbers and such.

That's what this chapter is about: the hard data that makes a business case for employee engagement. In this chapter, you discover the business areas that are most affected by employee engagement, the dangers of disengagement, and the importance of finding and developing engagement champions within your organization. Armed with the information in this chapter, you'll be able to explain to even the most hardened executive how employee engagement is not just good for the bottom line, but the very foundation of a healthy business.

What's the Big Deal? Why Employee Engagement Matters

Employee engagement results in lower absenteeism and turnover, as well as higher productivity and profitability. But don't just take my word for it. A 2012 Gallup study — which examined nearly 50,000 business or work units and roughly 1.4 million employees in 192 organizations across 49 industries and in 34 countries — concluded that employee engagement has a huge impact on these and other key organizational outcomes, regardless of the economic climate. Indeed, even during difficult economic times, employee engagement is a key competitive differentiator.

According to the Gallup study, titled "Engagement at Work: Its Effect on Performance Continues in Tough Economic Times," which measured the difference between the top 25 percent of employees and the bottom 25 percent of employees when it comes to employee engagement, employee engagement affects the following performance outcomes:

- **Absenteeism:** Organizations with the most engaged employees have 37 percent lower absenteeism than companies where employees are least engaged.

- **Turnover:** Even among high-turnover organizations, those with the most engaged employees experience 25 percent lower turnover. The number is even more impressive in low-turnover organizations: 65 percent.

- **Shrinkage:** On average, a highly engaged workforce results in 28 percent less shrinkage. *Shrinkage* refers to a loss of inventory that can be attributed to such factors as employee theft, shoplifting, administrative error, vendor fraud, damage in transit or in store, and cashier errors that benefit the customer. In other words, shrinkage is the difference between recorded and actual inventory.

- **Safety incidents:** Are safety incidents a concern in your organization? If so, it should interest you to know that organizations with the most engaged employees experience 48 percent fewer safety incidents than their least-engaged counterparts. And if you're in healthcare, where patient safety is critical, you'll be pleased to find that organizations with a highly engaged workforce experience 41 percent fewer patient safety incidents.

- **Quality incidents:** For many industries, quality — that is, lack of defects — is key. Not surprisingly, organizations with highly engaged employees experience 41 percent fewer quality incidents.

- **Customer metrics:** Organizations with highly engaged employees boast 10 percent higher customer metrics than those whose employees are least engaged.

- **Productivity:** Highly engaged employees are significantly more productive than their least-engaged counterparts. Indeed, organizations with a highly engaged workforce enjoy 21 percent higher productivity.

Considering all these points, it's probably no great surprise that business or work units that score in the top half of their organization in employee engagement have nearly double the odds of success of those in the bottom half. Moreover, those at the 99th percentile have *four times* the success rate of those at the 1st percentile.

Here are a few other interesting tidbits about employee engagement, these from a 2012 study published by Temkin Group, "Employee Engagement Benchmark Study":

- ✔ Compared with disengaged employees, employees who are highly engaged are 480 percent more committed to helping their organization succeed.
- ✔ Highly engaged employees are 250 percent more likely to recommend improvements.
- ✔ Employees who are highly engaged are 370 percent more likely to recommend their company as an employer (which, as discussed in Chapter 12, increases the chances of your organization hiring additional highly engaged workers).

In the following sections, I dig deeper into two key benefits of an engaged workforce: customer satisfaction and profitability.

Grow your own: Cultivating customer satisfaction with employee engagement

Have you ever gone into a restaurant, hotel, or retail outlet and encountered a disinterested or, worse, rude employee? If so, chances are, you have no plans to revisit that establishment — not now, and not ever. Often, the same employees who are rude and disinterested are also — you guessed it — disengaged. And if those employees are the ones representing your organization to the public, it can do a real number on your business. Conversely, employees who are engaged can serve as drivers for customer satisfaction and, by extension, profitable growth.

The bottom line? Engaged employees drive customer satisfaction. If your employees aren't engaged, your customers won't be either.

In any enterprise you can imagine, at any scale, if you can't satisfy the demands of your clients, you'll lose business. And the way to reach extraordinary levels of client and customer service is through engaged employees. Employees' dedication speaks volumes to clients and customers. A company's employees truly are its greatest asset. But don't just take my word for it. According to a study conducted by Serco, increased employee engagement was accompanied by a 12 percent increase in customer satisfaction!

Profit margin: Driving profits with employee engagement

Employee engagement and profit can seem like difficult metrics to square. As mentioned in this chapter's introduction, employee engagement is "soft," having to do with people and their investment in their jobs and their companies. Profit, however, is "hard" — it's all about the numbers. Most leaders (including many, *many* CEOs and CFOs) are highly analytical and are, therefore, more comfortable with hard data. "Soft" initiatives like engagement are rarely intuitive for the very people who need to be sold on them. No executive team will sign off on a plan to increase employee engagement without some assurance that the holy grail — discretionary effort, with its corollary increase in productivity and, ultimately, in profit — is a likely result.

To state the case plainly: Engagement leads to profit, and profit, when wisely publicized and distributed, leads to engagement. That said, it may take time for these two metrics to square satisfactorily. But having seen effects on the bottom lines of dozens of companies, I can tell you that having profit without employee engagement is very difficult. Moreover, engagement, once it's established, can see a company through leaner times and help to build it back up.

Want proof? How about this: That same Gallup study I mention earlier reports that organizations that enjoy high engagement among employees also boast 22 percent higher profitability. Another study, the 2010 Hewitt Associates Survey on Employee Engagement, reports that organizations with engagement scores above 65 percent outperformed the total stock market index, even in volatile times. In contrast, organizations with engagement scores below 40 percent saw a shareholder return that was 44 percent lower than average. And the 2008 WorkTrends Report by Kenexa Research Institute concluded that the top 25 percent of corporations, as measured by employee engagement, saw a five-year total shareholder return (TSR) of 18 percent. This was in contrast to the bottom 25 percent of corporations, which saw a TSR of –4 percent over the same period.

Danger, Will Robinson! The Dangers of Disengagement

As I outline in the previous section, engagement is good... and disengagement is bad. *Really* bad.

Unfortunately, disengagement is also quite prevalent. Since the Great Recession of 2008–2009, a "perfect storm" of company layoffs, marginal opportunities, minimal pay increases and bonuses, limited opportunities for promotion, and reduced training and development has resulted in rising levels of disengagement. According to a 2012 Dale Carnegie white paper, "What Drives Employee Engagement and Why It Matters," 45 percent of employees are only partially engaged, and a horrifying 26 percent are *disengaged*! This lack of engagement is costing companies billions of dollars in lost productivity and reduced levels of client service, resulting in declining profits and worsening client satisfaction.

In boom times, disengaged employees simply seek other opportunities. But in a recession, the disengaged have no place to go. They hunker down, fearful for their jobs. Although management may view the current economic circumstances as helping to separate the wheat from the chaff, rationalizing that the people who stay are the truly dedicated employees, this may not be the case. These people may well just be the employees who are the most disengaged.

To exacerbate matters, many people are postponing retirement to give their 401(k) plans and other retirement funds a chance to rebound. The result? A workforce composed of employees who don't want to be there and retirees hanging around for "one more year."

In a situation like this, it becomes even more urgent to increase employee engagement — and perhaps even more important, to capture the discretionary effort of the engaged before their frustration with their disengaged colleagues' apathy takes a further toll on the workplace and the economy at large.

Don't be afraid to prune. In fact, given the strong link between poor performance and disengagement, a good place to start may be the aforementioned staff who are disengaged but staying put!

Things won't get easier with a turn in the economy. Indeed, they could get harder, as employees take advantage of the rising tide and, well, jump ship. Indeed, there is a real threat that many businesses will soon be faced with a staff exodus, and the waste — in training and intellectual capital, but also in revenue — will be colossal. The war for talent will officially resume. And when it does, those companies that have continued to engage employees during the downturn will have a distinct advantage.

So, what does it matter if turnover is high? Well, at the most basic level, employee turnover is expensive. According to some industry sources, the cost of turnover is, on average, the annual salary of the person being replaced — or significantly higher (think 200 percent to 250 percent) if the employee who exits is part of your managerial or sales team. It's not just

Mythbusters: Five myths about employee engagement

The Greeks and Romans aren't the only ones with myths. You'll find plenty in the work world, too. For example, here are some myths about employee engagement:

✔ **Employee engagement is HR's role.** Most leaders, including many (and I mean *many*) CEOs and CFOs, are highly analytical. They're more comfortable with hard data than "soft" initiatives like employee engagement. That's why many of them delegate employee engagement to HR. The problem is, when they do, the result is merely an engagement program, not the cultural transformation that is needed to engage employees. *Remember:* Your leaders cast a huge shadow over your organization — you know, that whole "walk the walk" thing. Delegating employee engagement to HR will send a huge message to employees — namely, that employee engagement just isn't that important!

✔ **Employee engagement requires a large budget.** Although you can certainly spend all kinds of dough on engagement programs, you don't have to. In fact, some of the best engagement tools are free! Take recognition and respect, which are a huge part of engagement. Simply calling out employees for their accomplishments won't cost you a dime. Transparent communication, another key engagement driver, is also gratis.

✔ **Employee engagement isn't something to be focused on now.** When an organization faces economic difficulties, some managers inevitably subscribe to the notion that people are fortunate just to have jobs and dismiss any talk about the importance of engagement. But in times like these, it becomes even *more* urgent to increase employee engagement, before workers' frustration with their disengaged colleagues takes a further toll on the workplace.

✔ **Employee engagement is warm and fuzzy, and there aren't statistics to back it up.** Wrong. As I note throughout this chapter, there are plenty of statistics to support the idea that the more engaged your workforce is, the better it is for your organization.

✔ **Employee engagement is a trend.** Right. Kind of like the Internet. The truth is, if you run an online search for "employee engagement," you'll land over 37 million hits. Does that sound trendy to you? Look at it this way: Leadership never went out of favor, quality seems to have survived, and strategy has stood the test of time; similarly, employee engagement isn't going away anytime soon.

running ads and/or commissioning a recruiter that empties company coffers; the more difficult and more expensive outlay involves the loss of productivity while the empty position is unfilled. And that's not even counting the intellectual property that the person who leaves takes with her or the waste of the financial investment a company has made in that person, not to mention the very real likelihood of the employee leaving your business to join your competitor.

The damage doesn't stop there, however. Turnover has a Pied Piper effect. As people walk, others talk. They wonder, "Why did Jamie quit?" Even if an employee is leaving on the best possible terms, those who stay are bound to ask themselves, "What did Jamie know that I don't? Should I be looking around, too?" And if the terms of the parting of ways are less than ideal, or if people are quitting in droves, the impact on morale is even more detrimental. Even the sunniest internal communications spin on the situation can't entirely eradicate gossip, speculation, and skepticism.

Man overboard! Employees who "jump ship"

Recent research by Dale Carnegie shows that roughly one quarter of those employees who are fully engaged will jump ship for a 5 percent increase in salary. Sound like a lot? It is — until you consider that the number rises to 50 percent for partially engaged employees and spikes to a whopping 69 percent for disengaged employees. Put another way, improved engagement has a multiplier effect on lowering turnover costs! (That said, as the salary increase rises, so does the willingness of even the most engaged employees to jump ship, as shown in the following figure.)

Perhaps even more horrifying is when you flip that last number around — 31 percent of disengaged employees will stay, even when someone else is willing to pay them more. In other words, they're committed to remaining disengaged and making life miserable for everyone around them!

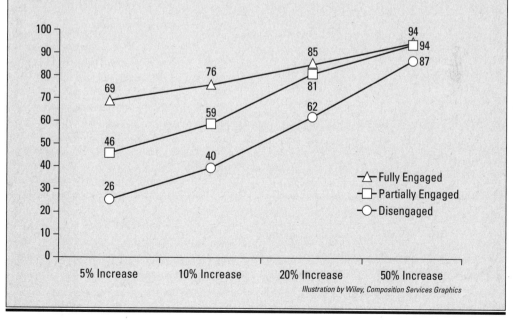

Illustration by Wiley, Composition Services Graphics

Not all turnover is created equal. In fact, losing your underperformers will strengthen your business. When disengaged employees or those who are known underperformers leave, you'll almost always experience a spike in engagement from remaining, hard-working employees. Companies that "get" engagement understand that to engage their top performers, they must prune their underperforming employees and address their disengaged employees.

Enlightened companies track *voluntary turnover* (employees who quit, often to seek opportunities elsewhere) and *involuntary turnover* (layoffs, termination due to poor performance, and temporary employees, such as interns, who leave because their assignments have ended). Some companies also track "key" employee turnover. Losing a superstar is significantly more painful than losing a "steady Eddie" employee. Identifying your top performers and tracking their turnover is a must for any company looking to build a high-performing business.

Breeding Ground: Engagement Breeds Innovation (Or Is It the Other Way Around?)

Too often, people think innovation is limited to research and development, technological advances, or filing a new patent. But really, innovation can occur in any industry, regardless of company size or maturity. It can also occur in any department, by any employee. Any change leading to a successful business process improvement constitutes innovation. The bottom line: Whether you realize it or not, innovation is critical to the health of your business.

Researchers overwhelmingly agree: Engaged employees drive innovation. Engaged employees are empowered to seek ways to innovate, whether that means improving the customer experience, boosting profitability, building the brand, improving marketing, improving quality, or simply being more creative. Indeed, recent research by Gallup found that 61 percent of engaged employees feed off the creativity of their colleagues, compared to a mere 9 percent of disengaged employees. In addition, it found that 59 percent of engaged employees believe their job brings out their most creative ideas, compared to only 3 percent of disengaged employees. This links to the customer side of the business as well; Gallup found that 74 percent of engaged employees give their customers new ideas, compared to only 13 percent of disengaged employees. And in an interesting chicken-or-egg type way, innovation also drives employee engagement.

Unfortunately, many leaders fail to create a safe environment for employees to contribute ideas. Worse, they create an environment in which new ideas are met with rejection. I often tell leadership teams that if they want to kill employee engagement and initiative, they should simply tell employees that they can't do something "because that's not how we do it here" or "because we've tried that before" or "because management will never accept that" or "because it isn't policy." This type of "because" culture ultimately maintains the status quo — and the status quo simply doesn't breed creativity or innovation. Companies fail when they stop evolving their product or service, become complacent, are afraid to fix what isn't yet broken, worry about the investment necessary to innovate, or worry about failure.

If your company has a "because" culture, odds are, it's lacking in innovation, empowerment, and engagement. I also suspect your firm's growth is lower than its peers, your client satisfaction levels are lower than the industry average, and voluntary employee turnover is higher than your competition. You're also most likely retaining only your marginally engaged employees.

All too often, leaders become protective of what they've created and fail to engage their employees to help them create or innovate. Countless leadership teams surround themselves with people who think just like them. Birds of a feather may flock together, but they don't innovate!

Instead of a "because" culture, why not try for a "why not?" culture? Instead of rejecting employees' ideas "just because," give them a whirl, just to see what happens. Even better, seek out those ideas. Sure, you'll have some misses, but you'll also have some hits! Continuous improvement is about challenging the norm. Besides, actually _listening_ to employees allows them to become even more comfortable about expressing their ideas, which naturally increases their level of engagement. (Of course, not all ideas will be winners. For some guidance on which ideas to pursue and which to set aside, check out the idea priority matrix in Figure 2-1. As you can see, it favors ideas that are low in cost and high in impact over all others.)

Idea Priority Matrix

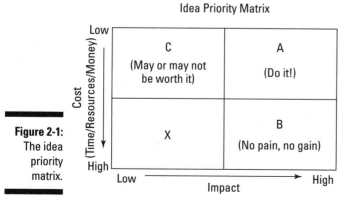

Figure 2-1:
The idea
priority
matrix.

Illustration by Wiley, Composition Services Graphics

"Because" companies

The annals of history are replete with now-defunct great companies headed by brilliant leaders who simply stopped innovating — in other words, companies with a "because" culture. Why did Digital Equipment Corporation founder and CEO Ken Olsen continue to produce minicomputers while competing startups built personal computers? Because. Why did *The New York Times* and *The Boston Globe* miss the boat on launching online job ads, giving Jeff Taylor space to launch Monster.com? Because. Why didn't Blockbuster deliver movies or offer streaming video, leaving that niche open for Netflix? Because. Why didn't the music industry latch onto digital music? Because. Why didn't Polaroid see the emergence of digital photography? Because. (Actually, folklore has it that Polaroid invented an early digital camera but was afraid to invest in a product that could cannibalize its film-based business.)

These are all examples of companies that failed to engage their employees to challenge the status quo. Innovation requires investing today's cash to discover tomorrow's new service or product offerings, technologies, or approaches. If you don't innovate, you'll end up with an old model that can't compete.

Why do so many companies settle into a "because" culture? To understand this, you need to recognize the business pressures to conform, exacerbated by the natural bureaucracies that develop over time as companies grow. Add to that the fact that people naturally become less creative as they grow older. In his book *What a Great Idea! 2.0: Unlocking Your Creativity in Business and in Life* (Sterling Publishing), author Chic Thompson cites a study that administered a test to compare the level of creativity of 5-year-olds with that of 44-year-olds. Incredibly, 98 percent of the 5-year-olds passed the test… compared to a woeful 2 percent of 44-year-olds. On a related note, according to Thomson, the average 5-year-old asks 65 "why" questions a day, compared to the average 44-year-old, who asks only 6. No wonder people have a hard time being innovative in the workplace! And no wonder recent Dale Carnegie research indicates that engagement levels are lowest with employees between the ages of 40 and 50. Coincidence? I think not!

Ask yourself: Does your culture underwrite creativity, or is it afraid of mistakes? Do risk takers get punished? Companies that foster a higher level of expression from their employees (and that accept that missteps are part of the creative process) will not only see more innovation, but also have more engaged employees.

When it comes to innovation, engagement is both a chauffeur and a passenger — that is, it both drives and is driven by innovation. Indeed, innovation is a key engagement driver. Employees want to create, be current, evolve, contribute new ideas and approaches, and work for the market leader.

Has all this talk about innovation and engagement gotten the gears in your noggin turning? Here are some tips to help you convert those thoughts into action:

- ✔ **It starts at the top.** Your leader and his or her leadership team need to become champions of innovation. Frequent and consistent company-wide communications must highlight innovation and recent successes and encourage employees to challenge the status quo.

- ✔ **Establish a "why not?" campaign.** Go big with posters, training, and supporting communication, all focused on helping leaders and employees recognize when they lapse into "because" thinking. Make it fun! Encourage your employees to catch others saying "because" and correct them with the appropriate "why not?" response.

- ✔ **Expand your definition of diversity.** As I discuss in Chapter 12, diversity is not simply about some Equal Employment Opportunity Commission charge to eliminate discrimination in the workplace due to gender, age, or race. Instead, it's about one's thinking style, culture, heritage, generation, tenure, organizational level… the list goes on. Diversity is about inclusion, and inclusion leads to innovation.

- ✔ **Budget and measure innovation.** The old adage "You get the behavior you measure" is certainly true with innovation. Are you establishing an innovation culture by budgeting for innovation? Some companies earmark a percentage of total profit or revenue or a set number of hours per employee per year. Regardless of your metric, reporting on progress and highlighting successes are essential. (For more on metrics in general, see Chapter 15.)

   Don't shoot down those who innovate and fail. A key ingredient of innovative cultures is the acceptance of failure. If your employees are afraid to fail, you'll never build a culture of innovation.

- ✔ **Establish a task force to oversee innovation.** Populate your team with left- and right-brain thinkers from both the full- and part-time staff, including recent hires. (***Remember:*** The "architects of the present" can rarely see what needs to change!) Also, make it a point to include Millennials (also known as Generation Y); they have great ideas on leveraging technology, using social media as a branding and communication tool, and the direction we're heading with mobile technology. Give the task force a budget to oversee and manage, and ask them to report on progress. You may even go so far as to establish your innovation task team as a permanent part of your organization, with one- to two-year rotating terms. Finally, consider instituting an idea process to encourage both guests and employees to suggest new ideas.

- ✔ **Look outside your own industry for ideas and talent.** I'm flummoxed by the fact that many firms continue to run in the same race as every other firm in their niche. That is, they do external benchmarking only against other firms within their same sector. If you want to come up with an innovative idea that is the first of its kind or is disruptive to your competition, you need to see what other industries are doing.

Don't be afraid to hire people from outside your industry. You want to surround yourself with people who think differently from you!

✔ **Provide an "innovation box."** I've never been a fan of suggestion boxes. In my experience, they tend to become clogged with complaints, often of the pettiest sort. A better approach is to use an innovation box — a feedback mechanism geared toward soliciting specific suggestions for innovation: How can we improve our proposal system? How should our technology evolve? Should our billing be centralized? What can we be doing better in terms of customer service? Are there new markets we need to penetrate? What technologies are we missing? An innovation box establishes a direct connection between the individual's contribution and the welfare of the organization as a whole. It further funds trust, and a sense that the individual is being heard. And perhaps most important, it provides a means by which new ideas — the fuel of a company's future — can flourish. This is engagement at its best.

At one company I worked for, we formalized this process by adding an "innovation light bulb" to our intranet home page and made it clear that we were looking for proactive, well thought-out ideas on how our employees could help the company innovate. Everyone who sent in an idea was recognized for it and rewarded with a small gift card. A committee, including members of the senior leadership team, reviewed all suggestions and responded to all submitters, letting them know if their ideas were or weren't implementable (and why). The cream of the crop were sent to the company's CEO. Many of these ideas made their way into our policies and processes, and even new and enhanced service offerings.

✔ **Follow the 125 rule.** Some experts claim that to foster a culture of innovation while avoiding bureaucracy, you must prevent your chain of command from exceeding 125 employees. Richard Branson, CEO of Virgin, keeps his profit units as small as possible to keep them fleet of foot, to foster innovation, and to encourage entrepreneurial drive.

✔ **Build a career lattice.** Most people think of careers as being a ladder — something you climb up. But enlightened organizations understand that engagement increases in cultures that support job rotation — that is, not just up, but across, like a lattice. The advantages are many:

- Continually promoting people upward is expensive; employees often look for more money as they advance in their careers.

- There are only so many promotional opportunities. Employees are far more willing to accept a lateral move if they feel they're learning a new skill that will help their careers.

- A job lattice increases not only engagement, but innovation as well. People who have been in the same department often struggle to develop new ideas, approaches, and process improvements. A career lattice minimizes job stagnancy and complacency.

We Are the Champions: Finding and Developing Engagement Champions

Just having your company leaders talk about engagement isn't enough. You must embed engagement champions throughout your workforce. Identifying the right employees as your engagement champions is key to building a culture of engagement. Failing to do so will severely hamper your engagement efforts.

To identify your engagement champions, first you need to understand your own culture. What behaviors and traits does your firm value? For instance, Southwest Airlines values a sense of humor, Apple values creativity, and Nordstrom values customer service. More often than not, your most engaged employees are those whose personal traits mirror the traits of the firm's culture. Those employees will make for great engagement champions.

Look, too, to your most respected and well networked employees. Malcolm Gladwell (author of such books as *The Tipping Point* and *Outliers,* both published by Little, Brown) calls them "connectors." You want to make sure your engagement champions are connectors within your firm, because you'll need them to serve as engagement ambassadors.

Although committees are often overused and improperly chartered, if you're new to engagement, you may consider bringing together a group of engaged connectors to help give the initiative some traction.

After you locate your engagement champions, it's on you to help them develop. Here are a few ideas:

- ✔ **Identify an organizational need or a problem that needs fixing and put your engagement champions in charge of a team aimed at solving it.** Give the group a budget, a voice at the leadership table, and a timetable to recommend a plan. Just remember that if your leadership team is unwilling to consider the team's solution, the result will be a disengaged champion.

- ✔ **Send your engagement champions to a conference or trade show to present a technical paper or work the booth.** Even if they're not marketing types, they'll be great brand ambassadors, representing you to your customers.

✔ **Invite your engagement champions to participate in your college recruiting program or at job fairs.** These standouts can act as brand ambassadors to potential employees in much the same way they can to customers. Also, invite them to mentor new hires or those who have been promoted.

✔ **Reward your engagement champions to a weeklong executive development program.** These programs are frequently offered at major universities. Also, ask them to participate in (or perhaps even present at) executive leadership team meetings.

Objective Case: Setting Goals and Objectives for Your Engagement Plan

This chapter is about making a business case for employee engagement, right? Well, you can't expect to make a credible business case for employee engagement if you don't include a set of business goals and objectives.

If your leadership team wanted to increase sales, they would put in place sales objectives. If they wanted to decrease defects in manufacturing, they would outline quality objectives. If they wanted to reduce shrinkage in the retail chain, they would outline your objectives to minimize theft and returns. But something funny often happens with employee engagement. Something happens in the firm — for example, employee turnover spikes — and someone cries, "Let's focus on employee engagement!" and off you go. No goal, and few objectives.

Employee engagement should be viewed as part of your overall strategic planning process. As such, it needs to be budgeted, tracked, and championed. Most important, it needs to follow a set of organizational objectives. Anything short of this, and you run the risk of turning employee engagement into a "flavor of the month"–type program. And as I make abundantly clear in Chapter 1, employee engagement is *not* a program!

Here are some engagement-related goals and objectives that would apply to most any firm:

✔ **Become an "employer of choice" in your industry.** Employers of choice — think Apple, Google, Southwest Airlines, Procter and Gamble, Whirlpool, Timberland, 3M, Starbucks, and so on — receive more résumés than their competitors. It follows, then, that these companies enjoy the benefit of choosing from more qualified candidates. Indeed, according to Dr. Wayne Cascio, author of *Investing in People: Financial Impact of Human Resource Initiatives* (FT Press) and a distinguished professor and instructor at the University of Colorado, firms that make *Fortune* magazine's annual "Top 100 Places to Work" list receive twice as many applications as firms that are not on the list. It's a simple concept, really: If you receive twice as many résumés from qualified candidates for a position as your competitor, you'll be able to select higher-caliber talent. Engaging your workforce is the first step in becoming an employer of choice — and of gaining all the associated benefits.

✔ **Improve employee retention.** Employee turnover is extremely expensive. Studies show that the cost to replace one person who resigns is, on average, equivalent to that person's annual salary, but can be much more depending on the person's role in the company. Fortunately, you can improve employee retention through engagement. Improving employee engagement will also help you retain your top employees, which will boost your image as a high-performing organization, which will help you draw even more engaged employees.

✔ **Build a culture of high performance.** Hopefully, you're beginning to see that an improvement in employee engagement leads to an increase in productivity and, over time, an increase in company performance (and profits)!

✔ **Improve customer satisfaction.** As you'll see throughout this book, engaged employees lead to improved customer satisfaction. Customers will always be put off by employees who are disengaged; it follows, then, that customers will generally respond more positively to employees who are engaged.

✔ **Increase shareholder value (for companies with shareholders).** Not to be all "broken record" about it, but the evidence is overwhelming. Companies with engaged employees outperform their peers. These companies enjoy increased revenue, reduced absenteeism, reduced shortages, improved safety, improved quality, stronger innovation, and reduced business costs. That translates to increased shareholder value!

✔ **Reduce absenteeism.** You should track by department your employee absenteeism and set goals to improve your metrics. Chances are, those business units that have high absenteeism also have higher disengagement.

Other objectives you might want to consider depending on need include increasing revenue, improving safety and wellness, increasing the number of innovative ideas, increasing the number of new hires that join the firm through employee referrals, and of course, improving the overall employee engagement survey metrics.

The ultimate goal here is employee engagement, not employee satisfaction. But of course, if done well, employee engagement can lead to employee satisfaction.

It's not enough to simply say, "Employee engagement is of critical importance to this company. We're going to invest in it and measure it." Even if you have the best intentions, this will sound to your staff like so much hot air because it's simply too broad. Chances are, your employees have some idea of the specific challenges your organization faces in terms of engagement, and will appreciate your acknowledgement of the specific mileposts that will help resolve them.

By the time you make any announcement of this sort, you should have identified your goals and decided upon how they will be measured, tracked, and reported. If you want to reduce turnover to single digits, tell your staff not only that this is an objective, but also how your performance and progress will be tracked. If your goal is to have 50 percent of new hires come from employee referrals, tell your staff what the benchmarks are both within your company and against competitors, if those are your metrics.

Sharing your plan in detail gives your message credibility. Employees can see the extent of thought and preparation that has been devoted to the specifics. This makes a much stronger impression than airy proclamations like, "Employees are our greatest asset." When you then follow up on these messages, you supplement your credibility much more than if you had reported successes that were not explicitly tied to your goals.

On a Budget: Budgeting for Engagement

While it's true that many engagement efforts involve little or no cost, engagement does require an investment of capital, just like financing a project or new product does. For example, if one of your goals is to reduce voluntary staff turnover, you might budget for the following:

- ✔ Specific recognition and spot bonus budgets
- ✔ Mentoring and cross-training opportunities
- ✔ External and internal training initiatives
- ✔ Increases to your bonus pool to reward performance

Key engagement items such as communication initiatives or talent management systems cost money and must be formally budgeted. And, as with any other budget, there must be accountability. Engagement cannot be the low man on the budgetary totem pole. Just as you would for "hard" programs, formalize your line items and track how your money is being spent. Make adjustments over time as appropriate.

Chapter 3

Engagement Gauges: Finding Your Employee Engagement Baseline

*Y*ou've probably heard the saying "That which is measured improves." Although its origin is ambiguous, its meaning couldn't be more clear: If you want something to be better in the future, you need cold, hard data on how it is *now*. The same holds true for employee engagement. If you're looking for a more engaged workforce down the road, the first step is to find out just how engaged your employees are in the here and now.

Perhaps the most obvious way to determine the level of your employees' engagement is to simply ask them. No, I'm not suggesting that you corner the next employee you see and inquire, "Hey! How engaged are you?" Instead, you'll want to use tools such as surveys and interviews to ask more specific questions, like the following:

✔ Would you recommend this as a good place to work?

✔ Do you have the tools to effectively do your job?

✔ Has anyone recognized you for doing a good job in the past week?

✔ Do your opinions seem to matter around here?

✔ Would you recommend this as a good place to do business?

✔ Do you believe the organization is going in the right direction?

✔ Do you believe the company's values are in alignment with your personal values?

✔ Are you proud of the contributions the company makes to the community?

✔ Do you believe all employees are respected and treated well in the company?

The only thing worse than never asking your employees what they think is to ask them, and then do nothing with the results. Asking employees what they think but doing nothing with the results will foster cynicism, skepticism, and mistrust among employees. Managers who ask for opinions must be prepared to listen to, evaluate, and prioritize suggestions, and then develop and communicate a plan. Even if the plan is to "do nothing" due to budget issues or competing priorities, you need to share this plan with employees.

One more thing: Don't seek out employees' opinions only when you know they'll tell you good things. Companies with healthy cultures seek feedback in good times and in bad. Ironically, struggling companies often avoid asking for feedback from employees for fear of hearing bad news. That's like not going to the doctor when you're running a fever, coughing, and feeling achy, because you're afraid you have the flu! Failing to acknowledge the reality of a negative situation doesn't make that situation go away. Unless you acknowledge the situation and seek ideas on what to do differently, things will likely get worse.

In this chapter, we walk you through a variety of tools you use can use to gauge employee engagement. With the answers these tools provide, you can strengthen your company and help to ensure its long-term health.

Survey Says: Conducting Employee Engagement Surveys

A companywide employee engagement survey is the most thorough tool for capturing your company's engagement baseline. Such a survey can help you determine where to invest first to increase engagement; it can also validate (or not) your employee engagement efforts down the road.

Employee engagement surveys also enable you to view engagement levels within various departments or business units in your organization in comparison with each other and with the company as a whole. And, assuming you opt to work with a consultant (more on that in a moment), you can use an engagement survey to get a sense of where your organization stacks up on the engagement issue compared to other companies, including companies you directly compete with.

Finally, if you measure engagement within your organization via surveys, you'll begin to see the connection between engagement efforts and profitable growth.

Measurement is critical to showing that engagement leads to improved performance.

Working with a consultant

To conduct a survey, I recommend partnering with a consulting firm. A consultant will create a survey that's specific to your organization and assist with the delivery and rollout of results.

You may think you have the in-house capability and IT support to design and implement your own survey. Shouldn't you save some money and take the DIY approach? If you do, just remember that your "savings" will be offset by the following:

- ✔ **A huge internal administrative effort:** If your IT department is like most, they're not sitting around playing solitaire all day. Adding a huge companywide survey to their already overflowing plates will have ramifications. How patient are you when your e-mail is down? Enough said.

- ✔ **Diminished trust with your employees:** When you ask the questions yourself, instead of bringing in a third party, there's a perceived lack of confidentiality among employees.

- ✔ **A lack of credible external benchmark data:** For example, suppose your survey respondents respond negatively to questions about compensation. Without the context of external benchmarks, you may think you have a compensation issue. But guess what? Employees *never* respond positively to these types of questions. ("Yup, I get paid too much to work around here," said no one ever.) Why? Because they're afraid that management will limit future pay increases. By putting your company's score in context with external norms, you may discover that your seemingly dismal score was actually high compared to the industry average.

When you're looking for a survey vendor, don't pinch your pennies, but do consider which features you truly need. If your employee engagement survey fails, it won't be because you didn't opt for the consultant with the most bells and whistles, or because that consultant failed to collect the correct data. It'll be because you didn't interpret the results properly, prioritize the go-forwards, or follow up.

Asking the right questions

The best surveys contain a blend of closed-ended questions and open-ended questions. In this section, I offer examples of both types, which you can use yourself or build upon to create your survey.

Don't ask too many questions, or you run the risk of survey fatigue. As a general rule, 10 questions is not enough, and 100 is too many. Shoot for something in between.

If you're bootstrapping an employee engagement survey (as opposed to working with a consultant), try writing survey items that measure traits of engaged employees. For more info, refer to Chapter 1.

Closed-ended questions

A *closed-ended question* typically gives people a list of responses to choose from. The answer choices could be as simple as Yes or No, or they may offer more options, such as Strongly Disagree, Disagree, Somewhat Disagree, Somewhat Agree, Agree, Strongly Agree, and Don't Know.

Following are some examples. *Note:* These examples are framed as statements to which respondents would choose from options such as Strongly Disagree, Disagree, and so on, but you could reframe these statements as questions, with a Yes or No response if you prefer.

- ✔ Management gets the best out of everybody at all our work locations.
- ✔ People within the company always treat others with respect.
- ✔ Management shows by their actions that employee training and development are important.
- ✔ Your manager respects your work–life balance.
- ✔ The communication between the company's management and people at your level is good.
- ✔ Promotions at the company are based on capability rather than tenure.
- ✔ You would like to be working for this organization one year from today.
- ✔ There are real opportunities at the company for meaningful career and professional advancement.
- ✔ Your opinions seem to count.
- ✔ Considering your contribution, you think you are fairly paid compared to others in the company.

✔ Someone has talked to you about your progress in the past six months.

✔ The company routinely hires the best people.

✔ The company tolerates poor performance.

✔ Enthusiasm and morale have never been higher.

Close-ended questions enable you to systematically tally up the results of your survey by leveraging technology, saving both time and money. Closed-ended questions also provide a consistent framework for collecting normative data, which is necessary if you're looking to benchmark against other firms (think "apples-to-apples" comparisons).

Open-ended questions

Open-ended questions, by their very nature, can't be answered in just one or two words. For this reason, they're sometimes known as *narrative questions.*

Here are some examples of open-ended questions:

✔ If you could change just one thing about working for this company, what would it be?

✔ What would make you consider changing jobs?

✔ Why do you love working for this company?

Your survey should contain only a few open-ended questions to minimize the time required not only to complete the survey but also to evaluate the survey results.

Complementing your closed-ended questionnaire with several open-ended questions (between two and four, max) allows you to seek more specific input on particular item — for example, "What's the one thing you would change about working here if you could?" Too many open-ended questions, however, will make it nearly impossible (from an administrative standpoint) to capture and assimilate the results. Also, surveys that include only open-ended questions can't be quantitatively compared with internal or external benchmark norms.

Analyzing the results

Obviously, simply conducting a survey isn't enough. You have to analyze the results to determine what to *do.* As you're analyzing the results, you may notice variations in several key areas:

- ✔ **Generation:** Engagement scores and needs often vary significantly across generations, and addressing these variances requires careful action planning. For more information on engaging different generations, whether Baby Boomers, Generation X, or Generation Y, see Chapter 7.

- ✔ **Tenure:** Employees typically join an organization filled with hope and enthusiasm, but their engagement level usually drops after the first year. Worse, they generally remain lower than year-one levels, with a corollary increase in turnover, until the employee reaches years four to eight (depending on the company). As you analyze your engagement results and consider where you want to concentrate your efforts, you'll likely want to focus at least some of your efforts on employees in this "valley of despair."

- ✔ **Business unit, department, and/or location:** The better leaders in your company most likely have more engaged employees and, thus, superior survey results, while the not-so-good leaders will usually see poorer results. The good news? You now have quantitative evidence to take back to the poorer managers, and they can no longer hide behind the argument that so-called "soft" skills aren't measurable.

As you analyze the results, think about the importance of corporate social responsibility (CSR) as an engagement driver. Employees want to work for a company that has a purpose and is committed to sustainability. Indeed, recent research by Dale Carnegie shows that this is one of two key factors to improving employees' pride in their organization and raising their level of engagement (the other being whether the company's values reflected their own). Look for ways to leverage this engagement driver as you build your action plan. For guidance, turn to Chapter 5.

Your engagement initiative is not about making your employees happy (although happiness is often a byproduct of engagement). It's about engaging your employees in your business in order to drive business success!

Hey, what about job tenure?

Many companies boast of having lots of long-termers, viewing long tenure as a sign of engagement. But length of tenure isn't necessarily a strong indicator of engagement. Especially in a down economy, it's important to make sure those people haven't plateaued; otherwise, you may be looking at an exodus when other opportunities present themselves to your staff. Worse, you may be providing job security for a group of complacent, satisfied, and perhaps underperforming employees. Job tenure may be an outcome of your engagement initiatives, but it shouldn't be a goal.

Communicating the results to your employees

After the results of your survey are summarized, invite your survey consultant to deliver an overview to your top leadership team. That person will be able to provide the proper context to minimize leadership anxiety — common among senior leaders, who often take less-than-positive results personally. After this meeting, work with your communication team and consultant to determine how and when to share survey results and next steps with employees. The goal is to build transparency throughout the communication process with frequent, open, and consistent messages. Employees need to know that their feedback was heard and analyzed, and that action is being taken. This will help to build trust and credibility.

You can find out more about broadcasting your communication efforts (and about the importance of communication in general) in Chapter 5.

Establish committees to review the results and make recommendations. You need two separate committees:

- ✔ **A cross-sectional committee to review overall company results and to make recommendations to management:** This committee should convene and make these recommendations shortly after your leadership team receives the survey results. The committee should be composed of 10 to 20 employees (depending on company size) and include an equal mix of leaders and respected rank-and-file employees. Consider keeping this task team together for a 12-month period to help guide and monitor the progress of key initiatives.

- ✔ **Cross-sectional subcommittees to review local results (departmental, by business unit, and so on) and appoint local senior champions:** You'll quickly learn that some departments and business units score significantly higher or lower than the company average, requiring an analysis at the local level and the establishment of local action plans. Consider having these local committees adopt a common action plan template, and post their plans on your intranet to encourage the sharing of best practices, collaboration, and consistency.

Going forward after a survey

The tendency after a survey is to overpromise and underdeliver. If you succumb to this temptation, you run the risk of creating a skeptical work culture. ("They told us they would do [fill in the blank], but we've seen nothing!") To avoid this problem, implement a rigorous priority review process that uses an idea priority matrix (see Chapter 2).

Provide the necessary funds to pay for what the company commits to. *Remember:* Engagement is not free. A well thought-out engagement action plan requires an organizational investment.

Often, the same leaders who were reluctant to endorse a survey at the outset become seduced by the results and push to change the culture overnight. But organizational change is like a dimmer switch, not an on/off switch. An engagement plan takes time to implement, and it competes with other organizational priorities, such as acquiring other organizations, launching a quality-control system, increasing business development, or upgrading your IT infrastructure. Organizational follow-up and follow-through are key in a successful implementation — and in how your employees will judge the success of your survey efforts.

Develop a feedback mechanism. How will you solicit ongoing input from employees? Your employee engagement survey task team, working in partnership with your HR or organizational development (OD) staff, will be invaluable for monitoring feedback while following up and following through on an effective action plan. I suggest managers include a "survey action plan" agenda item during their regular department meetings for a minimum of six months after an engagement survey.

Set the stage for the sequel: a follow-up survey. This means communicating specific actions, successes, and progress since the last survey. Summarizing your successes should be a key part of your overall survey communication plan and be led by your best internal communicators. Of course, if you've developed a vibrant and effective communication plan, you most likely are doing this already!

Don't commit to another survey for 18 to 24 months. Why? You need at least that much time to corral and review survey results, distribute them internally, and act upon them — let alone to see the results of your hard work. If you conduct a follow-up survey too quickly, your organization likely won't have enough time to digest the changes from the previous survey. You may even be setting yourself up for negative results on your follow-up survey. ("I've seen no change yet!")

If you absolutely must conduct a survey earlier — for example, after 12 months — then consider a pulse survey to quickly and inexpensively gauge trends. A *pulse survey* is a short questionnaire, usually 10 to 15 questions, that includes key questions from your larger survey — your "greatest hits," so to speak. Pulse surveys, which usually occur 12 months after a full survey, are primarily for those firms that want to track their progress (or lack thereof) since the initial survey.

Avoid introducing new questions in a pulse survey. Otherwise, you risk losing valuable comparisons with your first survey, which are necessary to gauge your progress.

Exit Only: Conducting Exit Interviews

Exit interviews (interviews conducted with employees who are leaving the company) have long been considered a "gold standard" tool for determining how happy, satisfied, or engaged employees are. Why? Because in contrast with many vague comments often heard in isolation — think "My boss John doesn't really communicate very well," or "Pam plays favorites" — exit interviews often reveal broader themes.

Plus, departing employees may show a greater willingness to share hard examples, such as "John's meetings are always just John talking and never include a chance for us to ask questions or give feedback," or "Did you know Pam is dating one of the employees she's managing? It's resulting in claims of favoritism. Don't be surprised if others quit, too!"

As useful as they may be, exit interviews are trailing indicators, not leading ones. In other words, by the time you uncover an issue in an exit interview, it's too late. The departing employee has already moved on. This metric, while important, assesses disengagement retroactively. That said, in conjunction with opportunities to solicit feedback from employees who are sticking around, healthy cultures have a process in place to conduct exit interviews with departing employees.

Who to interview and who should do the asking

Only conduct exit interviews with employees who have quit voluntarily. Don't conduct exit interviews with employees who have been laid off or terminated due to poor performance. Employees who have been downsized or fired aren't happy campers. Their feedback will be negatively, and perhaps inaccurately, skewed. It's just human nature.

Also, have HR or someone higher up than the employee's direct manager conduct the interview — don't have the employee's manager do it.

Research shows that the number-one reason someone leaves a company is the relationship with his manager. Asking said manager to take the lead in conducting the exit interview removes objectivity. Besides, it's often even more painful for the one being left behind — in this case, the manager. Managers often take an employee's resignation personally. Perhaps the manager was developing the departing employee as her successor and is now bitter about having "wasted her time" mentoring someone who went on to quit. On the other side of the coin, the departing employee understands that the "boss is mad" and doesn't want to risk saying anything to further anger the boss, such as providing feedback about his crummy leadership. Giving some time for emotions to settle down is a good idea in any breakup!

When to conduct an exit interview

Don't conduct an exit interview when emotions are high — that is, shortly after learning of the resignation. Separation is painful, whether between a married couple or a manager and an employee.

Consider conducting the interview 30 days after the employee leaves the firm, when the emotions surrounding the departure have dissipated for all parties. After a month, the employee will have settled into her new job and is more apt to be objective about her experience at your organization. Void of emotion, the feedback is often objective and intellectual.

You may also want to ask the former employee to fill out a written exit questionnaire 60 days after departure. A follow-up questionnaire sent to the departing employee's home address is often a safe way to solicit honest feedback.

If the employee was a valuable one, consider using a delayed exit interview as an opportunity to test whether the grass was, indeed, greener and to plant the seed for a return (and become a boomerang employee!). Former employees are often too proud to admit they've made a mistake in leaving and wouldn't think of picking up the phone and inquiring about coming back. Plus, employees who quit often think their former company is mad at them for leaving; because they're afraid of rejection, they don't reach out to see if a return is possible.

Smart companies understand these natural reactions and take it upon themselves to contact former top employees within 90 days of their departure to inquire about a return. Embedding this inquiry into an exit questionnaire is a safe way for the employer to explore a former employee's interest in returning. As for the former employee, being asked to return not only reveals that the former employer is not angry, but also enables him to save face (*"They called me!"*). The former employee won't have to worry about being perceived as begging to return, with his tail between his legs.

What to ask

Here are some examples of exit-interview questions:

- ✔ Would you describe your work as rewarding/challenging/interesting?
- ✔ Were goals and expectations clearly communicated?

✔ Did you understand how your job was connected to the organization's overall strategy?

✔ Did you understand how to operate successfully within the organization's structure?

✔ Did you understand how to complete your work assignments successfully?

✔ Was your work–life balance satisfactory?

✔ Did you have the materials and equipment needed to perform your job?

✔ Did your work team or colleagues create a positive environment?

✔ Did your co-workers treat you in a positive manner?

✔ Did you receive sufficient communication and information to successfully perform your job?

✔ Do you feel the organization demonstrates high integrity?

✔ Did your manager set realistic performance expectations?

✔ Did your manager lead your team in a positive direction?

✔ Was your manager willing to share relevant communications with you?

✔ Did your manager help find solutions to problems?

✔ Did your manager encourage and manage innovation?

✔ Did your manager demonstrate respect for you as an individual?

✔ Did your manager clearly articulate organization goals?

✔ Did your manager recognize your contributions/accomplishments?

✔ Did you receive timely and accurate performance feedback about your work progress?

✔ Did your manager demonstrate integrity and honesty?

✔ Did your manager adapt to changing circumstances?

✔ Did your manager encourage respect, teamwork, and communication?

✔ If you returned to the company, would you want to work for the same manager?

✔ Are you aware of any compliance issues with federal or state contracts that were not appropriately addressed by either your manager or others within the company? If so, please describe.

✔ Were you provided the necessary development to perform your job?

✔ Was there someone at work who encouraged your growth and development?

✔ Were you provided development opportunities to enhance your performance?

✔ Were advancement opportunities available to you?

✔ If your reason for leaving was a new job, what does this job offer that your position at this company did not? What is the name of the new company?

✔ What did you like best about working at this company?

✔ What did you like least about working at this company?

✔ What would make you interested in returning to work at this company?

Sit! Stay! Conducting Stay Interviews

Sure, exit interviews are helpful. But talking to employees *after* they've made the decision to leave is of limited use. By the time an exit interview reveals an issue, it's too late to correct it. Have you ever thought to yourself, "If only I had known — I could've done something before it was too late!" Well, smart managers avoid this situation by routinely asking their employees how they're doing, why they're staying, and how they might be further engaged.

You can even take things one step further and conduct *stay interviews,* in which a manager asks an employee specific questions relating to the employee's position, company, or level of engagement. Stay interviews enable managers to pinpoint issues *before* an employee decides to leave. Enlightened managers make it a point to conduct stay interviews to stave off resignations down the road.

Don't couple a stay interview with the performance appraisal process. Although some firms weave stay interview questions into performance appraisals for the sake of convenience, you're better off separating these processes, because they serve very different purposes. You may want to conduct stay interviews every year around an employee's anniversary date — perhaps over lunch.

Who to interview and who should do the asking

Conducting stay interviews with the top performers at your firm is particularly important. What drives these people to go above and beyond? This helps you not only to keep these top performers engaged, but also to pinpoint what traits and values these superstars share. This information can be helpful in lots of ways — for example, as you interview new hires. That being said, you shouldn't interview only top performers. You should conduct stay interviews with all your employees to avoid claims of favoritism or discrimination.

Don't outsource this task to HR, your boss, or another member of your team, and be sure to do it in person (as opposed to via e-mail). Your goal is, in part, to show your employees that you — yes, you — care about their well-being.

What to ask in a stay interview

Use a consistent set of questions in all your stay interviews so that you get the same information from each of your employees. The following questions can help you make the most of a stay interview:

- ✔ What about your job makes you jump out of bed in the morning?
- ✔ What about your job makes you hit the snooze button?
- ✔ What aspects of your job do you like the most?
- ✔ What aspects of your job do you like the least?
- ✔ What would make you leave this company for another job?
- ✔ Do you get enough recognition?
- ✔ What kind of recognition would be meaningful for you?
- ✔ Does this company allow you to reach your maximum potential?
- ✔ How can the company help you be more successful in your job?
- ✔ What three things could the company change that would help you realize your potential?
- ✔ If you were to win the lottery and resign, what would you miss the most?
- ✔ What would be the one thing that, if it changed in your current role, would make you consider moving on?
- ✔ What is something new that you'd like to learn this year?

Take a genuine interest in asking these questions. Any hint that you're just following a company form or checking off boxes will result in a lost opportunity.

Measuring Stick: Other Engagement Barometers

There are a few other ways to gauge employee engagement. One is to assess your training investment; another is to track employee referrals.

Assessing your training investment

When you invest in your employees, you generally see an increase in employee engagement scores. Indeed, according to recent research by Dale Carnegie:

- ✔ Fifty-five percent of employees who said they were encouraged to grow and develop new skills were highly engaged in their organization. Conversely, 75 percent of employees who said they were *not* encouraged to grow and develop new skills were fully *disengaged* in their organization.

- ✔ Forty-nine percent of employees who said they received the training needed to do a quality job were fully engaged, while 72 percent of employees who said they did *not* receive the training needed were fully *disengaged.*

- ✔ Sixty percent of employees who said they believe they have opportunities for personal development and growth are fully engaged in their organization. In contrast, 70 percent of employees who do not believe they have opportunities for personal development and growth are fully disengaged in their organization.

To confirm an increase in employee engagement in your own organization, establish a means to track your organization's investment in its employees — for example, training investment as a percentage of your payroll. Best-in-class companies routinely budget 3 percent to 5 percent of payroll for training, and they view this budget as an investment rather than a cost.

That's not to say that more training is always better. For one thing, not every employee warrants training or further investment. Additional investment in employees with attendance issues, on company "corrective action" plans, or with attitude issues may not be justified — at least not until their performance shows improvement.

On a related note, avoid promising a set number of training hours to all employees. ("Here at ABC Company, we provide 40 hours of training per employee per year!") Otherwise, employees may come to view training as an entitlement rather than something to be earned. Besides, promises like that can be difficult to keep, especially in tough economic times. Plus, there are the inevitable differences in potential among your employees. Some high-potential employees may require additional investment to maximize their potential, while others who have capped out in potential may not.

If possible, measure, track, and report training budgets at the department, business unit, store, and location level, and highlight the level of investment being made by business unit. Management should track and monitor training investment to keep an eye on those managers who don't see the benefit of training. These short term–focused managers may be tempted to pad their bottom lines instead of investing in training, kind of like the farmer who eats, rather than plants, his seeds. Some companies even budget and track training and development at the regional, national, and/or corporate level to prevent this from happening.

Tracking employee referrals

As I mention in Chapter 2, according to a 2012 study by the Temkin Group, highly engaged employees are 370 percent more likely to recommend their company as an employer. It stands to reason, then, that if your employees are engaged, they're more likely to refer you as a great employer than employees who are *not* engaged.

Track employee referrals by department or profit center. You'll likely find that departments with engaged employees spend less on recruitment advertising, search firms, and so on because they rely on their engaged employees to refer yet more engaged employees to join their department. Less engaged business units have to rely on more costly and less effective advertising and search techniques because they aren't getting good referrals.

Chapter 4

Motivation Nation: Engagement and Motivation

A key aspect of engagement is *motivation* — why people do what they do. A person may be motivated by any number of things: to attain status or money, to help others, to find meaning in life, or simply to express herself.

In this chapter, I explain the difference between someone who's motivated intrinsically and someone who's motivated extrinsically. Then I fill you in on key drivers of intrinsic motivation (in case you hadn't guessed, this is the kind you're after). I introduce you to Maslow's hierarchy of needs and tell you how you can use it to engage your employees. Finally, I show you how you can motivate your employees by fostering a learning culture. Motivated to find out more? Read on!

Outie or Innie? Understanding Extrinsic versus Intrinsic Motivation

According to psychology types, there are two types of motivation:

✔ **Extrinsic (external) motivation:** Extrinsic motivation comes from outside a person. For employees, the most obvious form of extrinsic motivation is money. Every paid job on this planet involves extrinsic motivation, whether in the form of salary, tips, commission, benefits, stock options, bribes, table scraps, or some combination thereof.

Another example of extrinsic motivation is the threat of punishment. For example, an employee who regularly shows up late will be fired; so, fear of being fired may serve as an extrinsic motivation.

Companies often use extrinsic motivation to encourage specific behaviors, such as competitiveness or punctuality. When people talk about engaged employees having both their heads and their hearts in their jobs, extrinsic motivation is the "head" part of that equation.

✔ **Intrinsic (internal) motivation:** Intrinsic motivation comes from within. It's driven by a personal interest or enjoyment in the task itself. For example, suppose you enjoy playing the pan flute, and you want to improve your skills. That's an example of an intrinsic motivation. You don't want to become a better pan-flute player so you can be a world-famous musician — you simply want, for your own personal reasons, to improve your pan-flute skills because you enjoy playing the pan flute.

With intrinsic motivation, the result is often growth — for example, growth as an intellectual journey or growth due to challenges that have been overcome. When people talk about engaged employees having both their heads and their hearts in their jobs, intrinsic motivation is the "heart" part of that equation.

Both extrinsic and intrinsic motivation play a role in building a culture of engagement. Obviously, extrinsic motivation (in the form of money) is important — after all, people need to be paid in order to put food on the table. But intrinsic motivation plays an even greater part in the world of employee engagement.

The fact is, intrinsically motivated employees are more likely to be engaged in what they're doing than their counterparts who rely only on extrinsic motivation

I second that emotion

Dale Carnegie research identified emotions that tend to raise levels of engagement, as well as emotions that tend to cause disengagement. Specifically, employees said their engagement levels were higher when their supervisors made them feel valued, confident, enthusiastic, inspired, and empowered. In contrast, employees also said their level of *disengagement* increased when their supervisors made them feel disinterested, manipulated, uncomfortable, irritated, upset, or intimidated. Emotions are intrinsic by nature, but much of what managers do extrinsically creates an environment that builds positive emotions (leading to engagement) or negative emotions (leading to disengagement).

Gordon Gekko was wrong: A word on organizational greed

Remember last month, when you drove to work in a downpour? You parked in the Siberia lot and scurried what felt like a quarter-mile to your building, umbrella turned inside-out by the wind, pelted by rain, dodging puddles the size of small lakes — only to see your company president ease his Porsche into a sheltered executive spot 12 feet from the front door. Did this make you want to rush to your work area and start cranking out discretionary effort?

If your goal is to increase employee engagement, you *must* stamp out any internal perception of organizational greed. Quite simply, your employees are fed up with executives receiving million-dollar bonuses, access to company jets, and other perks (read: executive parking spaces) that shout out, "We're more important than you are!"

Although employees understand that higher-ups will earn more than the rank and file, they resent the class systems that flourish as a result of organizational greed. Engaged cultures understand that organizational greed is not sustainable and will ultimately lead to an erosion of engagement and talent — or in extreme cases, the extinction of your business.

Oh — and those executive parking spaces? Eliminating those is sure to result in an almost instantaneous spike in engagement.

to put a spring in their step. Moreover, intrinsically motivated employees are more likely to go above and beyond — to put in that discretionary effort.

Interestingly, as noted by author Daniel H. Pink in his book *Drive: The Surprising Truth About What Motivates Us* (Riverhead), organizations that place too much emphasis on extrinsic rewards often discover their employees do *less*. In addition, over-reliance on extrinsic rewards often leads to undesirable behaviors and an erosion of any intrinsic behaviors. For proof, look no further than the financial market collapse of 2008–2009, during which there were countless examples of what happens when the focus shifts disproportionately to personal and organizational rewards. As we now know, at the root of the collapse of our financial institutions were countless examples of organizational greed made worse by a systematic lack of organizational and regulatory checks and balances.

Key Club: Identifying Key Intrinsic Motivational Drivers

The key to building an engaged workforce is putting in place the necessary measurement and reward systems to capture employees' extrinsic motivation, while also understanding the unique intrinsic drivers that motivate each of your employees. Often, these intrinsic motivational drivers will differ from person to person, so you need to get to know your employees well enough to understand their intrinsic motivational drivers.

In this section, I cover seven key intrinsic motivators, identified by combing through massive amounts of literature, studies, theories, concepts, and strategies on intrinsic motivation. (You may recognize some of these motivators if you're familiar with the work of Cynthia Berryman-Fink and Charles B. Fink, authors of *The Manager's Desk Reference* [AMACOM].)

Although all employees have some element of each of these seven drivers in their DNA, most have one primary motivational driver and one or two secondary motivational drivers. Some industries and/or occupations tend to draw certain motivational drivers. The example occupations listed here are not all-inclusive — you can find all types of drivers within all occupations and industries.

The seven motivational drivers are as follows:

- **Achievement:** Employees with this driver want the satisfaction of completing projects successfully. They want to exercise their talents to attain success. They're self-motivated if the job is challenging enough. Employees who are willing — in fact, *longing* — to take on that *stretch assignment* (a project or task given to an employee that is beyond his current knowledge or skill level, designed to "stretch" the employee in order to learn and grow) or to relocate for that promotion would most likely list "achievement" as their primary motivational driver, as would high achievers and many C-suite executives. Common occupations for people motivated by achievement include executive director, professional athlete, sales professional, CEO, inventor, scientist, and entrepreneur.

- **Authority:** Employees with this driver get satisfaction from influencing and sometimes even controlling others. They like to lead and persuade, and are motivated by positions of power and leadership. Individuals motivated by authority are those who volunteer to be project manager, lead the project team, and/or take on more direct reports. If you've ever served on a jury, the person who volunteered to be the foreman was most likely motivated by authority. Common occupations for people motivated by authority may include project manager, politician, and law enforcement officer.

- **Camaraderie:** Employees with this driver are satisfied through affiliation with others. They enjoy people and find the social aspect of the workplace rewarding. If you're looking for individuals to fill a task team, be on a committee, or participate in this year's charity campaign, your volunteers most likely will be those who are motivated by camaraderie. These are the same people who volunteer to be on your town's recreation committee or help plan the annual food drive for your local church.

(Of course, the person who volunteers to *lead* the food drive probably has camaraderie as a secondary motivational driver, with authority as the primary one.) Be careful if you're hiring or promoting someone who is motivated by camaraderie to start a new location as a one-person office or to work remotely. Odds are, he won't flourish. Common occupations for people motivated by camaraderie include HR professional, healthcare professional, hotel and restaurant worker, nonprofit professional, and other service industry positions.

✔ **Independence:** Employees with this driver want freedom and independence. They like to work and take responsibility for their own tasks and projects. When looking for employees to work at home, relocate to a remote location, or work in isolation to complete a project, you would be wise to select individuals whose primary motivational driver is independence. Common occupations for people motivated by independence include entrepreneur, freelancer, tradesperson (for example, electricians, plumbers, or carpenters), and research scientist.

✔ **Esteem:** Employees with this driver need sincere recognition and praise. They dislike generalities — they want praise for specific accomplishments. (Note that they don't necessarily require *public* praise.) You would want employees motivated by esteem on your new task team that will present its findings to the executive team. Experts who volunteer their time to share their knowledge via brown-bag luncheons, webinars, and so on are motivated by esteem. Common occupations for people motivated by esteem include training and development professional, politician, nonprofit professional, author, actor, and comedian.

✔ **Safety/security:** Employees with this driver crave job security, a steady income, health insurance, other fringe benefits, and a hazard-free work environment. These employees always worry about getting let go. They may even refuse pay increases for fear that their salaries will become so high that they'll be on the radar on the next round of layoffs. Common occupations for people motivated by safety and security include clergyperson, government personnel, military personnel, utility worker, and union worker.

✔ **Fairness:** Employees with this driver simply want to be treated fairly. They probably compare their own work hours, job duties, salary, and privileges to those of other employees to ensure they're getting a fair shake. If they perceive inequities, they'll quickly become discouraged. Employees motivated by fairness pay attention to how much you pay new employees, what their bonus was compared to others, and whose turn it is to be invited to the senior management team meeting. Common occupations for people motivated by fairness include accountant, payroll personnel, and human resources professional.

If you want to increase engagement among your employees, you'll want to develop a good sense of their internal drivers. How can you do that? Well, why not ask them? At your next department meeting, explain the seven motivational drivers (including how we all have elements of all seven within us), and ask them to write down what they believe to be their primary and secondary drivers. Then have them list what they think are the primary and secondary drivers of their teammates. Emphasize that there are no "wrong" answers. Finally, give team members the opportunity to share their drivers if they want. This entertaining and revealing exercise may lead to some surprises, and will enable the members of your team to better understand each other. After the meeting, follow up with team members individually to discuss their motivations in more detail. This will help you determine how best to engage them.

A No-Malarkey Hierarchy: Putting Maslow's Hierarchy of Needs to Work for You

Maslow's hierarchy of needs is a psychology theory posed by Abraham Maslow in his 1943 paper, "A Theory of Human Motivation." According to this theory, all people have needs that must be satisfied. Maslow used a pyramid to describe and categorize these needs, as shown in Figure 4-1. Needs on the bottom of the pyramid must be met before needs on the next level can be addressed.

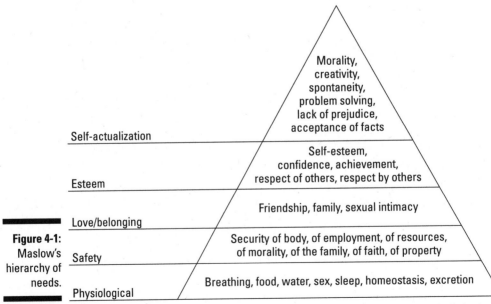

Figure 4-1: Maslow's hierarchy of needs.

Illustration by Wiley, Composition Services Graphics

Circular reasoning: Overlapping the three key circles

If your goal is to motivate employees and help them to become self-actualized, *and* you like a good Venn diagram, then you'll appreciate what I call a "three circles" diagram. As you probably guessed, this diagram has three circles (see the nearby figure):

✔ **The first circle represents what the employee likes to do.** Engaged employees sincerely like the job they're doing. They want to do a good job and grow in their positions.

✔ **The second circle represents what the employee is good at.** Beyond the need and desire to do a particular job, an engaged employee has or obtains — then continuously improves — the necessary skills.

✔ **The third circle represents what needs to get done.** Obviously, companies employ people to perform certain functions or duties, and those functions and duties must be fulfilled.

The more these circles overlap, the more engaged the employee will be. For example, if an employee really likes filing *and* the employee has a knack for it *and* it needs to get done, then you have a recipe for an intrinsically motivated employee who is reaching the top of Maslow's pyramid.

Of course, what a person enjoys may not always entirely coincide with what he's good at doing. Take me, for example. I love playing golf. However, I'm not any good at it. (As my three lifelong golf buddies would say, I stink.) Conversely, I don't particularly enjoy cranking through spreadsheets, but for whatever reason, I seem to have an aptitude for it. Add to that the fact that not many organizations really need a guy on staff to walk the back nine with a laptop open to Microsoft Excel, and you have three circles whose point of intersection is smaller than Bill Belichick's tie collection. In other words, if the goal here is to improve engagement, there's some work to do!

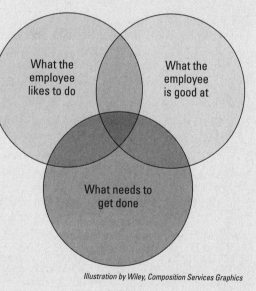

What the employee likes to do

What the employee is good at

What needs to get done

Illustration by Wiley, Composition Services Graphics

Here are the five levels in Maslow's hierarchy of needs, and how you can apply them to the workplace to engage your employees:

- ✔ **Psychological:** To survive, people need air, food, water, sleep, and so on. How does this relate to employee engagement? Employees need a comfortable work environment. If your employees work in conditions of extreme hot or cold, they probably won't advance to the next level in the pyramid — they simply won't have the motivation. Similarly, employees need access to such things as restroom breaks, food, drinks, and so on.

- ✔ **Safety:** People must feel that they, their family, their property, and other resources are safe. When it comes to the workplace, if employees have to worry about their personal safety (for example, getting hurt or sick at work) or their professional security (read: losing their jobs), morale will suffer. Ensuring a safe workplace may include providing ergonomic furniture and/or securing the building. Job security is also key.

- ✔ **Love/belonging:** Not surprisingly, creating a sense of belonging is a key aspect of building an engaged culture. In its highly regarded Q^{12}, which is a measure of employee engagement, Gallup includes the following question: "Do you have a best friend at work?" Why does this question matter? Because based on Gallup's research, employees who answer in the affirmative are more likely to be engaged than those who don't. This is directly attributed to Maslow's third level of love and belonging. Companies with a history of social and other camaraderie-building activities have higher degrees of employee engagement than companies that are all business, all the time.

Although employee perks like ping-pong tables and beer-cart Fridays are not employee engagement drivers in and of themselves (instead, they're satisfiers), they do help create an atmosphere of love and belonging.

- ✔ **Esteem:** Esteem is a person's belief that she is doing a good job and that her contributions are recognized. People want to feel that they're achieving and that their contributions matter and are recognized. Confidence is key. Any educator or coach will tell you, if a student or player has confidence, that person will shine. The same principle holds true in the workplace. If employees believe in themselves — and believe (thanks to recognition) that others believe in them — they'll be more engaged and productive.

Employee recognition is a key part of engagement. At its core, recognition builds esteem. Unfortunately, even though recognition has so much impact — and is often free — it remains low on most companies' list of priorities. (For more on employee recognition, see Chapter 17.)

- ✔ **Self-actualization:** In the workplace, self-actualization translates to maximizing one's true potential. Employees want to be the very best at what they do, and the manager's job is to help them realize that. With self-actualization, employees feel trusted and empowered — in control of their jobs and their futures.

A key aspect of self-actualization is ensuring that employees are only put in positions for which they are capable. Sure, employees should feel challenged, but you don't want them to be in over their heads. Ultimately, this erodes engagement, as employees begin to doubt themselves. The three circles discussed in the nearby sidebar are a great way for managers to ensure that their employees are positioned to excel and, therefore, become self-actualized.

You can't fully engage your employees if the employees' needs aren't being satisfied. For example, during a companywide layoff, engagement levels will be low. Even star employees who are at no risk of losing their jobs will worry. Why? Because the layoff has resulted in a failure to meet employees' level-two needs: safety and security. Employees don't feel secure. Even employees who know that their jobs are safe will worry about the company's future. (This explains why companies often see a spike in voluntary turnover after a companywide layoff. When people feel their jobs or employer is no longer secure, they often look for new opportunities to regain their sense of security.)

A healthy, fully engaged workforce is one that has collectively reached level five, or self-actualization. This occurs in organizations that have built a line of sight between where the company is going and each employee's job or role. Level five is where you win over employees' heads *and* hearts. *Fortune* magazine's annual Top 100 Best Companies to Work For is full of companies that have reached level five.

Unfortunately, we're not all so lucky to work for such enlightened companies. Therefore, it's incumbent on managers to really get to know their employees so they can maximize their engagement. The old "Treat people the way you want to be treated" rule no longer applies. These days, it's "Treat people the way *they* want to be treated." That means knowing what motivates them.

A Yearn to Learn: Fostering a Learning Culture

In 2013, SilkRoad, a cloud-based talent management solutions provider, asked 2,200 global clients, "What are the best mechanisms to foster employee engagement?" Not surprisingly, four of the top seven answers pertained to career development and learning opportunities. The power of career development, learning, and growth opportunities in improving engagement was also confirmed in the Dale Carnegie research referenced in Chapter 3.

It's quite simple: If you help your employees develop their skills by offering them learning opportunities, you'll increase employee engagement. Employees become engaged when they see a line of sight between where their career is today and where it's going. Managers who help employees get there will see a spike in the engagement of those being developed.

There's an old training adage that perhaps says it best:

> Non-enlightened manager: "If I train my employees, they might leave."

> Enlightened manager: "Would you rather *not* train them and have them stay?"

Managers who build a culture of learning understand that investing in employees today pays dividends tomorrow. A culture of learning can encompass many forms of education, including traditional classroom training and workshops, conferences and seminars, stretch assignments, job rotation, tuition reimbursement, internal transfers, and the growing trends of e-learning and web-based training.

Not only does a culture of learning improve employees' skills, but it also increases their engagement. Think back to your favorite job. Did you love it because you had a great boss? Possibly. Was it because you adored your colleagues? Maybe. Or was it because you weren't bored? Probably. The fact is, it's impossible for employees who are bored in their jobs, who feel they aren't advancing, or who aren't learning new skills to maintain high levels of engagement.

Organizations that invest in creating a learning culture are more likely to sustain high engagement. There is a reason General Electric has been a market leader for more than a hundred years: It invests millions of dollars in its various training and development initiatives. It isn't surprising that GE was again listed by *Fortune* as one of the "World's Most Admired Companies" in 2012, or by *Chief Executive* as one of the "Best Companies for Leaders" the same year.

In creating a culture of learning, it helps to assess the following:

✔ **Are employees challenged in their day-to-day work? What would provide more challenge?** In some occupations, continually thinking of new ways to challenge the troops is a constant struggle. Managers who oversee call centers or manufacturing environments often wrestle with challenging their employees. These managers need to introduce job rotation, incentives for process improvements, and task team involvement to minimize the boredom that often comes with these types of positions. Job rotation is particularly critical for Millennials, who are especially prone to changing jobs. If they're going to quit sooner rather than later anyway, why not let them "quit" but stay in the company? Job rotation allows them to do just that.

✔ **Are employees receiving the right amount of training?** To find out, conduct stay interviews (see Chapter 3). Employee engagement surveys are another great way to gauge how your employees perceive their development — especially if you benchmark your results against others in your industry. If you see that your competitors are investing more in the development of their people, that's a strong indication that they may be doing a better job than your firm of building their workforce of tomorrow.

✔ **Where do you see your employees in two to three years? What about in three to five years?** These questions are simple, yet powerful. Ambition is a competency that you should measure. Managers can often gauge their employees' level of ambition and whether they're being challenged in their current roles by asking these forward-looking questions.

Note, however, that some employees don't seek or need new challenges and opportunities in order to be engaged. These employees find enrichment in their current job, see no need to change, and have no hunger to take on new challenges. A perfect example is an enthusiastic and helpful receptionist who, despite 25 years on the job, is *always* engaged. This person is fulfilled by meeting new people, helping them as best she can, and being the "first face" of the company!

✔ **What nomenclature are you using to describe training in your organization?** Companies should swap the phrase *training and development* for the simpler *learning* to better describe the way employees develop in today's workplace.

✔ **Who else should employees be learning from within the organization?** Companies should communicate to all employees who their internal functional, technical, market, customer, and/or geographical experts are, and encourage those smarty-pants to host "lunch and learn" events. ("If you feed them, they will come" is a popular training adage that always holds true. Springing for pizza is a sure-fire way to increase attendance.)

✔ **Would a certain employee be a candidate for a company committee or task team?** Is there a national or international initiative in which an employee is interested in participating? As I've said, a great by-product of employee engagement is discretionary effort. Inviting employees to join internal task teams and/or committees is a great way to tap into this discretionary effort to solve a company problem or launch a new initiative.

Avoid appointing or assigning people to committees. Instead, have them volunteer. An employee is far more likely to be engaged in a committee if he really cares about the committee's charter. Also, avoid inviting the same people (a.k.a., your very best employees) to join every committee. If you do, you risk committee fatigue, which will tax their engagement. Chances are, they're already your busiest employees, and they may not positively perceive their nomination to your committee! That said, when seeking volunteers, do validate their capabilities by having their boss endorse their nomination. Nothing is more deflating for a committee than having fellow committee members be fired for performance issues or quit the company before their committee tenure is up.

Chapter 5

Talk to Me! The Importance of Communication

Saying communication is "important to engagement" is a little like saying Mardi Gras is "kind of exciting." It's an understatement. Indeed, communication is *so* important, I often call it the cornerstone of an engaged culture. There's no doubt about it: Communication helps drive most successful new company initiatives, ideas, and ventures. Unfortunately, it's also at the root of many organizational failures, boss–employee issues, and problems with disengagement.

This chapter focuses on the importance of communication both generally and in your engagement efforts, and the obstacles to achieving excellent communication. It also provides simple, practical methods for cascading the company message from upper management down through the ranks in ways that are clear, concise, and compelling — and that will result in higher engagement, and therefore higher discretionary effort, on the part of staff.

Mind the Gap: The Great Organizational Communication Fissure

In many organizations, there is a disconnect between leaders and employees. This fissure is at the root of many communication problems in organizations today. For management, the disconnect centers around the question "Why aren't employees onboard?" For employees, the question is, "What are those idiots doing now?" This disconnect is often a key factor in disengagement.

A few years back, while at the start of a 5K running race, I was reminded of this organizational fissure. Given my running prowess (or lack thereof), I was slated to start near the tail end of the field of 12,000 runners. I never heard the starting gun; I was too far back. I only learned we were off and running by rumor. Whereas the runners at the front of the pack hit the ground running (so to speak), those of us in the back merely shuffled forward.

It reminded me a lot of how information is communicated in some organizations. The CEO and other executives hear the starting gun — or, in many cases, are the ones firing it. Just like the elite runners at the front of the pack, leadership is at the front of the communication pipeline. When an important change is communicated, leadership has time to weigh alternatives, debate options, and digest the decision.

The rank and file employees, relegated to the back of the field, are not afforded the same depth of background, and may be unaware of how much time leadership has invested in the decision. When communication about a decision or change finally reaches them, employees inevitably wonder, "What are they thinking?!" They don't hit the ground running; they merely shuffle forward. Then, when employees are hesitant to jump onboard, leaders lose patience. They ask, "Why don't they get it?!"

Unfortunately, this communication pattern results in a lack of alignment. After all, if a company neglects to articulate a clear vision, it can hardly expect its employees to invest more than the bare minimum. In one oft-quoted study, conducted by Robert S. Kaplan and David P. Norton in 2001, a mere 7 percent of employees reported that they fully understood their company's business strategies and what was expected of them in order to help achieve the company's goals.

Companies that successfully engage their employees don't allow this to happen. Employers or leaders who articulate a clear vision and strategy will find that employees will help them reach their goals quickly and efficiently. Indeed, according to recent research by Dale Carnegie Training, employees indicated that working in a company that encourages open communication with senior leadership has a significant impact on their level of engagement. To cultivate an engaged culture, open and consistent communication must become part of the air your employees breathe.

Two-Way Street: Establishing Two-Way Communication

Communication starts at the top, with the CEO, president, or other appropriate executive. But in order for clear communication to become part of your corporate culture — and make no mistake, this is absolutely critical for engagement to take hold — there must be a process by which the message is cascaded down and reinforced by every level of management. The goal is to align what the CEO or other executives say with what line managers tell their direct reports. This takes time, repetition, and leveraging of available communication options.

In a *cascade communications strategy* (sometimes known as a *waterfall communications strategy*), the buck stops (or, more precisely, the message starts) with upper management. But the responsibility for communication is shared across every level, from the region to the district to the office to the line manager. No one individual, committee, or department should be placed in charge of disseminating information throughout the company (although there are many professionals who are highly skilled at greasing the gears of communication and finding creative ways to broadcast and publicize individual messages). The key is to make every leader a message ambassador, and every management level responsible for informing the next.

Eventually, this will happen as effortlessly as water pouring over a waterfall. But it will require some initial effort on your part, and ongoing vigilance. Keep these points in mind:

✔ **Identify your communications ambassadors.** Your initial recruits will be employees with management responsibility, and their duties will include transmitting company messages. Let them know that their performance in this arena will be evaluated — and follow up on that promise.

✔ **Enlist other engaged employees.** Provide a forum for their input and give them well-defined communications tasks within their peer groups (and beyond, if appropriate).

✔ **Supply direct channels and appropriate tools.** Every important message from the top should be accompanied, at minimum, by general talking points for managers at all levels, an (anticipated) FAQ, and a means by which unanticipated questions will be answered and publicized.

✔ **Scale your tools to fit the task at hand.** If a large-scale announcement or rollout needs to be communicated, look closely at the available vehicles and explore new options if necessary. Engage your communications ambassadors to find the most appropriate communication methods for your staff. And don't overlook the need to customize your communication approach depending on the audience. Your Gen Y staff members require a very different communication approach than your Boomers.

If you're worried that communication will add to the workload of already-harried line managers, the answer is to communicate effectively with *them*. Equip them with the information and tools they need to be effective message ambassadors, and let them know precisely what is expected: alignment with, and wide and frequent distribution of, the top-line message.

The bottom line? According to recent research by Dale Carnegie Training, employees are more highly engaged when their immediate manager communicates openly with them, recognizes their contribution, and gives feedback and encouragement that enhance their job performance.

"The Matrix is everywhere": Communicating in a matrix world

Does this sound familiar? "I have one boss who tells me one thing, and another boss who tells me something else!" Or, "Who reports to whom around here?" Or, "How do I get anything done when my team members all report to different people?" Or, "No one knows who is responsible anymore!" If so, you're likely living in the matrix. No, not the one with Keanu Reeves, where a malevolent cyber-intelligence harvests humans' essence to dominate the world. Instead, you're dealing with a matrix organization, in which employees may report to two or more bosses. For example, say you work as a cost accountant. You may report to a member of your regional leadership team, but also to someone in the corporate finance department.

How effectively a matrix organization functions often depends on how healthy the communication channels are between the key players. To ensure clear communication in a matrixed organization, keep these points in mind:

✔ Establish the "rules of communication" when the matrix is first established or when a new participant enters the matrix.

✔ Establish a schedule in which the three parties will meet to discuss goals, objectives, and so on.

✔ Everyone involved should make it a habit to copy all other parties on messages to ensure everyone is in the loop.

✔ Decide early on which boss will communicate key organizational changes. This person should also take the lead in performance appraisals.

In addition to communication waterfalls, for top-down communication, you also need *communication fountains* — that is, vehicles to propel communication from the bottom up. For engagement to truly take hold, employees must feel comfortable communicating upward.

Generally, this type of communication will come in one of two forms:

- ✓ **Questions:** Managers at all levels must answer questions in such a way that the overarching message is reinforced. If the answer is beyond a manager's knowledge, he must push the question to the next level while assuring the questioner that an answer is forthcoming. (Of course, it's important to deliver on this promise. The responsibility lies with the manager who has posed the question to his superiors.)

- ✓ **Feedback:** Whether it's positive or negative, managers must be provided a means by which to funnel employee input to the people responsible for processing and, if warranted, incorporating it. Employee engagement surveys, conducted biannually, with a pulse survey in the alternative years, are one mechanism to ensure that this happens. Communicating those results back is the way to complete the loop. Companies that establish a continuous feedback loop between themselves and their employees virtually guarantee alignment.

Communication cannot be one way, and calls for feedback must be genuine. A company where employees feel comfortable participating in a dialogue with anyone, anytime, however senior, is a company well on its way to an engaged culture. If individuals are afraid to approach higher-ups with questions or feedback, or if they sense that their questions and feedback are not being addressed at the appropriate level, engagement will suffer. Moreover, having good feedback mechanisms in place is the only way to ensure that any engagement initiatives you've undertaken are the right ones, are progressing, and are embraced and supported by management and staff.

Bob the Builder: Building a Communication Protocol

I've never met a manager who says they shouldn't communicate openly and frequently with their employees — but often they don't. See, for many managers, communication falls in the category of "should do" rather than "must do." And when we're busy, "must do" trumps "should do" every time.

Implementing innovation boxes

Here's one great idea that, by itself, will make your purchase of this book worthwhile: Eliminate suggestion boxes. See, suggestion boxes often lead to complaints. In other words, people don't use them to suggest ways to improve your business; instead, they use them to carp about receiving too many e-mails, criticize the cafeteria fare, or grumble about having too many layers of management. Instead, provide innovation boxes. You'll quickly find that instead of receiving complaints, you'll wind up with innovative ideas and suggestions for improving processes.

To close the loop, assemble a cross-sectional group of junior-level to midlevel employees to evaluate ideas from the innovation box (have them use the idea priority matrix discussed in Chapter 2) and send the best ones up the ladder. Assuming the organization's leadership actually listens to these ideas and implements them when possible, this can be a great engagement driver! And in time, membership on the committee will be seen as a great honor.

That's where a communication protocol comes in. A *communication protocol* is a formal process that outlines the types of information to be communicated to an organization, as well as identifying the person(s) responsible for communicating particular topics. The protocol also outlines the audience, frequency, and suggested communication vehicles.

A communication protocol, which should be displayed in all common areas such as lobbies and conference rooms and distributed to all new hires, ensures that communications align with the company's key strategic priorities, whether they be related to engagement or some other initiative. As importantly, the protocol represents a set of company commitments to employees. These include the following:

- ✔ Leaders will be held accountable for fulfilling their communication responsibilities, and will be assessed on the effectiveness and timeliness of their communication.

- ✔ Employees will receive regular updates about the progress, initiatives, and changes that affect them.

- ✔ Most important from an engagement perspective, each communication milestone provides opportunities for employees to ask questions, contribute ideas, and give or receive feedback.

In turn, the expectations for employees are clear. All employees are responsible for sharing information and giving feedback to help the company reach its goals, thereby reinforcing the desire for employees to communicate "up" and bolstering the mutual commitment shared by employer and employee.

There are several benefits to implementing a communication protocol. A communication protocol does all the following:

- ✔ Defines communication expectations for both employees and leaders.

- ✔ Builds consistency in communicating the firm's mission, vision, values, and strategy.

- ✔ Creates alignment with employees at all levels.

- ✔ Builds in circular communication. Circular communication includes communication between those in a traditional hierarchy, such as the boss and subordinate, as well as communication between business units and departments and communication that leverages task teams and focus groups. In a healthy circular communication culture, you're also including 360 feedback assessments (discussed in Chapter 16), customer feedback, and feedback within the matrix relationship.

- ✔ Ensures shared accountability, from top to bottom.

- ✔ Helps ensure that messages are communicated 13 times, which is the number of times some experts believe an employee needs to hear something to absorb it.

- ✔ Helps to leverage different communication venues and tools — for example, town hall meetings, e-mails, vlogs (video blogs), department meetings, and so on. (You can find out more about these venues and tools later in this chapter.)

- ✔ Helps connect all levels of your organization with your brand.

To build a communication protocol, you need a cross-sectional team of executives (preferably including the "top dog") along with a cross-sectional group of key influencers, or *connectors*. The first thing this team should do is assemble a draft of the communication protocol. (This will take the group anywhere from two to eight hours.) Figure 5-1 shows a template for teams in this phase to help guide them in their efforts.

	Message	Communicator	Audience	Frequency

Figure 5-1: A communication protocol template.

When drafting the protocol, the team should consider the following:

- ✔ How can we build in the communication of metrics that are key to our strategic plan (for example, growth, profit, employee engagement, customer service, quality, and so on)?
- ✔ How can we ensure that staff are given an opportunity to communicate up?
- ✔ How can we build in redundancy in messaging between each level?

When the draft is complete, it should be sent to those who report up through the CEO (and perhaps their direct reports as well) to obtain additional input. This key step will also help you get buy-in. Once the input has been received and appropriated, the protocol can be finalized (see Figure 5-2).

	Message	Communicator	Audience	Frequency
Day-to-Day Operations	Strategic plan Regular business reporting	CEO	All	Monthly Quarterly Annually
	Strategic plan Strategic activities Regional news Performance to date	Regional manager	Regional staff	Monthly Semi-annually
	Strategic activities Office news Performance to date Information sharing	Office managers and managing directors	Office/department staff	Quarterly
	Strategic activities Department news Performance to date Information sharing	Department manager/team leader	Department staff	Weekly
	Project news and updates Technology and innovation sharing	Project managers	Project team	Weekly
Corporate/Strategic Direction	Strategic plan	CEO	Executive committee	Bi-monthly
	Strategic plan Market updates	CSO	All	Semi-annually
	Market updates Strategic actions Information sharing	Market/service leaders	Market/service practitioners	Quarterly
	Strategic plan Senior strategic direction Business health	CEO/operations group chair Corporate leaders (finance, legal, HR, IT, marketing, facilities)	Operations group	Quarterly
Governance	Governance issues	Board of directors	Stockholders	Annually

Figure 5-2: Sample communication protocol.

Illustration by Wiley, Composition Services Graphics

A word on charisma

Of course, some people are just naturally better at communicating than others. For every charismatic Steve Jobs at the helm, there may be ten more introverted Bill Gateses. This is not to say that charisma is the be-all and end-all of great leadership. Indeed, there are plenty of examples in every field — even politics — where quiet brilliance and a keen business sense has served better than any amount of charm or eloquence. Still, in successful enterprises of all sizes, more often than not, leaders who know communication is not their strong suit still find ways to leverage their talent to disseminate big messages at all levels.

Smart leaders know that what they themselves may not be able to articulate in the most compelling way can gain power as it filters through the ranks of the passionate. All that being said, while certain people are better communicators than others, this does not diminish anyone's responsibility to communicate. Those for whom consistent, frequent, and genuine communication do not come easily must be given the tools to succeed — and held accountable regardless of their personal preferences or comfort zones.

With a finalized protocol in hand, the team's next move is to build a plan to roll out the protocol. This rollout should involve significant fanfare to generate excitement. *Remember:* The launch of a communication protocol is great news, and will be embraced by employees as, to quote Martha Stewart, "a good thing." That being said, you'll likely meet resistance from middle management, who will likely view the protocol as "one more thing to do that takes time." To overcome this roadblock, educate them on the protocol's benefits as well as on how to be an engaged participant in the protocol. Over time, they'll see that the administrative effort involved in maintaining a robust communication protocol will be offset by the gain in their employees' alignment and engagement.

Tool Time: Maximizing the Various Communication Tools

Never before in the course of human history have we had more communication tools available to us. Where before we were limited to grunting and sharing our thoughts via cave paintings, now we have any number of ways to express ourselves. This section covers the myriad communication vehicles available to you, and helps you determine which vehicle is most likely to engage your employees.

Face to face

At the end of the day, nothing beats good, old-fashioned, face-to-face communication. Why? Because face time eliminates assumptions, allows for body language, and enables real-time give and take.

This medium is almost always the most effective way to communicate. It's especially important for receiving feedback, performing annual employee reviews, and resolving conflicts. And it's the *only* way to communicate when delivering bad news. (I've heard plenty of horror stories of managers firing employees via a voice mail or e-mail. Ouch!) Face-to-face communication is also a wonderful way to share good news. Once, I received a bonus check accompanied only by a yellow sticky note on the envelope with the word *Thanks* on it. Talk about an opportunity lost!

Engaged managers can leverage face-to-face communication by implementing an open-door policy, engaging in drop-bys, having face-to-face meetings with direct reports, and planning periodic face-to-face meetings with remote or telecommuting employees. Face-to-face meetings can be one-on-one, with the entire team, or in a town-hall format, and can be ad hoc, formal, scheduled, and/or unscheduled.

One-on-one meetings

One-on-one meetings are a time for you to focus on an employee and his or her needs. As such, you should follow the 80/20 rule: Listen 80 percent of the time, and talk 20 percent of the time. To ensure the employee doesn't feel she's being given short shrift, schedule more time than expected. For example, if you think the meeting will take 30 minutes, put 45 minutes on your calendar. And of course, make sure there are no distractions. Meet in a private room (an office or a meeting room with a door), and turn off your phone and computer. If time and logistics allow, perhaps meet for lunch offsite.

For best results, prepare an agenda beforehand, with objectives for the meeting. Key topics may include the employees' roles and responsibilities on the team, performance goals, strengths and challenges, concerns and issues, and professional development and opportunities.

Team and department meetings

For many organizations, weekly or bi-weekly team and department meetings are the communication bloodline for employees. They help establish department expectations and goals, and provide an opportunity to celebrate good news and recognize staff.

If possible, these meetings should be face to face. If you have remote employees, make sure they participate, even if only virtually. If possible, schedule time for remote employees to occasionally attend in person.

On the topic of virtual meetings, be aware that these lack the visual cues found in face-to-face meetings, even when conducted using such visual services as Skype. (Sure, people may be able to see your face, but your body language may be hidden.) As such, they require more concentration when listening, more care when speaking, and more rules for structure.

A great way to boost engagement at department meetings is to rotate the meeting "chair" among department employees. The meeting chair establishes the agenda (with guidelines from the boss, of course), runs the meeting, and captures minutes and actions. In addition to boosting engagement, this is a great way to evaluate the leadership capabilities of staff and to foster innovation.

Town hall meetings

Whenever a manager needs to deliver a consistent message to a large number of employees, town hall meetings are a great way to go. That being said, the town hall format often discourages employees from participating in any sort of Q&A. Indeed, in large town hall–type settings, I'm hard-pressed to think of a circumstance in which honest, insightful questions are likely to result.

To avoid hearing crickets when you open up the floor for questions, try soliciting questions in advance. That way, if they aren't brought up during the course of the meeting, you can address them anyway. Also, before you show up, do what you can to learn about the specific concerns of your audience.

One more thing: Consider leaving your executive entourage behind. A CEO by herself in a folksy town hall venue can more effectively convey to staff that she's "one of us," and thereby increase their engagement.

Phone

If meeting face to face is not an option, and a video service such as Skype is not available, then a phone is the way to go. Communicating via phone is also great for answering questions, gathering information, and having discussions not involving the whole team.

When using the phone, be sure to turn your entire attention to the caller. Don't multitask! Also, answer the phone only if you have time to talk. Otherwise, let calls go to voicemail.

Speaking of voicemail, be sure you check yours regularly, and return calls promptly. If you're going to be out, consider recording an outgoing message to communicate this. And when it comes to leaving messages on other people's voicemail, keep things brief.

Meet market: Tips for running a great meeting

Do you feel like your organization holds too many meetings? Perhaps. But my guess is, it's not the *quantity*, but the *quality* of these meetings that's suspect. To ensure your meetings are productive and, dare I say, engaging, keep these points in mind:

- **Stick to the schedule.** Start and end meetings on time, and make sure they don't last more than two hours — but preferably one hour. To stay on track, use meeting time for discussions, not presentations. In addition, keep conversations concise and quick.

- **Prepare for the meeting.** Create and distribute an agenda 24 to 48 hours in advance. Identify participants, but don't invite more than you need. Assign roles to participants, such as facilitator (usually the team leader), note taker (to jot down meeting minutes), timekeeper (to keep things moving), and assessor (to provide feedback on the meeting's effectiveness). If you're rotating the leadership of the meeting between team members, this week's chair will assume most of these duties.

- **Develop a solid agenda.** This may include a discussion of general "housekeeping" issues, actions taken since the last meeting, ongoing reminders and updates, and a list of key topics in order of priority. Consider involving your team in this process, as a team-building activity.

- **Set up the room.** Ideally, arrange to meet in a private meeting room. Arrive early enough to rearrange the seating, if needed. Also, be sure you have all the necessary equipment — phone, projector, flip chart, markers, and so on.

- **Set the ground rules.** These may include no multitasking, no smartphones, limitations on speaking times, and expectations of confidentiality.

- **Stay neutral.** As the leader, your opinion can sway the discussion and decisions made. Don't show your hand until you've heard all members' thoughts. I always advise leaders to speak last when seeking feedback from others.

- **Listen actively.** Listen for words and emotions; then paraphrase what you hear back to the group to clarify your, and their, understanding. Also, ask questions. Push the group to clarify positions and react to challenges.

- **Manage digression.** Make sure the discussion remains focused on the agenda items. If it starts to stray, rein it in with a simple "I'm not sure this applies to the topic. Let's go back to. . ."

- **Assess the meeting's effectiveness.** Did you meet your objectives and desired outcomes? Did you achieve the desired level of participation? Did the technology add value? Did you manage your time well? Did participants demonstrate confidence and trust in the process and results? Will participants look forward to attending another one of your meetings, given the choice?

- **Follow up.** After the meeting, send out the meeting minutes, along with a summary of decisions made and subsequent task assignments. Also, survey meeting participants to gauge their impressions of the value of the meeting.

Technology-aided meetings

I recently saw a hilarious FedEx commercial in which a boss is talking via videoconference to his project team, who appear to be back at the office. To the project team's horror, the "office" is revealed to be a backdrop, which tips over to reveal their true location: a beautiful golf course.

Humor (and scheming employees) aside, only managers stuck in the Dark Ages fail to leverage technology as a meeting tool, whether said technology is inexpensive (read: free), such as FaceTime or Skype, or an elaborate enterprise-wide solutions, such as TelePresence from Cisco Systems. For sharing and viewing information across geographies with many meeting attendees, technology tools such as GoToMeeting (www.gotomeeting.com) are a great resource.

E-mail

Although my Millennial daughter insists that "E-mail is so yesterday," it remains the communication form of choice for many businesses today. E-mail is particularly well suited for information-only communication that must be conveyed to a group — for example, to schedule meetings and phone calls, to distribute materials for meetings, and to gather input between meetings. E-mail is also a great tool for maintaining a written record of key points.

E-mail is not great for everything, however. For example, you should never use e-mail to communicate bad news or to relay sensitive or confidential information. It leaves too much unsaid. Also, never send an e-mail when your emotions are running high. The 24-hour rule is a great check and balance; save the e-mail as a draft and wait 24 hours before you send it.

 If you wouldn't want an e-mail message to be posted on a public bulletin board, don't send it. Moreover, *never* make any libelous, sexist, or racially discriminating comments in e-mails, even if meant as a joke.

Social media

With the assimilation of Generation Y into the workplace, adding social media to your communication toolkit is moving from a "nice to have" to a "must have." This generation — which will soon be the dominant generation at work (if it isn't already), and which by 2025 will comprise half the workforce — depends heavily on technology to communicate. It's incumbent upon you to "speak their language," so to speak. That means getting hip to such communication platforms as Facebook, Twitter, YouTube, and blogs.

Baby Boomers, members of Generation X, and members of Generation Y communicate very differently. To engage members of Generation Y, leaders must communicate using their tools: tweets, blogs, vlogs, and related social and mobile tools, such as texting. A message that you text or tweet to one of your Gen Y employees will almost certainly be read right away. But a message sent via e-mail? Maybe, maybe not.

Don't commit to maintaining a blog, a YouTube channel, or a Twitter feed and then fail to follow up. You must have the staff and resources to handle any new communications program. The popularity or "sexiness" of a new vehicle is not, in and of itself, sufficient justification for utilizing it.

Putting it all together

Not sure what communication format to use when? Table 5-1 should help. It contains at-a-glance info on each form of communication.

A word on corporate blogging

In recent years, many companies have begun publishing blogs authored by their CEOs, presidents, or other top-level executives. This idea has considerable merit if the executive in question is truly committed to the idea and the process, and if the communication strategy incorporates checks and balances to ensure that both entries and comments are communicating productive things.

If, however, an executive is *not* committed to blogging, or expects his or her entries to be ghostwritten or excessively vetted, then a blog is ultimately of negative value. A disconnect will result between what the blog is saying and what the executive "knows." Once this is discovered, the credibility of the project — and of corporate communications as a whole — will be undermined.

If a senior-level employee doesn't have the time or motivation to blog, consider spreading the responsibility among several midlevel employees who have a passion for it. Ideally, this will include a roster of bloggers who are representative of your firm's diversity in terms of discipline and cultural background, but first and foremost, you should recruit on the basis of passion and commitment. For some companies I've worked with, blogging is a perfect vessel for discretionary effort by midlevel or junior-level staff for whom self-expression and new technologies are motivators.

Channeling Emily Post: A word on e-mail etiquette

Here are a few tips to ensure you don't accidentally annoy anyone over e-mail:

✔ **Include a subject line.** Try to use one that will be meaningful to the recipient as well as to you. That way, the recipient will have some idea what your message is about even before he reads it. In addition, including subject lines makes it easier to find e-mails later.

✔ **Be concise.** Don't make an e-mail longer than it needs to be. No one wants to read a message that rivals *War and Peace* in its length.

✔ **Use proper spelling, grammar, and punctuation.** Yes, sending an e-mail riddled with errors in spelling, grammar, and punctuation makes you look like an idiot. Worse, messages with these types of errors can be easily misinterpreted. Grammatical rules exist for a reason: to ensure clear communication. Follow them, and you'll minimize misunderstandings! Also, avoid the use of abbreviations (think "BTW" for "by the way," and so on).

✔ **Reply swiftly.** Try to reply to all e-mails within 24 hours, and preferably on the same working day. If you aren't able to provide the necessary information within that time frame, then drop the sender a line to let her know you're working on it.

✔ **Don't write in ALL CAPS.** IF YOU WRITE IN ALL CAPS, IT SEEMS AS IF YOU ARE SHOUTING. THIS IS VERY ANNOYING.

Table 5-1	Forms of Communication	
Form of Communication	*Best Used For*	*Tips for Success*
Face to face: the best communication tool available	Team meetings (discussions, decision making, problem solving)	Look the person or people you're talking to in the eye.
	One-on-ones between managers and supervisors	Listen to words and tone of voice, and observe body language.
	Conflict resolution	Listen more than you talk (observe the 80/20 rule).
	Annual employee reviews	
	Feedback	Paraphrase what you hear to clarify your understanding.

(continued)

Table 5-1 *(continued)*

Form of Communication	Best Used For	Tips for Success
Telephone: the best communication tool to use when face-to-face communication isn't available	Answering questions Gathering information Discussions not involving the whole team	Answer the phone only if you're willing to talk. Give all your attention to the caller. Don't multitask. Set your outgoing message to notify callers if you're out for the day. Check your voicemail often and return calls promptly.
E-mail: great for group communications that are simply informative in nature	Messages for more than one person Distribution of materials for team meetings Scheduling meetings and phone calls Gathering input between meetings Messages that need a thread or record	Don't send an e-mail when your emotions are running high. Use descriptive subject headings. Be brief. Use good grammar, punctuation, and spelling. Reply swiftly. Use a mixture of uppercase and lowercase letters. DO NOT USE ALL CAPS.
Smartphones, mobile applications, and social media: excellent for communicating with younger employees	Younger employees Quick communication (texting) Communication that you aren't worried about going public (or that you'd *like* to go public, as with tri-branding, discussed in Chapter 10)	Leverage your junior-level employees' knowledge and social media expertise. Establish baseline rules and guidelines of what is and is not appropriate. Link to both your marketing and employer branding (HR) efforts.

Form of Communication	Best Used For	Tips for Success
Videoconferencing	Conference calls with remote employees or communicating with telecommuting employees Sharing documents	Learn how the technology works. Nothing is more painful for meeting attendees than having to sit around for 15 minutes while the meeting organizer fiddles with the technology, trying to get it to work.

He Said, She Said: Resolving Conflict

Is there such a thing as a workplace that's free from conflict? Yes. It's called a "one-man shop." The minute you introduce a second person into the mix, conflict is inevitable. It's also natural (see Chapter 9). The key with conflict is to recognize your own conflict-management style, and to resolve the conflict before it becomes personal.

Resolving conflict is important to maintaining engagement. If you've ever played team sports, you know that dealing with teammates who are in constant conflict can really affect team morale, not to mention the team's ability to work. The same goes in business. If Mary and John are always in conflict, it will ultimately erode everyone else's level of engagement. Yes, conflict is a normal part of life. But prolonged conflict is bad karma ... and bad karma is like kryptonite when it comes to building engagement.

Identifying your conflict-management style

To determine your own conflict-management style, complete the following questionnaire. To fill it out, read each statement, and then circle the answer that applies most to you. ***Remember:*** There are no wrong answers!

1. When I have a difference of opinion with other people, I usually:

   A. Try to convince others of the merit of my positions

   B. Try to find a solution that will benefit everyone involved

   C. Try to be sure that others get what they want

   D. Try to smooth over the differences quickly

2. When my goals are different from another team member's goals, I usually:

    A. Stand firm in pursuing my goal

    B. Try to negotiate common goals

    C. Sacrifice my goal for the goals of others

    D. Ignore the problem

3. When I'm involved in an emotional, interpersonal dispute, I usually:

    A. Press hard to get exactly what I want

    B. Consider both my concerns and the concerns of others

    C. Try not to hurt anyone's feelings

    D. Leave as quickly as possible

4. When a group of people are trying to solve a problem, I usually:

    A. Firmly demonstrate the benefits of my solution

    B. Listen to all and propose a middle-ground solution

    C. Support other people's solutions

    D. Stay quiet and let others solve the problem

5. When my views are different from another person's views, I usually:

    A. Firmly stick to my viewpoint

    B. Try to see the value in all views

    C. Support others' views to keep them happy

    D. Don't express my views at all

6. When tension develops between another person and me, I usually:

    A. Confront the tension directly

    B. Work with the person to reduce the tension

    C. Give the person what he or she wants to reduce the tension

    D. Try to avoid all tension

7. When negotiating a position on an issue different from others, I usually:

    A. Try to get my position accepted immediately

    B. Work with others to find a middle-ground position

    C. Give in quickly to the other's position

    D. Try to postpone dealing with the issue

8. When my wishes conflict with the wishes of others, I usually:

   A. Assert my wishes very clearly

   B. Try to satisfy all our wishes

   C. Sacrifice my wishes so others can have their wishes

   D. Don't express (or even know) my wishes

9. When someone is actively hostile toward me (yelling and so on), I usually:

   A. Respond with equal hostility

   B. Listen, try to understand, and try to calm the other person down

   C. Do all I can to placate the other person so he or she will calm down

   D. Shut down and/or walk away

10. The feedback I get about how I cope with conflict is that I usually:

   A. Find it challenging and actively try to influence others

   B. Find it creative and try to work out differences cooperatively

   C. Find it quite uncomfortable and tend to give in easily to others

   D. Find it very difficult and avoid at all costs

Count the number of A's you circled, the number of B's you circled, the number of C's you circled, and the number of D's you circled. If you circled the most A's, your conflict style is "confronting." If you circled the most B's, your conflict style is "cooperating." If you circled the most C's, your conflict style is "adapting." Finally, if you circled the most D's, your conflict style is "avoiding."

For more on these styles, read on:

- **Confronting (win-lose):** This style is based on the belief that "might makes right." It's power-oriented, focused on controlling situations and people, and involves competing in order to win. This conflict style is appropriate when you're facing a crisis, when the issue is very important to you, if you're an expert, and if the enforcement of guidelines is essential. A high score here indicates you have a tendency toward fighting for your own concerns, sometimes without considering other needs. A low score indicates a feeling of powerlessness, and that you may never get what you want.

- **Cooperating (win-win):** This style is based on the belief that two heads are better than one. It tries to reach a solution that satisfies each person's needs and addresses issues directly. For this style to be effective, a commitment of time and energy is required. This style is appropriate when the needs of each person are important, when the best solution is needed, when a high level of commitment to the solution is needed, when no one person has the best answer, and when there is sufficient time. A high score here indicates a tendency to both stand up for yourself and consider others' needs. A low score indicates you may not get other people's ideas and support, and that you may not reach the best solution.

✔ **Adapting (lose-win):** This style is based on the belief in "killing your enemies with kindness." It may take the form of giving in to others' wants. It tends to be self-sacrificing and overly cooperative, requiring you to back down on issues. This style is appropriate when the outcome is not important to you, when it's very important to preserve harmony, when the other person's position is right, when the other person has all the power, and when adapting to another's needs now will increase your chances of getting what you want later. A high score here indicates a tendency to consider the needs of other people above your own. A low score indicates that you may frustrate others, and may find it difficult to get along with people because you aren't willing to let them have what they need. You may seem either overpowering or unconcerned.

✔ **Avoiding (lose-lose):** This style is based on the belief in "leaving well enough alone." It takes the form of diplomatically sidestepping an issue. Often, this style merely postpones the inevitable. Suppressed feelings and desires are common with this style. This style is appropriate when the issue is trivial, when people need to calm down, when no one actually wants a resolution, when others believe they can resolve the conflict better than you can, when there is no way to win, and when there is not enough time to resolve the issue. A high score here indicates a tendency toward withdrawing in a conflict situation and avoiding conflict. A low score indicates that you may find yourself overwhelmed with conflict, hurting others' feelings, and feeling emotionally drained from not choosing which issues are worth fighting over.

There is no right or wrong style. In fact, effective leaders incorporate a blend of all four. Like a mechanic selecting the appropriate wrench, savvy leaders deploy the conflict style that best fits the situation. For instance, using a confronting style with an employee who is about to commit a safety violation is entirely appropriate. In contrast, someone working with senior leaders in conflict would be wise to leverage a cooperating conflict style. A leader who is asked to arbitrate a disagreement between employees he doesn't lead or within a task team may opt for an adapting style. Finally, although avoidance is usually the least appealing style, it would be appropriate if you're dealing with such a minor infraction that addressing it would be worse than avoiding it. (Don't sweat the small stuff.) Avoidance is also appropriate when dealing with a hot-headed employee in the moment, because confrontation may worsen an already-heated situation. In this scenario, you're often better off revisiting the situation when tempers have abated.

Resolving conflict with ease

When faced with conflict, remember this acronym: EASE. It stands for the following:

- ✔ **Empathy:** Identify and understand the emotions of the person with whom you're in conflict. You don't have to agree with his or her position, but you do need to respect his or her right to have an opinion that is different from yours.

- ✔ **Appreciation:** Recognize and appreciate that the other person is coming from a position of good intentions.

- ✔ **Search for solutions:** Think of alternative positions that may represent a compromise.

- ✔ **Explore:** If conflict is still present, explore ways to have a productive discussion.

If you're in the "explore" phase, which centers around discussion, try following these steps to resolve the conflict:

1. **Open the conversation with a positive tone.**

2. **Express the desire to preserve the working relationship, and explain that you need the other person's help to solve a problem that threatens it.**

3. **State the facts as you see them, avoiding rumors or passing judgment.**

4. **Ask the other party for help in understanding his or her behavior.**

   For example, say, "Can you help me understand why. . . ."

5. **State the ideal behavior (from your perspective).**

6. **Let the other person know what he or she can do to restore the relationship.**

7. **State the consequences.**

   What will happen if the conflict is not resolved?

8. **Open negotiations.**

   Be willing to listen, and to make a change yourself.

Of course, if you're in a leadership role, you may need to mediate others' conflicts from time to time. In that case, you'll want to follow these steps:

1. **Meet with both parties in a closed room.**

2. **Review the rules for the discussion.**

For example, one rule may be that only one person is allowed to talk at a time. Another may be that both parties will show respect by listening to what the other has to say. A third rule could be that the focus of the discussion will be issues, not personalities.

3. **Identify the problem or conflict.**

4. **Ask each party to explain the conflict.**

    As each party speaks, listen to his or her answer. Then ask the other party to repeat what the first party said.

5. **Discuss solutions.**

6. **Agree on a solution and on actions to take.**

7. **Follow up.**

As a leader, you should also take time to teach team members to resolve conflict among themselves. You can do this by coaching team members through conflicts and by acting as an observer. By actively dealing with conflict, you can help avoid disengaging employees.

Dealing with difficult people

Let's face it: Some people are just difficult. They're hard to deal with. Worse, over time, difficult people erode engagement among other employees. See, engagement is about creating a culture in which employees are motivated to perform their best. Any obstacle that prevents employees from doing their best will erode their engagement over time. And there's no doubt about it: Difficult people are obstacles.

If you find yourself dealing with a difficult person, keep these points in mind to minimize conflict and perhaps even engage them. (Hey, even schmucks can be engaged!)

- ✔ **Help build their confidence.** Try going out of your way to recognize a difficult person's expertise. (That person is good at *something*, right?) You may be surprised what a little stroking of egos will do to soften difficult employees.

- ✔ **Establish parameters.** When dealing with difficult employees, there must be non-negotiables. Establishing your non-negotiable boundaries early on will make everyone's life easier.

- ✔ **Establish clear deadlines.** The key word here is *clear*. It's amazing how many times I've had to arbitrate a meeting between a manager and an employee in conflict, only to discover that expectations with respect to deadlines were never clear. And it's usually the manager's fault!

✔ **Partner them with peers to build skills.** We often perceive people as difficult simply because we don't know them. Try partnering a difficult employee with someone who has complementary skills. More often than not, the difficult person will seem far less difficult when he or she starts working with someone else. Plus, if you select the right partner — someone who is friendly, kind, and patient — he or she may just rub off on your problem employee.

✔ **Redirect conversations back to work.** Often, people are described as "difficult" when really, a different word applies: *whiny.* In other words, they complain about everything — including things that can never be fixed or that are outside their control. Refocusing the conversation on things that can be fixed or that are within their control is a great first step to nipping all that whining in the bud.

✔ **Establish a communication routine.** Scheduling check-ins will often help you avoid more painful conversations. Although it sounds counterintuitive to suggest spending *more* time with a difficult employee, it's often the best fix.

✔ **Don't take the bait.** Some people are like alpha dogs, just waiting for someone to challenge them. Pick your moments, and remember: Avoidance is often the best approach when dealing with difficult people.

✔ **Brainstorm new processes as needed.** Difficult employees are often difficult because they believe they have more to offer than they're being asked to contribute — but no one will give them the chance. Soliciting their opinions can turn them from feeling frustrated ("No one listens to me around here!") to empowered. . . and engaged.

✔ **Go to them when you need help.** President Lyndon Johnson was known for inviting difficult people into his inner circle. As he said, "I'd rather have them inside the tent pissing out than outside the tent pissing in." Inviting difficult people into your inner circle will often make them less difficult. *Remember:* People are often difficult because they feel they have more to offer than they're being asked to contribute.

✔ **Discuss ways to redistribute the work.** Sometimes, employees are simply overwhelmed with work, and their way of coping is to lash out, making them difficult. To minimize this, try redistributing their workload.

✔ **Invite 360 feedback.** When a manager confronts a difficult employee, said difficult employee often thinks it's simply because the manager doesn't like her. Inviting others to chime in via 360 feedback — or better yet, a "more of/same as/less of" feedback session (both are discussed in Chapter 16) — will lend much-needed credibility to the manager's observations.

✔ **Document issues.** If all the aforementioned suggestions fail, and one of your direct reports continues to be so difficult that he's affecting the engagement levels of the entire team, it's time to start documenting the issues. The endgame may well be formal corrective action (see Chapter 18).

Ch-Ch-Ch-Ch-Changes: Communicating Change

As you're no doubt aware, people resist change. Why? Lots of reasons. Often, it's simply fear of the unknown. Sometimes, it has to do with lack of trust. On occasion, it may simply be due to bad timing. In a work setting, people resist change because they're afraid of losing job security or control. And some people don't like change "just because" — even when it's a change for the better.

And yet, change is everywhere — and with good reason. If we didn't undergo change, we'd be at a considerable disadvantage. After all, "changing" often translates to "keeping up with the times." We've all survived significant change in the past, and we'll survive it in the future as well.

Communication is never more important than during a period of change. That's because people tend to assume the worst during a change event. During times of change, employees tend to be less trusting and less direct. They're more careful when choosing their words. Often, they're fearful of disagreeing with management, whether said management is old or new. Fear also causes them to expend more energy looking after their own self-interests, and to be more open to messages that reach them via the rumor mill — especially in the absence of actual information.

To stave off anxiety among the troops, leaders must increase the level of communication during a change event such as a merger, reduction in force, reorganization, change in strategic direction, or change to the leadership team.

If you're facing a change event in your organization, keep these points in mind:

✔ **As a leader, you go first!** Make sure you fully embrace the change initiative and its implications before attempting to persuade others. Be cognizant of the influence you have on those around you.

✔ **Talk the talk, and walk the walk.** Be a positive role model and an ambassador for the change. Support it both publicly and privately, and demonstrate the behaviors that you expect from others in the face of change.

✔ **Overcommunicate.** Whether good news or bad, sharing information as often as you can and being forthright with the truth are critical. Communicating is the number-one way to maintain trust and employee engagement. As you do, assess your employees' understanding of the change initiative. Do they grasp the change initiative's goals and pertinent details? If not, provide any missing information and clear up any misconceptions.

✔ **Check in with your staff and encourage candid feedback.** In your role as leader, you must check in with your people to see how they're doing — especially during times of change. Allow and encourage employees to candidly express their feelings. Get any resistance to change out in the open so it can be dealt with.

✔ **Establish crystal-clear priorities.** Going through change can be confusing and stressful. Be ultra-specific with regard to team priorities and staff expectations throughout the change initiative.

✔ **Delegate.** Move less important tasks off your plate so you can focus on leading through the change. When possible, delegate tasks to staff members to further their skills, knowledge, and abilities.

✔ **Be there.** Make yourself available to your people. You're undoubtedly busy, but don't close your door and stay in your office all day. *Remember:* These are the times when your staff needs you the most.

✔ **Make your employees feel valued and give positive reinforcement.** During times of change, motivating your employees and making them feel appreciated are especially important. Reward positive behaviors as often as possible, and celebrate accomplishments whenever you can. Pay extra attention to your top performers!

✔ **Re-skill your employees (and yourself) as needed.** Determine what competencies will be required to work in the "new world" and provide relevant training and development opportunities for your team.

✔ **Pass information up as well as down.** Be sure to pass questions, issues, and feedback up to your manager or leadership team in addition to conveying information down to your team.

✔ **Stay sharp!** Leading change is hard work. Keep your change leadership skills finely tuned. Take advantage of the resources at your disposal to build your knowledge and abilities in this important competency.

✔ **Get help.** Don't underestimate your own need for assistance during change. Reach out to a peer or seek advice from your boss on how best to handle your own situation during change.

To help your employees through the change, advise them to keep the following points in mind:

✓ **Adopt a proactive mind-set.** You make things happen; things don't happen *to you*. Don't assume a victim mentality, in which you perceive your life to be controlled by others. Yes, some things will be out of your control during change. But your attitude is always entirely within your control.

✓ **Think evolution, not revolution.** It may not always feel like it, but change is never a conscious attempt to make our lives more hectic! Change is rarely introduced to tear everything down. Most changes are initiated to improve and build on results.

✓ **Focus on what is *not* changing.** Few change initiatives change *every-thing*. Let the stable aspects of the situation give you a sense of security as you adjust to what *is* changing.

✓ **Ask questions.** Get the facts about the change. Speak up and find out more about the things that aren't clear to you. Try not to fill in your own blanks; often, you'll be wrong.

✓ **Keep doing your work.** Chances are, many aspects of your job are not changing. Keep doing what you do best. Onward and upward!

✓ **Use the change as a development opportunity.** Change often brings new opportunities and prospects. Leverage the change to your advantage by identifying ways to improve your skills, knowledge, and abilities to help you meet your career goals.

✓ **Be prepared for mental fatigue.** Change can be challenging, unsettling, and exhausting, even for the most experienced employees. Don't be surprised if mental fatigue sets in — especially during larger change initiatives. Expect it, normalize it, and find ways to deal with it.

✓ **Be forgiving and tolerant.** Change is difficult, and people are bound to make mistakes. Be forgiving and lenient with others (and yourself) during times of change.

✓ **Ask for help when needed.** Nobody can read your mind. Be vocal about your needs and about how the company, your manager, and your co-workers can support you.

Talking It Up: Communicating Your Engagement Efforts

Long ago, I worked for a company whose management decided it wanted to be an "employer of choice," which would naturally involve improving employee engagement. Like many organizations, we knew we had a lot of work to do to get there.

A chief concern was how our employees would react to this goal. We worried that cynicism might trump our efforts. In fact, we were so concerned about this, we considered not even telling employees about our aspirations.

Thankfully, we came to our senses. We realized that we were embarking on a multi-year journey, and that if we were *truly* committed to being successful, we were going to have to communicate exactly what we were trying to do and why. We were going to have to report on milestones, regardless of whether we were proud of the results. In addition, we were going to have to make ourselves accountable. That was the only way we could command the respect and trust of the very people we needed to make our culture shift a success.

Yes, employees *were* skeptical. But this didn't take us by surprise or dampen our resolve. We stuck to the plan. Our CEO made employee engagement one of the eight key elements of his strategic plan and issued monthly progress reports. In addition, all ten members of the leadership team spoke continually about employee engagement. They became true ambassadors of an employee-focused culture.

Your senior leaders — up to and including the president, CEO, COO, and/or CFO — must communicate the business strategy every month, especially with regard to how engagement fits in. This communication can be via newsletter, e-mail, report, video, or presentation — just don't let it fall by the wayside. The communication protocol discussed earlier in this chapter (in the section "Bob the Builder: Building a Communication Protocol") is a great first step!

Welcome criticism and deal with it transparently. This in and of itself helps to defuse the more vocal skeptics. It's hard to maintain a sour outlook when you're clearly being heard and when management is openly fessing up to missteps and seeking ways to correct the course. Even the most ardent skeptics will have to acknowledge the evident effort on the part of management. They won't be able to deny when gains, however small, are made. Again, the key is communication. Skeptics who continue to grumble in the face of clear progress will quickly find themselves without an audience.

How did the story end? Well, engagement became the foundation of our business culture, ultimately leading to best-in-class performance in profit, growth, client service, and yes, employee engagement survey scores. The company even promoted the head of engagement (yours truly), proof of the pudding that engagement drives business results!

Communication Don'ts

Throughout this chapter, we fill you in on communication "do's" — establishing two-way communication, developing a communication protocol, maximizing communication tools, resolving conflict, communicating change, and broadcasting your engagement efforts.

To ensure you don't put your foot in it, here are some communication don'ts:

✔ **Don't underestimate the importance of communication.** I said it earlier: Communication is the cornerstone of employee engagement. Communication should never be viewed as anything but essential in engaging your employees.

✔ **Don't be afraid to overcommunicate.** "Gee, I left that company because management just communicated *too much*," said no one ever. Simply put, your employees want to know what is going on, and proactive communication is your way of keeping them in the loop. Key messages, especially those pertaining to progress or success, must be queued up and pushed out with the highest possible frequency using a variety of communication tools.

✔ **Don't focus on the negative.** The vast majority of the time, your employees are doing something right. But too many managers focus the majority of *their* time discussing the few times employees did something wrong. (And more often than not, the "something wrong" wasn't really "wrong" at all. It was just "different.") Although it's certainly important to let employees know when they've made a mistake, you'll find that focusing on the positive will pay long-term engagement dividends.

✔ **Don't be afraid to communicate setbacks or losses.** Yes, I know I just said that focusing on the positive will pay long-term engagement dividends. But that doesn't mean you should refrain from sharing bad news. Many managers are hesitant to communicate news of setbacks or losses, fearing employees will grow demoralized. But for employees to feel invested in their work, they must know how the business is doing with respect to its goals. Simply put, you can't improve if you don't know you're underperforming.

✔ I once worked with a company in which one regional manager shielded employees from negative news about their performance in an effort to maintain morale. But by doing so, he failed to create any impetus for change or any channel for constructive input from the ranks. Fortunately, the company replaced this manager. The new boss kicked off his tenure with a frank conversation with his staff about their performance (or lack thereof). In doing so, he tapped into the staff's innate urge to be competitive and to excel. As a result, engagement scores, revenue growth, and profitability all improved. Indeed, the region went from *losing* $1 million per year to *making* $1 million per year — a $2 million swing!

✔ **Don't shoot the messenger.** Too often, I've seen top-level executives become angry in the face of unflattering feedback. This attitude, especially when displayed in a public forum, will effectively stifle any benefits that may arise from the sharing of employees' opinions. In other words, if executives get mad at people who tell them things they don't want to hear, people will stop telling them things, period. When you create feedback mechanisms, you must accept the bad news with the good. That means creating an environment in which people are comfortable speaking truth to power. Otherwise, all you're doing is creating a culture in which people tell you what you want to hear — which is *not* a model for business excellence.

Part II
Strategies for Driving Engagement

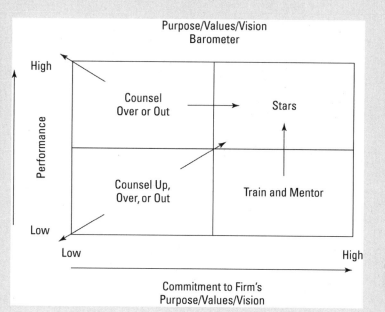

Purpose/Values/Vision
Barometer

Find out more about driving engagement through training by establishing a "corporate university" in an article at www.dummies.com/extras/employeeengagement.

web extras

In this part...

- Win over employees' heads and hearts to drive engagement.
- Identify leadership-based engagement drivers because engagement starts at the top.
- Drive engagement across generations because the drivers are different for each generation.
- Team up to drive engagement because dysfunctional teams will erode your engagement efforts.
- Identify your employment value proposition to tell the world why you're a great place to work.
- Use game mechanics to drive engagement because fun is an engagement driver.

Chapter 6

Winning Their Hearts and Minds: Driving Engagement with a Sense of Purpose

In This Chapter

▶ Connecting your employees' behavior to your mission statement

▶ Engaging employees' heads and hearts

As I mention in Chapter 4, money is not always a primary engagement driver — although the perception of unfairness or an organizational caste system (in which there are clear "haves" and "have nots") is certain to lead to disengagement. Purpose, however, *is* an engagement driver. Indeed, organizations that build their cultures around purpose generally have higher levels of engagement than those that don't.

These companies are in on a powerful secret: Companies that know their own purpose, values, vision, and strategic plan (what I call their "line of sight"), and that believe in corporate social responsibility, are better positioned to win over the hearts and minds of their employees. And not surprisingly, employees who are duly won over are significantly more likely to be engaged.

Sightseeing: Building Your Line of Sight

One morning, while staying at a hotel in Portland, Oregon, that was part of a national chain, I stepped into the hotel elevator on my way to a meeting. In the elevator were two hotel employees actively engaged in conversation. By their feet was a piece of crumpled-up paper, which was clearly trash.

Neither employee greeted me with a "Good morning!" or even made eye contact. Worse, they made no attempt to pick up the piece of trash on the floor. Seeing an opportunity for a social experiment, I calmly picked up the piece of paper before exiting the elevator on the ground floor. "Gentlemen," I said, "can you tell me why you didn't pick up this piece of paper?" The first employee fibbed: "I didn't see it." The second answered, "Sir, they don't pay me enough money to pick up trash."

A few months later, I was staying at the Four Seasons in Philadelphia, where I was speaking at a conference. When I returned to the hotel from my morning run, the valet was waiting for me with a bottle of water and a towel. I thanked him, and without missing a beat, he replied: "No need to thank me, sir. Here at the Four Seasons, it's all about the customer experience!" Afterward, I reflected on my earlier experience at the Portland hotel chain. I couldn't help but notice the difference in customer service.

I decided to conduct another social experiment. I grabbed a tissue, crumpled it up, headed to the elevator, and tossed it on the floor. Feeling a bit foolish, I rode up and down for several minutes, waiting for a hotel employee to enter the elevator car. Finally, one did. "Good morning, sir!" he said cheerfully. He then quickly picked up the crumpled-up tissue and hid it behind his back. Wow, what a contrast!

When I arrived home, I did some research about these two hotel chains. Believe it or not, the pay for hotel employees was similar at both chains. So, why was the customer experience at one so different from the other? Well, one reason is that the Four Seasons is renowned for its service culture. This is underscored by its mission statement, which includes the following components:

- ✔ **What we believe:** Our greatest asset, and the key to our success, is our people. We believe that each of us needs a sense of dignity, pride, and satisfaction in what we do. Because satisfying our guests depends on the united efforts of many, we are most effective when we work together cooperatively, respecting each other's contribution and importance.

- ✔ **How we behave:** We demonstrate our beliefs most meaningfully in the way we treat each other and by the example we set for one another. In all our interactions with our guests, customers, business associates, and colleagues, we seek to deal with others as we would have them deal with us.

In other words, the Four Seasons has been very successful in building a "line of sight" between its mission statement and the behaviors of its employees.

For organizations to develop a "line of sight," they must answer the following questions:

- ✔ Why do we exist (purpose)?
- ✔ Who are we (values)?

✔ Where are we going (vision)?

✔ How will we get there (strategic plan)?

In addition, organizations must assess how they are doing — in other words, develop a scorecard of sorts. (For more on developing a scorecard, see Chapter 15.)

How does building this "line of sight" boost engagement? Simple. It all has to do with aligning your organization with its purpose. When people care deeply about something, or are invested in an activity, cause, or job — intellectually and emotionally — they're generally more passionate about the outcome than when they are *not* invested. If you don't believe me, consider people who donate their time to their community food kitchen, their church, local youth sports organizations, or charities. Do they get paid? No. So, why do they do it? Why do they invest time and energy in something that doesn't pay the mortgage? They do it because it has a purpose. It's a higher calling.

As an aside, just as it's important to create a company-level line of sight, it's also critical to create a personal-level one — that is, to help individuals develop a clear picture of where they are today in their careers and where they're going. You want employees to understand the company's strategic plan, and to know where they fit in that plan. For more information on this personal-level line of sight, see Chapter 16.

Identifying your firm's purpose

Okay, stop reading for a minute. Go to your company's website, and try to find out why it's in business. Not what you do, make, or sell — but *why.*

Most companies know what they do, make, or sell. But they struggle when they try to define their reason for being — what I call their "why" — even though being able to do so makes business sense. In his excellent book *Good to Great: Why Some Companies Make the Leap . . . And Others Don't* (HarperBusiness), author Jim Collins notes that companies that focus on purpose outperform their peer group by a factor of six. You read that right: They do *six times* better than their peers.

Despite this, most companies struggle when it comes to identifying their why. Indeed, very few companies are able to identify a purpose that resonates with their employees both intellectually and emotionally. Why? Well, for starters, identifying an organization's why is often difficult. Sure, identifying the purpose of a charity for the homeless is easy. Most likely, it's something along the lines of "providing jobs for the homeless" or "providing shelter to those in need." But not every firm's purpose, or mission, is so readily understood or so easily articulated.

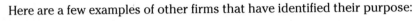

Take Raytheon, a large global defense company. My son works for Raytheon, in its Patriot missile division. It's easy to identify what Raytheon does, makes, and sells. But its reason for being? Its purpose, mission, or why? Identifying that is a bit more difficult. Even so, Raytheon's Patriot missile division *has* crystalized its purpose. As my son puts it, "We protect those who protect us."

Here are a few examples of other firms that have identified their purpose:

- ✔ **3M:** "Our purpose is to solve unsolved problems innovatively."

- ✔ **Merck:** "Our purpose is to preserve and improve human life."

- ✔ **Disney:** "Our purpose is to make people happy."

- ✔ **Mary Kay Cosmetics:** "To inspire women to transform their lives, and in doing so, help other women transform their lives." (Note that Mary Kay Cosmetics refers to its purpose as its "dream.")

- ✔ **The Coca-Cola Company:** "To refresh the world, inspire moments of optimism and happiness, create value, and make a difference."

Unfortunately, the very people who most need to understand a company's purpose — CEOs, COOs, CFOs, managing directors, and other key executives — are often the last to grasp its importance. These left-brain types typically spend their time worrying about numbers rather than "soft" issues like purpose and values. Ensuring that these stakeholders understand and appreciate your firm's purpose is critical. Otherwise, you'll likely be unable to build a line of sight around your purpose.

Need help pinpointing your organization's purpose? Try following these steps:

1. **Send out a quick survey to a sampling of employees from all representative groups, including generations, tenure, background, levels, culture, and departments.**

   You can build the survey using SurveyMonkey (`www.surveymonkey.com`). It's free!

   Ask the following questions:

   - Why do we exist as an organization?

   - In 100 years, what do we want to be remembered for?

   - How are we different from our competitors?

   - What is the one thing we do as an organization that everyone admires?

   - What inspires you about working here?

2. **Assemble a "Purpose" task team to evaluate the answers to these questions, with the goal of developing two or three draft purpose statements.**

   This team should include owners, key leaders, and a cross-sectional group of high performers.

3. **Distribute the top purpose statements to all employees for further input and perhaps to vote for the statement that resonates the most.**

4. **Have the company leadership select the best purpose statement using the input provided and begin the communication and branding outreach.**

Organizations that build their culture on purpose, and that hire people with the behaviors and traits that match their culture (see Chapter 12), understand that employees are more likely to give if there is a bigger purpose worth rallying behind. This purpose is key to getting your employees to contribute above and beyond what's expected of them (in other words, apply discretionary effort), which can be a competitive advantage. Having a purpose is like magic dust for organizations.

Defining your firm's values

Values are beliefs that are shared among the stakeholders of an organization. They drive an organization's culture and priorities, and provide a framework in which decisions are made. Examples of values include the following:

- ✔ "Innovation is the cornerstone of everything we do."
- ✔ "Collaboration is the hallmark of our culture."

If you want your people to behave in a certain way or produce specific outcomes, you have to define, communicate, and then model those behaviors and outcomes. The same is true for your core values. In order for your people to live and embody them, three critical actions must occur:

- ✔ **Your leadership team must define and commit to a set of four to eight core values.** These values should represent the "rules of the tavern," or the organizational behaviors you most value. If your company has no stated values, the leadership team should begin with a short list of key values that they believe are representative, such as innovation, collaboration, respect, teamwork, fun, quality, service, creativity, and so on. This short list should be sent out to employees with a request that they rank them.

> ✔ **The agreed-upon values should be communicated on an ongoing basis.** A fun way to do this is to have employees use their smartphones to film their interpretation of your values. Post the top videos on your intranet page or perhaps even choose a winner and showcase his or her video on YouTube or on your firm's website.
>
> ✔ **If you're going to talk the talk, you have to walk the walk.** Make sure that whatever values you identify, your leadership team lives them daily.

When articulating their values, some organizations are able to inject their own personalities. For example, the e-commerce firm Zappos espouses the following values (referred to as the company's "Family Values"):

- ✔ Deliver WOW Through Service
- ✔ Embrace and Drive Change
- ✔ Create Fun and A Little Weirdness
- ✔ Be Adventurous, Creative, and Open-Minded
- ✔ Pursue Growth and Learning
- ✔ Build Open and Honest Relationships With Communication
- ✔ Build a Positive Team and Family Spirit
- ✔ Do More With Less
- ✔ Be Passionate and Determined
- ✔ Be Humble

On a more traditional level, you can see the power of simplicity of the Kellogg Company's values: Integrity, Accountability, Passion, Humility, Simplicity, and Results.

Identifying your organization's vision

An organization's vision, expressed in the form of a vision statement, outlines what the organization wants to be and/or how it wants the world in which it operates to be. As author Andy Stanley notes, vision is "what could be and what should be, regardless of what is. Vision creates possibilities and inspires people to behave and take action in ways that allow the vision to become a reality."

It should be a longer-term view with a focus on the future. For example, a charity that works with the poor might have the vision, "a world without poverty." As another example, consider Amazon's vision statement:

Our vision is to be earth's most customer centric company; to build a place where people can come to find and discover anything they might want to buy online.

A successful vision statement has six key characteristics:

- ✔ **It's imaginable.** Does it prompt employees to think about the future? Is it part inspirational and part aspirational? Is it unique to your firm?

- ✔ **It's energizing.** Is it exciting, captivating, and engaging? Does it make employees want to jump out of bed in the morning?

- ✔ **It's feasible, yet bold.** There is a fine line between inspiring employees to reach for new heights and creating jaded skeptics. A vision that is too bold risks cynicism ("Are they kidding?"). A vision should be bold but achievable.

- ✔ **It's focused.** For example, Amazon's vision explicitly states that its business model will continue to be built around online shopping. A vision that's too vague can result in employees and customers not understanding who you are or where you're going.

- ✔ **It's flexible.** Successful visions allow for flexibility in chasing and responding to shifting market and labor forces. If Amazon's vision started as "online bookstore," the company would have struggled with its subsequent diversification strategy.

- ✔ **It's easy to communicate and remember.** Can a stranger remember your company's vision statement after spending 40 seconds with you in an elevator? If not, it needs work. This is never more true than today, with the increasing prevalence of social media and mobile applications.

Also, the vision, which can be emotional, should be a source of inspiration. To quote the great Walt Disney, "A vision is a picture of the future that captures the imagination of others and inspires them to follow."

Building your strategic plan

Of course, it's not enough to say where you want to go. You also have to develop a strategic plan to get there. This includes allocating the necessary resources — people, money, paper clips, what have you — to get where you're going. Most organizations develop a new strategic plan every three to five years. Building a strategic plan involves the following key steps:

1. **Conduct a SWOT (short for "strengths, weaknesses, opportunities, and threats") analysis of your current business position.**

2. **Identify the market(s), customer(s), and geographical area(s) you're focusing on.**

3. **Outline the objectives — between three and eight — you want to accomplish over the next three to five years.**

4. **Decide on the specific goals and actions to accomplish your objectives.**

5. **Budget for and allocate your resource needs, including human resources, capital resources, system requirements, acquisitions, and so on.**

6. **Develop your measurement tools. (See Chapter 15 for more information.)**

7. **Install a communications protocol. (Refer to Chapter 5.)**

Promoting your purpose, values, and vision

Okay, you've identified your purpose, values, and vision, and developed your five-year strategic plan (see Chapter 15). Now what? Promoting, that's what. Promoting your purpose, values, and vision is key to developing your line of sight and fostering engagement.

Remember those Four Seasons employees I mention earlier? Those guys did not accidentally stumble upon the fact that the Four Seasons has a service culture. Instead, the Four Seasons understood the importance of promoting its purpose, values, and vision.

So, what is your company's purpose? What are its values? What is its vision? Can all your employees articulate these? Is there consistency? To boost the stickiness of your organization's purpose, values, and vision, consider adopting these best practices:

- ✔ **Build an internal promotion campaign with your purpose, values, and vision as the theme.** The campaign should be repetitive (employees don't "hear" something unless they've been exposed to it 13 times) and employ all forms of communication: written, oral, videos, blogs, social media, mobile applications, town hall meetings, lunch and learn, posters, and so on. Depending on your culture, make the campaign fit who you are. For example, Harley Davidson might include themes of adventure or rebellion, use earthy tones, and so on.

- ✔ **Sponsor a "Why We Work Here" video contest, in which employees create their own short films that incorporate the firm's purpose, values, and vision.** Generation Y will love this idea.

- ✔ **Print your company's purpose, values, and vision on the back of everyone's business cards.**

- ✔ **Boost your co-branding efforts by combining your marketing and sales efforts with your employment branding efforts.** For more information, see Chapter 10.

✔ **Leverage tri-branding, linking employees, customers, and other key stakeholders.** Again, see Chapter 10 for more info.

✔ **Create a four-quadrant value barometer with "Performance" on one axis and "Commitment to the Firm's Purpose/Values/Vision" on the other (see Figure 6-1).** Use this barometer when evaluating an internal candidate for a promotion, raise, bonus, or pay increase.

✔ **Hire people who display specific behaviors and traits that reflect your values and culture.** For more about pinpointing these key behaviors and traits, see Chapter 12.

✔ **Make your firm's purpose, values, and vision the centerpiece of its onboarding/new hire orientation program.** Chapter 14 discusses onboarding in more detail.

✔ **Incorporate questions in your employee engagement survey that not only reinforce your purpose, values, and vision, but also gauge employees' familiarity with your purpose, values, and vision.**

✔ **Suggest that all organizational meetings include a "line of sight" agenda item, with purpose, values, and vision embedded into a discussion of the firm's business results.**

REMEMBER

Identifying your organization's purpose, values, and vision is an important part of defining your employee value proposition (EVP), which I cover in Chapter 10.

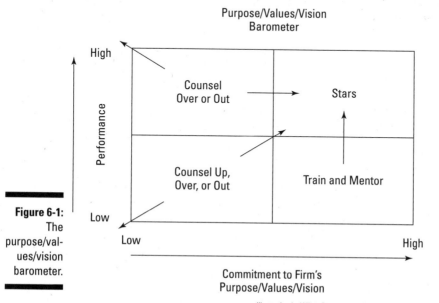

Figure 6-1: The purpose/values/vision barometer.

Illustration by Wiley, Composition Services Graphics

Be Responsible! Engaging Employees through Corporate Social Responsibility

Remember the movie *Wall Street?* In it, Gordon Gekko, played by the incomparable Michael Douglas, famously declares, "Greed is good."

Well, with all due respect to Mr. Gekko, I'd argue that seldom in the course of Western history has greed been less popular. These days, many people give the stink-eye to corporate policies and practices that enable an elite group to accrue wealth at everyone else's expense. They demand a higher level of responsibility — namely, corporate social responsibility (CSR).

Corporate social responsibility is the idea that organizations have moral, ethical, environmental, and philanthropic responsibilities above and beyond their responsibility to legally earn a fair return for investors. You can bet that your clients, vendors, stakeholders, and especially your employees are assessing your level of CSR — things ranging from your carbon footprint to your level of volunteerism to your efforts to give back to your community. In addition to their paycheck and benefits, a large portion of your staff will want to see that the company they work for is making a difference in the world. With every passing day (and every depressing headline), this engagement driver becomes even more important.

Don't just take my word for it. As I once heard Andrew W. Savitz, author of *The Triple Bottom Line* (Jossey-Bass), say, "To stay focused on business alone is no longer sustainable . . . People want to work for responsible companies." Thomas Friedman, author of *The World Is Flat* (Picador), concurs, noting that tomorrow's companies will need to have "the brains of a business school graduate and the heart of a social worker." And in his book *Built to Last: Successful Habits of Visionary Companies* (HarperBusiness), author Jim Collins summarizes the importance of CSR by noting that it provides purpose above and beyond profit. "In a truly great company," Collins writes, "profits and cash flow become like blood and water to a human body: They are absolutely essential for life, but they are not the very *point* of life."

Successful companies will be those that make CSR part of their DNA. It's been proven that socially conscious organizations outperform those solely committed to beating the competition.

Warby Parker is one organization that takes CSR seriously. A web-based eyeglass company, Warby Parker launched a "Buy a Pair, Give a Pair" program. For each purchase made, Warby Parker donates glasses to someone in need. So far, the company has donated more than 150,000 pairs. Toms, a shoe and eyewear company, has a similar program, donating one pair of shoes or glasses for each pair bought.

Of course, a "buy one, give one" model is only one way to go. Other options include donating employees' time. This approach is used by Salesforce.com, which donates 1 percent of each employee's time for community service — 350,000 hours at last count. Salesforce.com goes two better, though, also donating 1 percent of the company's equity (we're talking $40 million so far) to charitable and related organizations in the form of grants, and donating 1 percent of the company's products to nonprofit organizations.

Microsoft is another great example. Although the ascension of Google, Facebook, and other high-tech companies has made it tougher for Microsoft to recruit and retain top employees and engineers in recent years, the Redmond-based software giant believes its philanthropic efforts are attracting talent now more than ever. Indeed, this is one area where Microsoft sets the pace for the entire technology sector. As noted by Brad Smith, Microsoft's general counsel, at the conclusion of the company's 30th annual Employee Giving Campaign, "When you're living through a time when unemployment is up and when people see more human needs, there is a greater focus now on what companies and employees are doing to address those human needs." Smith, who believes that Microsoft's reputation as a charitable organization is a key recruiting tool, continued by saying that he "frequently hears from young interns and employees that Microsoft's broad citizenship efforts are part of what people find attractive to the company. "The opportunity to work on great products and services is hugely important and always will be," Smith said, adding "but [prospective employees] also really value the broader connections that a company has in the community."

Some companies even go so far as to build their mission around CSR. Take Patagonia. It's mission statement is as follows:

> Build the best product, cause no unnecessary harm, use business to inspire and implement solutions to the environmental crisis.

Whole Foods has a similar mission:

> Whole Foods, Whole People, Whole Planet.

And then there's the Starbucks mission statement:

> To inspire and nurture the human spirit — one person, one cup, and one neighborhood at a time.

A company whose very mission is CSR will be very attractive to many engaged workers!

Many CSR activities are inexpensive or free to launch, and pay significant engagement benefits. If you're looking to incorporate CSR into your organization, consider these tips:

- ✔ Allow employees to take one paid service day per year with an approved nonprofit or charitable organization.

- ✔ Establish a matching contribution program with a charitable organization such as the Red Cross in the aftermath of a natural disaster or national emergency, when funds are needed.

- ✔ Establish a CSR committee to communicate, suggest, and solicit ideas.

- ✔ "Brand" any CSR programs in your organization. Obviously, this includes formal CSR programs launched by your company, but it should also include any informal CSR programs that may exist. Believe me, they're there — you just may not be aware of them! You can bet that your employees are already championing activities like walks for hunger, corporate challenges, food drives, and other forms of volunteerism. Consider forming a task team consisting of a cross-section of volunteers to hunt down these ad-hoc activities.

- ✔ Establish a "green" program with a focus on recycling, water conservation, and other environmentally sensitive initiatives.

- ✔ Launch a "chain reaction" initiative in which you ask for volunteers (they're out there!) to identify, promote, and coordinate location-specific community events — for example, planning a walk to raise money for cancer research, participating in a charity road race, or working at the local soup kitchen.

- ✔ Use CSR initiatives to reward employees. For example, you might give employees who win your Innovation Idea of the Month contest a free day for community service or a nominal cash award (say, $100), which they can donate to their favorite charity.

- ✔ In the spirit of "walk the talk," schedule time at the next executive offsite meeting for the executive team to work on a socially responsible activity. For example, the team could partner with Habitat for Humanity to help rebuild a community hit by a tornado or flood.

The great thing about CSR programs is, you get as much as you give — if not more. Jonathan Reckford, CEO of Habitat for Humanity, notes: "The one consistent takeaway I hear from all company volunteers is that they receive more than they give when they work on one of our homebuilding projects."

Interestingly, CSR is important across the generational spectrum. As I discuss in Chapter 8, Generation Y workers are purpose-driven by their very nature. But Baby Boomers, too, have demonstrated a growing interest in social responsibility as they enter the "back nine" of their careers. Having attained hierarchical and monetary success, many Boomers are asking, "How do I give back?" Even better, because many of these Boomers are now in executive leadership positions, they're even going so far as to ask, "How can I persuade my company to give back?" Increasingly, Baby Boomers are pushing their employers to donate to charities, reduce their carbon footprint, and support volunteerism. This cross-generational interest in social responsibility is a powerful means of staff cohesion, as well as a key engagement driver — one that you cannot afford to neglect.

To get the most bang for your CSR buck, be sure to publicize your investments both internally and externally. You can also embed CSR efforts into your organizational metrics — again, reiterating the connection between measurement and results.

Be warned: CSR isn't just some program you can cut when the bottom line slips. It must be embedded in the very essence of your company. If your leadership sees it as a "flavor of the month" initiative, your employees will quickly detect its transitory nature. Implementing a policy of social responsibility means following through. If you don't, the internal perception — and maybe even the *external* perception — will be negative, to say the least!

Chapter 7

People Who Lead People: Engaging Employees through Leadership

Recent research by Dale Carnegie shows that employees' engagement levels rise when they believe in their senior leadership. Indeed, they feel most engaged when the company's leadership clearly communicates strategy and plans, connects with employees, and helps everyone feel part of where the organization is going. Leadership, then, is a key engagement driver! To find out how leadership begets engagement, read on.

Vice Versus: Management Versus Leadership

Often, people confuse the term *leader* with the term *manager*. But there's a big difference between them. A manager manages process, programs, and data. Leaders, on the other hand, guide people, build fellowship, and steer organizations to success (read: make money and grow). Leaders set the direction; managers follow the plan to get there. Yes, managers are indispensible when it comes to creating and monitoring policy. But it's leaders who define and uphold an organization's principles. And it's leaders — more specifically, *engaged* leaders — who really drive engagement in an organization.

Don't misunderstand me. I'm not denigrating the essential role that management plays in the stability of a company. In fact, it's critical for leaders to be effective managers as well as effective leaders. But because employee engagement entails a pervasive change in corporate culture, it unfortunately cannot be simply assigned to just any manager or management team.

Before you can get a handle on how leadership drives engagement, it's important to understand the difference between a leader and a manager. For help, see Table 7-1.

Table 7-1	Management versus Leadership
Management	*Leadership*
Management is about control.	Leadership is about trust and empowerment.
Management is about authority and hierarchy.	Leadership is about alignment and expertise.
Management involves discrete tasks.	Leadership's focus is on vision.
Management involves one-way communication.	Leadership involves two-way communication.
Management is characterized by following the plan.	Leadership is characterized by experimentation.
Management assumes a dominating perspective.	Leadership invites multiple perspectives.
With management, there is often one decision maker.	With leadership, team input is emphasized.
Management is about measurement.	Leadership is about personal accountability.
Management focuses on quick decision making.	Leadership focuses on wise decision making.
Management sticks with the tried and true.	Leadership seeks innovation.
Management assumes the role of director.	Leadership assumes the role of coach and counselor.
Management seeks to satisfy employees.	Leadership seeks to engage employees.

Table 7-2 offers another way of looking at the difference between managers and leaders.

Table 7-2	Managers versus Leaders
Managers	**Leaders**
Take care of where you are	Take you to a new place
Deal with complexity	Deal with uncertainty
Are efficient	Are effective
Create policies	Establish principles

The Big 12: Identifying 12 Leadership-Based Engagement Drivers

How, exactly, does a strong leader engage employees? One way to answer that question is to mention three things a strong leader *doesn't* do: spread negativity, cynicism, and skepticism. Instead, strong leaders engage employees by offering the following:

- **Trust:** You don't *get* trust unless you *give* trust. Strong leaders trust their employees. When employees feel trusted by their leaders, they're more likely to trust their leaders and be engaged. If employees don't feel trusted, they won't trust in return — and engagement will take a dive.

- **Authority:** For employees, feeling confident that someone is in charge can lay the foundation for engagement. If employees are worried that no one's at the helm of the ship, engagement will suffer.

- **Security:** Especially when the economy is suffering, security is key to engagement. Strong leaders leave their employees feeling like things will turn out okay, and in doing so, they boost engagement.

- **Direction:** A key part of leading is knowing where you're going — you can't expect people to follow you if you lack direction. Engagement suffers when leaders lack direction.

- **Vision:** Employees will be more engaged when their leaders have and convey a clear vision — one that inspires them to follow.

- **Structure:** The organization's structure must be such that everybody knows the organizations' boundaries. A lack of structure will quickly result in false assumptions, leading to disengagement.

- **Clarity:** Employees must understand what's expected of them.

✔ **A role model:** Employees need someone to look up to. Role models enable employees to pinpoint — and then emulate — behaviors that result in success.

✔ **Reassurance:** All employees seek reassurance. They want to feel as if someone is looking out for them. Failure to provide this can lead to a reduction in both confidence and engagement.

✔ **Cohesion:** Think of your team as a symphony. Although each person has her own part to play, everyone must be playing from the same musical score. This cohesion plays a big part in employee engagement.

✔ **Inspiration:** Chapter 6 discusses the importance of a sense of purpose. Giving people a sense of purpose inspires them, enabling them to feel good about what they're doing.

✔ **Recognition:** All employees want to feel that what they do matters. That's where recognition comes in. Chapter 17 covers recognition and rewards, and how they can help foster engagement.

Top It Off: Leadership Starts at the Top

It's not enough for line managers to work to engage employees. When it comes to engagement, leadership must come from the top.

Most CEOs are far more comfortable working their left (analytical, sequential, objective) brains than their right (random, creative, subjective) brains. As a result, many CEOs attempt to delegate the primary responsibility for engagement to HR or some "soft skill" function instead of championing the cause themselves.

Unless you want your employees' engagement levels to go the way of the dodo, you must do all you can to prevent top leaders from delegating engagement efforts. With all due respect to HR, if it owns engagement, engagement will likely be perceived by employees as just another "flavor of the month" program. Senior leaders *must* support engagement to prevent employees from assuming it's a touchy-feely, lip-service-only, employee-satisfaction initiative.

If the CEO lacks the time or talent to champion engagement, your firm must identify someone else at the senior level to take up the charge. This person must be senior enough to lend credibility to your engagement efforts, and preferably have the ear and support of the leader. Regardless of personal preferences, all senior leaders must speak the language of engagement and behave in demonstrably committed ways. Top leaders must believe in and be able to articulate engagement.

Holding leaders accountable for engagement levels in your firm is critical. Measurement is an important driver. Unless a CEO's board measures the CEO on engagement, the CEO may not have an impetus to lead any differently. Only when senior management is regularly measured and judged on engagement criteria (by reporting on engagement every quarter and communicating the CEO's performance metrics throughout the company) will they be motivated to measure up. For more on measuring engagement, see Chapter 15.

Although it's critical that senior leaders make the push for engagement, the things that drive engagement (see the preceding section) are largely the province of an organization's visionaries, role models, innovators, and counselors. These leaders may not be the most senior staff, hold the loftiest titles, or pull down the biggest salaries. But they make their mark on the company culture, inviting multiple perspectives and team decisions while retaining — and communicating — a strong sense of personal accountability.

Creative + leadership = creativeship

These days, mere leadership may not be enough. What's often needed is a little something I call *creativeship* — that is, creative leadership necessary to build a sustainable business model and culture. Creativeship enables businesses to engage employees and thrive in this new world of unprecedented technological advances, globalization, shifting economic drivers, government intervention, changing workforce demographics, widespread generational differences, and the emergence of corporate social responsibility as a motivational driver.

Briefly, creativeship involves focusing on six key priorities:

✔ **Purpose:** As discussed in Chapter 6, organizations must articulate both what they do and why they do it if they want to attract, hire, and retain top employees.

✔ **Engagement:** According to Gallup research, companies with high engagement levels are more than 200 percent more profitable than organizations with low engagement levels — which is why more and more leadership teams are asking their HR and OD staff to build engaged workforces.

✔ **Performance:** Creating sustainable cultures of performance at both the company and individual level is key.

✔ **Innovation:** Creating cultures of *innovation* fosters both engagement and sustainability. Companies fail when they stop evolving their product, service, and internal processes. That means investing today's cash to discover tomorrow's new technologies, products, services, geographies, and approaches.

✔ **Tri-branding:** Tri-branding, discussed in Chapter 10, occurs when organizations link their employment brand with their product or service brand, while at the same time leveraging third parties, including customers and suppliers, as brand ambassadors. The results are astounding!

✔ **Global growth:** The old business adage, "grow or die," is at the core of creativeship. In this era of globalization and technological advances, companies need to understand that they'll perish if they don't evolve, grow, expand, and morph. Companies that are local need to think regional; companies that are regional need to think national; companies that are national need to think global. (Shameless-plug alert: Creativeship is the topic of my second book, *Creativeship: A Novel for Evolving Leaders* [BLKB Publishing].)

Purple People Leader: Identifying the Behaviors and Traits of Engaged Leaders

Does this sound familiar? Mary is an exceptional engineer, so you promote her to be the department manager, and she fails miserably. Or, John is an outstanding nurse, so you promote him to be the nursing supervisor, and all the other nurses hate him. Or, Stephanie is your top salesperson, so you promote her to be the sales manager, and the sales team's quotas drop, big time.

Fact: It is actually quite rare for an outstanding employee in his job to also be an excellent *succession candidate* (that is, someone who could take over his boss's or his boss's boss's job). Why? Because the traits and behaviors needed to succeed as a engineer, nurse, or salesperson are often quite different from those required to be a successful leader. (You can find out more about key behaviors and traits in Chapter 12.) For example, an engineer probably doesn't need to be empathetic. But the person who manages the engineering department? That person probably does.

Strong people skills transcend technical capability. It's possible to successfully lead engineers, for example, without being one. For me, this point hits close to home. At one point in my career, I was asked to serve as chief operating officer of a global environmental consulting company, overseeing 2,000 engineers and scientists. I resisted, saying, "But I'm not an engineer!" My boss responded, "We have 2,000 engineers and scientists who all think alike. You, on the other hand, possess the behaviors and traits necessary to *lead.*"

The challenge facing many companies is that salaries and rank increase based on individuals' ability to leverage others to get things done. That's why upper managers make more money. In part because of this, a lot of people have aspirations to become leaders of people. But that doesn't mean everyone's good at it.

If you're considering hiring or promoting someone as a "people leader" in your organization, evaluate whether that person possesses the following traits:

- ✔ Caring
- ✔ Empathy
- ✔ Energy
- ✔ Equitableness
- ✔ Expressiveness
- ✔ Fairness

- ✔ Honesty
- ✔ Humility
- ✔ Neutrality
- ✔ Optimism
- ✔ Passion

In addition, great people leaders

- ✔ Communicate a clear vision for their part of the organization
- ✔ Translate their vision into motivating strategies and implementation plans
- ✔ Help people set short-term priorities in line with long-term goals
- ✔ Help direct reports understand how they contribute to the vision
- ✔ Recruit and hire talented, high-performing employees
- ✔ Clearly communicate performance expectations
- ✔ Manage and evaluate performance (including making the tough decisions)
- ✔ Focus on *how* results are achieved as much as on *what* results are achieved
- ✔ Recognize and reward achievement when performance surpasses expectations
- ✔ Base pay fairly on both quantitative and qualitative results
- ✔ Provide clear, specific direction and give open, honest feedback — including positive feedback, when deserved
- ✔ Place a high priority on coaching people
- ✔ Create a continuous learning environment
- ✔ Help others prepare for increased responsibility
- ✔ Proactively look to promote from within
- ✔ Work with employees to identify career-growth plans that link with business-growth plans (known as cross-training or professional development)
- ✔ Help less-experienced employees gain experience interacting with clients
- ✔ Look to eliminate unnecessary work or obstacles to productivity
- ✔ Proactively identify and develop a successor

- ✔ Maintain open communication
- ✔ Create an environment and culture that motivates and inspires, and enables others to succeed
- ✔ Inspire people to follow
- ✔ Willingly share their best individual talent with others
- ✔ Create and facilitate productive teams
- ✔ Delegate and empower
- ✔ Remain distant enough to be objective
- ✔ Keep their promises and honor their commitments
- ✔ Seek input before making key decisions
- ✔ Encourage feedback
- ✔ Listen
- ✔ Treat people with dignity and respect
- ✔ Respect the importance of other people's time
- ✔ Work cooperatively with others to achieve common goals
- ✔ Successfully manage conflict
- ✔ Assess issues and come up with shared solutions to improve performance
- ✔ Work effectively with peers and colleagues
- ✔ Strengthen employee/manager relationships and build a stronger team
- ✔ Work effectively in a cross-cultural environment
- ✔ Appreciate the value of diversity (race, nationality, culture, age, gender, sexual orientation)
- ✔ Adapt to cultural differences

If you need to assess someone's leadership capabilities — or your own — try using a scale of 1 to 10, with 1 meaning "not at all" and 10 meaning "excels at this," to rate that person on each of these items.

Take a hard look at your organization. Who are your best managers? What are the traits and behaviors that make them so good? These are the traits and behaviors that define success in your firm, and the traits and behaviors you must cultivate in each and every line manager. Be prepared to make an investment in the development of people skills in the same way you would in the development of technical skills. For more on assessing traits and behaviors, see Chapter 12.

Here Comes the Train Again: Training Managers to Become Engaged Leaders

If you want to be a doctor, you have to attend years of medical school. If your goal is to be a pilot, flight school is likely in your future. Yet, people often receive zero training — zip — when tapped by their firms to start leading people. Incredibly, we act like anyone can do it!

Guess what? They can't. Sure, some people are natural leaders. They just have it. But most people need a little training . . . even if they think they don't. (Unfortunately, the ability to lead others is a trait that almost everyone thinks they possess. For example, someone who would never venture an opinion on a technical issue often has completely misplaced confidence in his or her communication and team-building skills.)

"Sure," you say. "In a perfect world, we'd provide training for every new manager. But here at XYC Corp., we're too busy trying to get product out the door. We don't have time!"

Wrong. You have to make time. Practically every research study in the history of the world lists people's relationships with their leaders — or, more precisely, their managers, who *should* be their leaders — as a leading engagement driver (good manager) or *dis*engagement driver (bad manager). (One 2012 study, by *Parade* magazine, revealed that 35 percent of U.S. workers polled would trade a substantial pay increase for seeing their direct supervisor get fired.) Heck, there's even an adage about it: "People join great companies, but they leave bad managers." And yet, organizations put scant resources in training these most-valued assets — the people we entrust to lead, motivate, and engage our employees.

These people leaders can truly make or break your overall engagement efforts because they're perfectly positioned to transmit key information up and down the ranks.

The proper development of your firm's people leaders is one of the first "must do" items on your list. This should include supervisory training for first-line people leaders, who are often being asked to manage people for the first time. I've long been baffled by the fact that employees who need the most attention and leadership — entry-level staff — are often entrusted to managers who have, on average, the least experience, and who often lack the communication skills required to establish trust and create alignment.

Trust is the first step toward capturing discretionary effort — the invaluable byproduct of great leadership. If leaders withhold trust, they can hardly expect employees to trust the leadership in return. Leaders who trust their employees will soon see this trust reciprocated.

On the other side of the spectrum, senior leaders, who have honed their communication skills over the years and have loads of practice leading people, are most likely directing executives who are self-sufficient and independently motivated. In other words, those with the highest level of leadership skill and experience are leading people with nominal need, while those who lack leadership skill and experience are leading those with the greatest need. This situation can be a tremendous stumbling block to engagement. Clearly, if your first-line leaders are not in alignment with your company's engagement goals, your chances of success are slim to none.

Compounding this problem is the fact that line managers often achieve their position for the wrong reasons — chiefly tenure, technical ability, and personal ambition, rather than leadership ability. Few organizations consider "people skills" a core competency — let alone a requirement for advancement. But in order for your engagement efforts to work, these "soft" skills must be seen as a job requirement for managers. In addition, managers' effectiveness in engaging their staff must be measured. Otherwise, they simply won't make engagement a priority. Managers must be trained in, and evaluated on, leading people.

An organization needs talented, skilled leaders of people at the line-manager level. If a person doesn't like to lead people or isn't good at it, that person should not be in line for promotion to management, period, end of story.

Of course, for a leader to be able to engage others, she must also be engaged. Indeed, according to a 2009 study by Sirota Survey Intelligence, Inc., disengaged leaders are, on average, three times as likely to have disengaged direct reports. A key first step to building engagement among first-line leaders is to treat them as part of the leadership of the company. That means making sure that even first-line leaders receive critical communication in advance of the general population. They need thorough information on the issue, policy change, or strategic plan in play, including what has already been challenged or debated. They also need the opportunity to ask questions of their own. And they may need time to digest a policy change and to think through how it should be incorporated into their group's work. Most of all, they must appear informed when they pass along the information to their staff. Otherwise, their authority is diminished.

If line managers disagree with a corporate mandate, the proper forum for discussion is with his superiors, not with those lower in the chain. Agreeing to serve as a leader means forfeiting the right to vocal cynicism! That being said, effective managers also happen to be authentic, real, and transparent. Employees can see through a manager who engages in "corporate speak." Bottom line: Enthusiastically embracing a mandate is often a struggle when you know it may cause a disconnect with your employees. This is a fine line that managers have to walk.

Put Me In, Coach! Coaching for Engagement

A key aspect of leadership and engagement is coaching. Coaching may be provided by a manager, by a team leader, or by a formal or informal mentor. A coaching session could be an organized meeting or occur during a brief, informal conversation.

What is coaching, exactly? Simply put, coaching is about ongoing change and development. It's about helping others gain knowledge, information, and perspective to improve performance, develop competencies, build better relationships, enhance communication, enable different perspectives and insights, and identify and recognize strengths and potential.

A coach can help others explore new approaches to a problem, challenge them to take a risk, help them think of things differently, assist them as they strive to complete a stretch goal. Coaches regularly provide direction, instruction, feedback, recognition, support, and encouragement to the individuals or groups they lead.

A quick guide to coaching

Coaching is a continuous process, consisting of three primary steps:

1. **Set expectations and confirm a plan of action.**

   Countless times in my career, I've been brought in to arbitrate a conflict between a boss and an employee. More often than not, these issues have their roots in a lack of expectations and objectives, and no plan in place to ensure regular follow-up. Typically, the boss has been vague with instructions, and then becomes upset when the employee interprets the vague instructions incorrectly. Almost always, the manager coaching the employee through the process would have resulted in a productive outcome. Chapter 16 discusses why this practice is so important!

2. **Observe performance and provide developmental opportunities.**

   Part of the plan of action should be to build in regular check-in points to make sure the employee has a go-to person for questions and input, and to ensure the employee is being developed to succeed. A manager who is willing to provide a stretch assignment can really engage an employee, but ongoing coaching will be required to ensure development.

Formal versus informal coaching

Throughout this chapter, you see references to formal and informal coaching. *Formal* simply refers to coaching or mentoring that occurs as part of the line organization (in other words, by "the boss"), by design (for example, as part of a formal mentoring program), or using company-approved tools (such as performance appraisal forms or 360 feedback instruments). *Informal* refers to coaching that a protégé seeks on her own or to coaching offered by a manager or mentor outside the official tools and process of the company.

3. **Solicit or offer feedback and provide direction, instruction, or perspective as needed.**

    This step is so critical in coaching. Engaged managers create cultures where it's safe for an employee to ask for help, instructions, clarifications, and insight. People respond to positive recognition; an employee who receives positive reinforcement through coaching is more often than not going to excel.

All three steps apply whether the coaching is formal or informal.

A key to coaching for performance and development is creating dialogue that encourages the "coachee" to self-reflect and disclose information about his or own performance. Honest, two-way discussion about progress toward goals and feedback on specific behaviors is the aim. Effective two-way dialogue involves the following:

✔ **Speaking:** Asking questions and giving feedback

✔ **Checking:** Checking for a response

✔ **Listening:** Using active listening skills

Coaching is not about "fixing" people, or about the coach having all the answers. It's a give and take.

Effective coaching requires the following core communication skills:

✔ **Active listening:** This is a set of skills — namely, attending, following, and reflecting (that is, briefly restating, in your own words, the core of what the speaker has communicated) — that demonstrate that you understand the thoughts and feelings being communicated by the other person from her frame of reference.

✔ **Soliciting self-feedback:** To solicit self-feedback, you must ask questions to get the other person to reflect on his own performance. This helps the person think critically, leading to increased self-awareness and ownership of one's performance and development. Key questions include, "Specifically, what did you do well?" and "What would you do differently next time?"

✔ **Giving feedback:** You must give feedback to reinforce or correct behavior, leading to greater results and effectiveness.

✔ **Asking questions:** Asking the right questions can be incredibly powerful. Doing so can help people to think more critically, help them explore and solve their own problems, and lead to self-discovery — or, to quote Oprah, that "a-ha" moment. For best results, use *open-ended questions* (that is, questions whose responses tend to be sentences, explanations, or insights) to solicit self-feedback and facilitate insight and learning. Use *closed questions* (that is, questions that require no explanation or insight, and often result in single-word answers) to focus a conversation or to clarify information.

✔ **Providing perspective:** A key aspect to coaching is helping your coachee find and understand additional information — to take a broader view of issues and challenges. You can use several lenses to view problems or opportunities. For example, you may discuss how other people or groups may view the situation. Also, discuss the multiple aspects and impacts of an issue — for example, by running "what if" scenarios.

When it comes to coaching, keep the following tips in mind:

✔ Before you start coaching, make sure there are shared expectations for the coaching discussion.

✔ Keep the conversation focused and on track, and create two-way dialogue.

✔ Solicit information from the coachee to find out how she self-assesses her own behavior, strengths, and areas for improvement.

✔ Listen to truly understand the other person's unique points of view. Be an effective listener.

✔ Provide feedback that is timely, specific, and objective.

✔ Be able to deal with difficult situations, such as defusing and addressing defensive reactions to corrective feedback.

✔ Ask effective, open-ended, clarifying questions, followed by silence, to allow your coachee to reflect and answer the question completely before moving on to the next question/subject.

✔ Facilitate the process of brainstorming and problem solving in coaching discussions instead of just giving the coachee the answer.

✔ Help others to understand and explore alternative perspectives when considering different actions or solutions to an issue.

✔ Help others to feel re-energized, focused, and committed as a result of a coaching discussion.

✔ Support your coachees in helping them develop their own action plan for their development. This should include setting short-term and long-term goals.

✔ Instill a sense of accountability with employees by coaching them on success measures and following up on their progress.

To better understand your current coaching skills and capabilities, try ranking your skill level with regard to each of the preceding tips, assigning a score of 1 to your weakest skill and a score of 12 to your strongest skill. Use each number only once. After you've ranked yourself, look at the skills you ranked the lowest. These are the ones you probably need to work on. Don't forget about the other skills, however. Even the ones you ranked highest may require attention.

Using the GROW model

When planning a coaching session, whether formal or informal, consider using the GROW model. GROW stands for the following:

✔ **Goal:** What is your goal? What do you want to achieve? To determine this, you might ask the following questions:

- What would you like to discuss?

- What do you really want?

- What is stopping you?

- What is important to you about this?

✔ **Reality:** What is the current reality of your situation? You might assess this by asking the following questions:

- What's going on/getting in your way?

- What have you tried so far?

- What worked or didn't work?

- What decisions do you need to make?

✔ **Options:** What are your options? To establish these, try asking the following questions:

- What might you do to reach your goal?

- What if that course of action doesn't work?

- What is another way of looking at this?

- What else do you need to take into consideration?

- What is another possibility or option?

- What is the upside or downside?

✔ **Will:** What will you do or commit to? To tease out this information, consider the following questions:

- What will you do?

- When will you do it?

- What support do you need to accomplish it?

Do This, Not That: Identifying Leadership Best Practices

There are countless leadership best practices and traps to avoid. Indeed, whole libraries are filled with books on how to effectively lead people. Following are just a few practices that can make an immediate difference, are free to implement, and can be used by leaders at all levels with little training or skill. As you work to improve leadership skills, consider the "best practices" in this section.

I feel you, man

Know what your employees like — and hate — both inside and outside of work. If you take away nothing else from this book, take away this: A top engagement driver is showing your employees you care about them as people. It takes all of two seconds to ask an employee how his weekend was, or how his daughter's dance recital went, or if his wife recovered from the flu. It's probably no coincidence that my favorite boss ever also happened to know the names of my kids. Obtaining and weaving this knowledge into your daily chit-chat with employees goes a long way toward engaging them.

If what your employees love (or hate) is different from what you love (or hate), suck it up. Act interested. Sure, it's a basic thing, but it goes a long way toward earning their devotion and ensuring their continued engagement. Besides, you may learn something!

Offering a hand up

Make employees feel as though you really care about their careers. Part of your job is to give your employees experiences at your firm that they couldn't have elsewhere — experiences that will make them more valuable. Sure, you hope your employees stay with your firm for a long time, but if the day comes when they need to move on to another company, that's okay. That concept may feel scary. After all, you're basically saying that your employees should feel free to take what they've learned with your organization and move on — maybe even to a competitor. But working to grow your talent, and communicating your efforts, is a great way to foster engagement.

Chapter 6 talks about developing a "line of sight" for your organization. In addition to this "macro" line of sight, there's also a "micro" line of sight that exists on an employee level. This line of sight is all about "What job do I currently have?" and "Where am I going?" The more concern you show for your employees' growth and development in their careers — their personal "lines of sight" — the greater the probability you'll have engaged employees.

You're not the boss of me!

Stop telling employees what to do. Instead, force them to help come up with solutions. Often, when managers spot a performance issue, they simply tell the employee what she needs to do to improve. There's no interaction, no dialogue, nothing. A better approach is to make an observation and then shut your cake hole and let the employee talk. Whatever the solution turns out to be, you'll almost certainly get better buy-in with this approach.

Also, avoid describing how to do a project or task. Give your employee the destination, but leave the driving directions to her. Employees often have their own ideas about process, and those ideas are often quicker, more innovative, and more efficient than the "tried and true."

Recognize, recognize, recognize

When it comes to engaging employees, recognition is one of the most effective weapons in a leader's arsenal. Experienced managers have learned what neuroscientists and child psychologists have known for decades: Positive reinforcement and recognition lead to the replication of positive results. This is such a key leadership best practice, I've devoted an entire chapter to it — namely, Chapter 17.

Chapter 8

Talkin' 'Bout My Generation: Driving Engagement across Generations

Do you have teenagers or kids in their 20s? If so, have you ever tried leaving them a voicemail? Assuming your kids are like mine, they probably texted you back with a one-word response: "What?" Don't bother asking if they listened to the message — I can promise you, they didn't. See, young people today communicate differently than, say, Baby Boomers.

People of different generations don't just communicate differently. They also have different motivational drivers. Smart managers adjust their communication, leadership, oversight, recognition, and patience levels when leading a department populated by people of different generations.

Just who comprises each of these generations? And what do they want? For a run down, read on. This chapter focuses on the unique differences between the three generations that dominate today's workplace — Baby Boomers, Generation X, and Generation Y (also known as Millennials) — and how you can best drive engagement with each group.

The descriptions that follow are merely generational generalizations. Expect some exceptions to the rule. That said, most employers (and employees) will recognize the truths in the traits associated with each generation.

Boom Baby: Attracting, Training, Engaging, and Rewarding Baby Boomers

Generally identified as being born between the years of 1945 and 1964, Baby Boomers are idealistic and have a tendency toward personal and social expression. The first generation to earn and possess more than their parents, Baby Boomers are typically ambitious, materialistic, and prone to being workaholics.

Questioning authority — a tenet for masses of young people in the 1960s and 1970s — is still very much a part of the Boomer approach to life and to work. Boomers are far more apt to challenge leadership than those who came before them, and also to embrace change. Boomers also remember when getting e-mail was a good thing, and not overwhelming.

Unlike their predecessors, Baby Boomers have largely opted against retiring at age 65. Why? For one thing, they like their jobs. Sure, if they'd worked in a coal mine or an assembly line for the last 30 years, they might feel differently. But many Baby Boomers work in knowledge-based positions, which are often quite engaging. Besides, with the demise of traditional pension plans — plus the fact that people are, on average, living longer — many Boomers have found that retirement at 65 is not financially feasible.

Traditionalists (a.k.a., "The Silent Generation")

Don't assume that Baby Boomers comprise the oldest members of your employee roster. There may remain a few "Traditionalists," or workers born between 1925 and 1944 (though not many, given their age). Traditionalist workers are motivated by conformity, stability, security, and upward mobility. They tend to pledge allegiance to the company that employs them. They identify with the statement "I will give my all to my company" with nearly the same fervor they might once have felt for "I will fight for my country." This theme was popularized in Tom Brokaw's book *The Greatest Generation* (Random House). This generation is also characterized by a respect for authority. As such, their fidelity to the company often blends seamlessly with their loyalty to superiors and co-workers.

Traditionalists take pride in doing their work consistently, dependably, and well, but they likely aren't interested in the latest technological tools or the hottest trends in management. With retirement looming, many Traditionalists are motivated by the desire to leave the workforce in security and comfort, and pleased that they fulfilled their employment obligations to their companies. Due to today's difficult economic conditions, however, some Traditionalists, like many Boomers, have postponed retirement until their savings recover. This can lead to tensions with the younger staff, who are looking to move up.

Attracting and hiring Boomers

Boomers are ambitious — always have been, always will be. That said, an emerging trend is Boomers' increasing interest in corporate social responsibility (CSR). Having successfully climbed the corporate ladder and accumulated the things their parents couldn't afford, Baby Boomers seem to have experienced a resurgence of concern about social and environmental issues. This reawakening is due in part to the importance of CSR among Generation Y workers. Indeed, working alongside this younger generation seems to have inspired Boomers to levels of activism they may associate with their youth.

Smart organizations include CSR activities as a hiring hook to lure Baby Boomers. Many older workers who view themselves as being "on the back nine" of their careers are more inclined than ever to bypass the big paycheck (and related pressure) to take on a job with a more altruistic theme. Other recruitment hooks for this generation include job variety, travel, opportunities to learn new skills, and opportunities to teach and mentor younger workers. For more on CSR, see Chapter 6.

Training Boomers

Everyone knows the saying "You can't teach an old dog new tricks." But the thing about that saying is, it's wrong. You *can* teach an old dog new tricks. You just have to know what training method to use!

When it comes to training Boomers, you'll want to keep these points in mind:

- ✔ **Include team activities.** Yes, everyone says they hate team activities, role playing, and experiential exercises. But in course evaluations, team activities almost always get the highest marks. See, people *say* they don't like these activities, but I promise you: They dislike sitting in a chair for hours, being lectured to, and looking at PowerPoint slides even more. If done well, team activities can be incredibly effective ways to teach and engage Boomers (as well as other generations). In fact, based on research by the National Training Laboratories in Arlington, Virginia, hands-on training is effective with 75 percent of people, second only to teaching others.

- ✔ **Let participants experience different team roles.** Job rotation, even on a temporary basis, is a great way to reinforce learning with Baby Boomers. It will also build greater understanding of and appreciation for others' jobs — the "walk a mile in her shoes" thing.

- ✔ **Align training with the company's strategic plan.** Boomers are goal driven. The more a company can link learning with organizational goals, the better. If employee engagement is a strategic goal of the company,

Boomers are far more likely to embrace engagement-training initiatives. Having led employee-engagement workshops all over the world, I can say firsthand that training "stickiness" is greatly enhanced when the engagement workshop is connected to the organizational goals. Decoupling from organizational goals turns the learning opportunity into a "flavor of the month."

✔ **Allow time after training for participants to evaluate.** The best evaluations to weigh the effectiveness of training occur 60 to 90 days *after* the learning event. Waiting two or three months provides you with feedback on whether the participants are applying the learning in their jobs.

Engaging Boomers

To engage Baby Boomers on your staff, you'll want to consider the following:

✔ **Foster a non-authoritarian work environment.** Boomers don't like being told what to do. An authoritarian culture will meet resistance at best, and disengagement at worst. At this stage of their careers, Boomers are set in their ways. They have — or believe they have — accomplished a lot. Not surprisingly, a democratic leadership style goes a long way toward engaging Boomers.

✔ **Tap into their experience.** Ask questions like the following:

- "So, what do you suggest?"

- "How have you done this in the past?"

- "What has worked best when you've tried to do this?"

- "How would you recommend we proceed?"

Asking these and related questions will engage Boomers. It shows respect for their years in the trenches.

✔ **Offer fresh assignments and other development opportunities.** After years of climbing the corporate ladder, Boomers may be interested in lateral or even lower-level positions — *if* the positions will allow them to do new jobs or learn new skills. Shifting assignments will also boost innovation, because it invites new and different perspectives.

✔ **Be aware of the challenges they face.** Many Boomers wrestle with various personal challenges, such as paying college tuition for their children, subsidizing older children, and/or taking care of aging parents. In addition, some Boomers may be experiencing their own medical issues for the first time. Managers who are empathetic about all the things Boomers must juggle in their complex lives will be rewarded over time with above-and-beyond effort.

✔ **Foster collaboration.** The idealism that encouraged many of this generation to boycott the Vietnam War still kindles a desire to be part of "something bigger." As such, Boomers tend to be highly engaged by working in partnership or as part of a team.

✔ **Encourage expression.** Boomers enjoy opportunities for expression. They're among the ranks of workers who are truly engaged by meetings — especially when said meetings involve the exchange of ideas that intrigue them.

✔ **Engage in CSR.** To engage Boomers, encourage social activism, volunteerism, and CSR activities. As Chapter 6 discusses, Boomers are looking for ways to give back.

Rewarding Boomers

Boomers respond well to the following types of rewards:

✔ **Key assignments:** Although people tend to associate the term *reward* with something monetary, that's not always the case. Why not reward a Boomer with an international assignment, a transfer, or a key slot on the company's five-year strategic planning committee? Leveraging and acknowledging Boomers' experience is a benefit to both the company *and* the deserving Boomer!

✔ **Acknowledgment of their accomplishments and their years of service:** Chapter 17 discusses employee recognition as a key engagement driver. Public recognition, handwritten notes, saying "Job well done!", and similar acknowledgments of an employee's accomplishments and/or tenure are important engagement drivers for all generations, including Boomers.

✔ **Promotional opportunities:** Baby Boomers are the wealthiest generation ever, and they didn't build that wealth by accident. They are, and remain, quite ambitious. Many organizations fail to understand that ambition is a competency that must be leveraged among employees who demonstrate it. In this world of work–life balance, organizations often struggle to find the employee who is willing to take on a key position that requires above-and-beyond effort. Thankfully, Boomers have a history of climbing the next rung of the ladder, and many continue to be motivated by that next great promotion.

✔ **CSR activities:** Rewarding Boomers by enabling them to give back is a great engagement driver. For example, many Boomers would respond very positively to a paid week to build homes for the homeless with an organization such as Habitat for Humanity.

X Marks the Spot: Attracting, Training, Engaging, and Rewarding Generation X

The first generation to insist on work–life balance, this group, born between 1965 and 1980, includes more women, as well as men who have assumed more home and family responsibilities. Not surprisingly, Generation X was also the generation that pushed for paternity benefits and support for stay-at-home dads. This generation was the first to rely heavily on technology.

After watching their parents and older siblings get laid off or fired by an increasingly un-loyal corporate America, Generation X brought free agency to the workplace. What do I mean by "free agency"? Let's use a sports analogy. It used to be that a top-level athlete would play his whole career for a single team. Carl Yastrzemski, Al Kaline, Magic Johnson, and Dan Marino are but a few examples. These days, however, these athletes are in the minority. More and more athletes follow the money. At the same time, the franchises they play for are quick to trade or cut players. Loyalty is dead in sports, and in many ways, it's dead in business as well. Cradle-to-grave employment has been replaced by business free agency. Employers no longer offer the same long-term benefits and security to their employees, and employees are quick to quit a job to follow a boss, to pursue a new opportunity, or to stay home to raise their children.

Caught between Baby Boomers and Generation Y, Gen X workers are experiencing growing unrest. Because their Baby Boomer predecessors have delayed retirement (or opted out altogether), members of Generation X have been denied opportunities to advance. Their situation has been made even worse by the Great Recession of 2008–2009, which has resulted in fewer growth opportunities. And of course, there's Generation Y — soon to be the largest demographic in the workforce — breathing down Generation X's neck. It's no wonder many Gen Xers, who often view their younger cohorts as spoiled, lazy, and the recipients of way too much attention, feel stuck with no place to go! Nonetheless, they do represent the next generation of senior leaders. Figuring out how to attract, develop, and engage Generation X will be key to any organization's success.

Attracting and hiring Generation X

Members of Generation X have been frustrated by their career progression — or lack thereof. Having been pummeled by a deep and painful recession, Gen X is waiting for its next big opportunity.

In the years ahead, money will be more of a driver for Generation X than for its Boomer and Gen Y counterparts. More than any other generation, Gen X has borne the brunt of the collapse in the mortgage industry, and many still owe more on their homes than those homes are worth.

Fairness is also important to Gen X. Many Gen Xers feel that the cards have been stacked against them, and they're looking for an opportunity that evens the score — at least financially. (As you'll learn in later chapters, the perception of unfairness is a major *dis*engagement driver.) Other recruitment hooks for this group include technology, benefits (after all, they're the ones now having babies), and development opportunities.

Training Generation X

Training is important to Generation X. They're all about development opportunities. When training members of this generation, you'll want to consider the following:

✔ **Include lots of activities and individual report-backs.** As with Boomers, building experiential exercises and activities into training opportunities is important. However, unlike their Boomer predecessors, Gen Xers are still looking to prove themselves and itching to show their stuff. It's a good idea to give members of Gen X opportunities to co-lead the training, take the lead on report-backs, and otherwise shine in front of their peers. "Teaching others" is the top way in which people learn; Gen Xers are primed to take the lead in teaching others while boosting their own learning during training events.

✔ **Have more than one solution to case studies.** Now more than ever, Gen X wants to be heard, seen, and given an opportunity to make its own footprint. Pressed between two sizable generations, Gen X has ideas and wants to share them. If you expect Gen Xers to follow suit or go along with the tried and true, you risk disengaging them and losing out on a significant learning opportunity. Best-in-class organizations bring together their high potentials (often disproportionately made up of Gen X) and invite them to tackle organizational challenges, explore new markets, or evaluate the business case to expand their product offerings.

✔ **Align training with the company's mission.** Members of Generation X are similar to members of other generations in that their training time can best be leveraged if they see a "line of sight" between the time necessary to train and the relationship of the training with the company's overall mission.

✔ **Allow participants to provide feedback during the training session.** Whereas Boomers are often more comfortable providing feedback after a training event, members of Generation X are more "instant" in their willingness (and desire) to provide feedback on the training they're receiving. Consider it "real-time" quality improvement for your training program.

Engaging Generation X

If you're tasked with engaging Gen Xers, consider these points:

✔ **Don't pile it on.** Boomers may be motivated by a heavy workload, but the opposite is often true of Generation X. Instead, *independence* and *free agency* are watchwords for Gen X. If they sense that these values aren't being honored, they'll likely become cynical about their jobs.

✔ **Avoid meetings.** Generation X was the first generation to grow up with technology. As a result, members of this group often prefer to communicate via e-mail (or electronic bulletins or newsletters) rather than attending meetings.

✔ **Flexibility is key.** Despite a perception on the part of some of their elders that they work less, Gen Xers usually make up for the time they've taken to attend a child's play or soccer game by working nights or weekends.

✔ **Offer training and development opportunities.** Right now, members of this generation are quite career oriented. They see themselves as next in line to take the reins. But as older workers stay on in the workplace, Gen Xers may grow impatient. To keep them engaged, you need to make them feel that they're learning and growing. Thus, training and development are huge engagement drivers for this group.

Looking to attract and engage more Gen Xers (and Gen Yers) to your firm? Use the sheet in Figure 8-1 to note what you do now in terms of CSR, workforce flexibility, innovation, rotation of assignments, and branding, and what you *could* do in each of those categories.

Rewarding Generation X

Here are some rewards that will help motivate members of Generation X:

✔ **Time off:** Gen X brought the concept of work–life balance to the workplace, and today they're at the age where they're working parents with dual responsibilities. Companies should occasionally offer the option of a financial reward or an enhanced vacation or time-off benefit.

✔ **Professional development opportunities:** Gen Xers see themselves as next in line and are often hungry for the necessary stretch assignment, executive education course, job transfer, or other opportunity to enhance their personal and professional development.

Attracting Gen X and Gen Y

What do you or could you do right now to be more attractive to engaged Gen X and Gen Y employees?

	What do you do now?	What could you do?
Corporate Social Responsibility		
Workforce Flexibility		
Innovation		
Rotation of Assignments		
Branding – "We're great!"		

Figure 8-1: Attract and engage Gen X and Gen Y.

Illustration by Wiley, Composition Services Graphics

✔ **Accelerated promotions:** Early in their careers, it was common for Boomers to wait their turn for a promotional opportunity. For example, at one engineering company I worked for, project managers were required to have ten years' experience. Generation X — and Generation Y, for that matter — will not and should not wait a certain number of years for a promotion. Instead of "putting in their time," they'll simply quit and go elsewhere. Accelerating Gen X into stretch assignments will go a long way toward engaging this generation.

✔ **Technology upgrades:** Generation X grew up with technology and is tech savvy. If you saddle a Gen Xer with yesterday's technology, it will become an irritant. Giving a Gen Xer a laptop (instead of a desktop) may not, in and of itself, make her feel satisfied, but if you *don't* provide it, she'll feel unhappy. In other words, technology may not be critical to Gen Xers' overall engagement, but not having it may lead to their *dis*engagement.

✔ **Participation on a prestigious committee:** If Gen X represents the next generation to lead your firm, why not ask them to lead the next strategic planning committee or other high-profile organizational subcommittee? Not only will this help engage them, but you'll also benefit because their insights are different from those of their Boomer predecessors.

✔ **Opportunities to present to the senior leadership team:** Want to engage a high-potential Gen Xer? Ask him to attend — or better yet, present at — the next board meeting, senior management offsite, or executive leadership team monthly meeting. Presenting to the bosses will be highly engaging to your high-potential Gen Xers.

Y Ask Y: Attracting, Training, Engaging, and Rewarding Generation Y

Born between 1980 and 2002, this highly computer-oriented group is characterized by hope about the future, social activism, family-centricity, and the desire for diversity. Before the recession of 2008–2009, the average tenure of Generation Y, or Millennial, workers at any given job was a mere 20 months — significantly shorter than their older cohorts. Experts predict this behavior will likely recur as the economy picks back up.

Generation Y workers — which will soon be the largest workforce demographic (if they aren't already) — require a continuous flow of positive feedback. *Remember:* Members of this generation were somewhat pampered by their Baby Boomer parents. For this generation, trophies were awarded to both winning *and* losing teams; seat belts and car seats were *required* car accessories; and in some cases, the traditional A through F school grades were replaced by the gentler "below/meeting/exceeding expectations" metric.

Attracting and hiring Generation Y

Chapter 6 discusses the importance of purpose and the notion of CSR. Gen Y in particular wants to work for a "company that cares" — one that donates to charity, is concerned about the environment, and supports volunteerism. That means that if you're looking to recruit the best of the best among Gen Y, you really need to crystallize your company's "why" as part of your company's employee value proposition (EVP; see Chapter 10).

Millennials are also quite receptive to branding, and they're willing to work for a cool brand for lower pay. If you don't believe me, walk into any Apple Store. You'll see the highest engagement with the lowest pay anywhere. These store associates are willing to accept low wages for an opportunity to work for one of the coolest brands and cultures around.

Training Generation Y

As the youngest members of the workforce, Generation Y is perhaps most in need of training. When training members of Generation Y, keep these points in mind:

- ✔ **Use technology and lots of variety in teaching methods.** If you're speaking to members of Gen Y in a class setting, don't even think about using bulleted PowerPoint slides as your mode of delivery. Today's training professionals understand the importance of incorporating videos, movie clips, video blogs (*vlogs* for short), music, and other media into their presentations. For example, when training on team development and cohesion, you might show the movie *Miracle,* about the U.S. men's hockey team, which won the gold medal in the 1980 Olympics, followed by a highly interactive debrief. Your Gen Y attendees will respond far more favorably than the standard (and oh-so-Boomer) data-intensive PowerPoint slides.

- ✔ **Don't have just one solution to case studies.** Gen Yers, like their Gen X predecessors, feel they have lots to offer (no doubt due in part to the fact that their parents have been telling them how wonderful they are since birth). And in reality, they do. They'll push you to include in your case studies solutions that are rich in technology, mobile applications, cloud computing, social media, gamification (see Chapter 11), and other key trends that Boomers may just be reading about.

✓ **Align training with the company's values and positive image.** Members of Generation Y want to work for a purpose-driven organization. Linking training to your firm's values and brand will have longer-term leverage.

✓ **Allow participants to provide feedback during the training session.** Be aware that participants will expect praise for providing this feedback. Consider leveraging the many real-time feedback tools available to enable your employees to be active participants in the training event.

Engaging Generation Y

Are you tasked with engaging Millennials? If so, here are a few ideas:

✓ **Harness technology for communication.** Where Gen Xers are technologically *savvy,* Gen Yers are technologically *dependent.* Having grown up well after the advent of computers, the Internet, and mobile phones, Gen Y is accustomed to enjoying instant communication and having information at their fingertips. Note, however, that they increasingly eschew both phones and e-mail in favor of text messaging — important to consider if your company's communication protocol involves lengthy missives from the CEO.

✓ **Allow for mobility and flexibility.** Millennials are attracted to new technologies, especially those that grant them increased mobility. If your Gen X workers looked at the desktop computer as a dinosaur, preferring a laptop computer in its stead, don't be surprised to see your Gen Y employees take things a step further and request tablets to get their jobs done. Trust me: You'll recoup the cost by capturing their discretionary effort during non-work hours. And if telecommuting and/or flextime is an option, all the better.

✓ **Allow for job rotation.** Earlier generations saw job rotation as nice to have. For Millennials, however, job rotation is a must. Unlike some older employees, Gen Y is not particularly concerned with permanence or security. Instead, many view abruptly changing career directions to be perfectly acceptable solutions if they're dissatisfied with their jobs. If you want your Millennials to stick around, you must allow them to take on different jobs or do the same jobs differently.

✓ **Give frequent feedback.** Boomers may happily go years between performance appraisals. But recognition, praise, and constructive criticism are not only welcomed by both younger groups, but are means to motivate them. Gen Xers require a little more attention in this area, but will likely be satisfied with mid-year performance feedback in addition to their annual performance review. Millennials, however, are likely to ask, "How am I doing *today?*" When you have Millennials on staff, be prepared to offer constant feedback!

✔ **Don't restrict Internet or social media use.** Many organizations restrict employees' use of the Internet and social media, citing employees who "waste time" using these technologies. But if your employees are downloading the latest Muse video off YouTube or socializing on Facebook four hours a day, you have a *performance* problem, not an Internet or social media problem. Too many IT departments look at the Internet and social media as a hardware issue ("They'll shut down our server!") and block the use of these invaluable communications tools. The Internet, along with social media, can be amazing research, communication, branding, and engagement enablers. Plus, if you restrict their use, employees — particularly Gen Yers — will simply obtain access via their own mobile devices during work hours. Trust your employees to do the right thing, and more often than not, they will!

✔ **Invite Millennials to serve on social committees.** If Gen X brought work–life balance to the workplace, Gen Y is bringing work–life *blending.* Millennials are a social and networked generation, accustomed to connecting with a wide universe. For them, the walls between work and play are porous. They're hungry to bring their work colleagues into their social sphere. Engage them to participate and perhaps even lead your social committees, CSR initiatives, and so on. They're a ready and able committee waiting to be asked to help socialize your business.

Looking to attract and engage more Millennials to your firm? Refer to the sheet in Figure 8-2 and note what you do now in terms of CSR, workforce flexibility, innovation, rotation of assignments, and branding, and what you *could* do in each of those categories.

Engagement and globalization

Experts predict that in the United States and other parts of the Western world, Gen Y will be the first generation that *won't* make as much money as their parents did. For developing nations, however, it's a different story. Young workers elsewhere around the world — for example, in India and China — will likely see opportunities that their parents were never offered. It's no surprise, then, that these workers behave more like Baby Boomers than their Gen Y counterparts. Many are even Traditionalist in nature, feeling nearly as committed to their companies as they are to their families. Less important is work–life balance, which is such a priority among younger generations in the United States. My point? If you work for a global organization, you'll need to be aware that the "regular" generation-based engagement drivers may not apply.

Next up: Preparing for the next generation

So far, we don't know much about the next generation — the "Net Generation," or "Generation Z," or whatever else society decides to call the generation that follows Gen Y. All we know is, they *will* be different from all generations that preceded them. Born after 2002, the next generation will primarily be children of Gen X parents and will be the most connected generation ever. These kids, some of whom played with iPads as babies, believe having access to all things electronic is a way of life. They don't view technology as a tool or a device; instead, they view everything in instant and connected terms.

Rewarding Generation Y

The following serve as excellent rewards for Millennials:

- ✔ **Professional development opportunities:** According to a 2011 PricewaterhouseCooper study, training and development is the most highly valued employee benefit among Millennials. In fact, the number of Millennials who cited this as their most prized benefit was *three* times higher than those who chose cash bonuses.

- ✔ **Tangible rewards:** Millennials have received trophies, ribbons, and other awards their whole lives — even when they lost. That makes them particularly amenable to tangible rewards, such as certificates.

- ✔ **Regular feedback:** As far as Gen Y is concerned, your annual performance appraisal process is, like, so yesterday. Instead, they need — indeed, they *require* — frequent feedback. They expect to be told they've done a terrific job, time and time again. In fact, some experts say that to truly engage members of this generation, they need to be recognized eight times a day.

Putting It All Together

As you develop your organization's engagement plan, you'll want to take all these generational differences into consideration. First, however, you should get a sense of how many Millennials, Gen Xers, Boomers, and even Traditionalists you have in your firm. Use a form like the one in Figure 8-2 to write down your numbers.

	Traditionalist	Boomer	Gen X	Gen Y
National average	4.7%	38.6%	32.2%	24.7%
Total				
By location				
Location #1				
Location #2				
Location #3				

Figure 8-2:
Track your generational demographics.

Illustration by Wiley, Composition Services Graphics

For help juggling the various priorities of each generation, see Table 8-1.

Table 8-1	Generations at Work		
	Baby Boomers (Born 1946–1964)	**Generation X (Born 1965–1980)**	**Generation Y (Born 1980–2002)**
Values	Workaholic	Life balance	Team player
	Competitive	Global thinking	Enthusiasm for change
	Innovative	Diversity	Respect for authority
	Questions authority	Unimpressed by authority	Tempered hopefulness
	Materialism	Fun	Sociability
	Personal/social expression	Self-reliance	Optimism
	Skepticism	Cynicism/ pessimism	
Work Is	An exciting adventure	A difficult challenge	A means to an end
Leadership Style	Consensual Collegial	Challenges others	To be determined

(continued)

Table 8-1 (continued)

	Baby Boomers (Born 1946–1964)	Generation X (Born 1965–1980)	Generation Y (Born 1980–2002)
Communication	In person	Direct	Text message
	In meetings	Immediate	Direct message
		E-mail	Twitter
		Voicemail	Instagram
			YouTube
Feedback	Doesn't appreciate it	Asks, "How am I doing?"	At the push of a button
Rewards	Money	Freedom	Meaningful work
	Title	Independence	
	Recognition		
Motivation	The need to feel valued and needed	Do it "my way"	Work with bright staff
		Work–life balance	Work–life balance
			Social interaction through technology
Engagement Strategies	Establish non-authoritarian environment	Allow time for questions	Provide interaction with colleagues
	Offer fresh assignments	Provide references	Bring up to speed quickly
	Provide developmental experiences	Use time-efficient approaches	Encourage mentoring
	Tap into their expertise	Keep up a quick pace	Use technology
	Ease pressure of complex life	Be specific about growth	Nonparental approach
		Allow time to earn their respect	

Knowing the traits commonly found among members of a particular generation can help you pinpoint what drives the individuals in your firm. One Gen Y woman I supervised was incredibly driven by recognition. Money was practically irrelevant to her. So, I made sure she had plenty of face time with executives whenever the opportunity arose. On the opposite end of the spectrum was a Boomer in his late 50s, who showed signs of becoming disengaged during a period when layoffs were necessary. Recognizing that this man's various financial responsibilities likely made security a key driver, I frequently went out of my way to reassure him that his job was safe.

The generations do have very different views on authority, teamwork, development, and work–life balance, but everyone — regardless of age — wants the following:

- ✔ **Achievement:** Taking pride in one's work

- ✔ **Camaraderie:** Having positive, inclusive, and productive relationships

- ✔ **Equality:** Being treated fairly in matters such as pay, benefits, and developmental opportunities

Smart bosses know that to boost engagement, they must build cultures with these three values in mind.

Chapter 9

Go, Team! Driving Engagement through Team Development

*O*ne of my all-time favorite jobs was working as a grocery clerk at a neighborhood grocer throughout high school and college. Over the years, when I've bumped into former co-workers, we've often reflected on what an amazing experience we had working there. I've come to realize that stocking shelves is not in and of itself terribly engaging. But working with great co-workers, helping each other out, and having great camaraderie, trust, and love for one another *is* engaging. In other words, a great team environment can engage a person as much as a great job can! For the details on how team dynamics can act as a significant engagement driver (or a big-time driver of disengagement), read on!

Yay, Team: Identifying Characteristics of an Engaged Team

Early in my career, when facilitating supervisory training, I used to tell the participants the characteristics of an engaged team. Eventually, however, I figured out this was something most people already know. After all, every-one's been on a sports team, a dance team, in Boy Scouts or Girl Scouts, on church committees, or in a play group, and has seen what works and what doesn't. In fact, I'm so confident you're already familiar with the characteristics of an engaged team that I'm tempted to just move on to the next section. But in the interest of being thorough, I'll spell it out here. Engaged teams demonstrate the following:

✔ Accountability

✔ Authority

✔ Clarity of roles

✔ Decisiveness

✔ Direction

✔ Mutual commitment

✔ Open communication

✔ Performance

✔ Productivity

✔ Respect

✔ Selflessness

✔ Transparency

✔ Trust

✔ Vision

But that's not all. For a team to be *truly* engaged, focused, and motivated, it must also demonstrate the following:

✔ Accessibility

✔ Agility

✔ Appreciation

✔ Balance

✔ Celebration

✔ Collaboration

✔ Complementary skills

✔ Diversity

✔ Drive

✔ Empowerment

✔ External focus

- Flexibility
- Fun
- Morale
- Ownership
- Pride
- Recognition
- Sense of purpose
- Visibility

Unfortunately, many teams don't demonstrate these characteristics. In other words, these words describe what characteristics teams *should* have, not what they *do* have. Why? For one, people get busy, and they don't always feel they have the time to exhibit these ideal behaviors. Additionally, some people are just mistrusting, cynical, or skeptical by their very nature. They're not bad people — these traits are just part of their DNA.

For many, the default is to assume the worst of people, or that people have bad intentions. But perhaps the most significant hallmark of a successful team is that members assume good intentions. In addition, people on successful teams hold each other accountable when they see their teammates demonstrating less-than-ideal characteristics.

Stormin' Norman: Exploring Tuckman's Stages

In 1965, psychologist Dr. Bruce Tuckman proposed a model of group development that he called "Tuckman's Stages." This model included four stages:

- Stage 1: Forming
- Stage 2: Storming
- Stage 3: Norming
- Stage 4: Performing

To help you understand this model, let me give an example: Suppose you and your partner decide to have a child. Fast-forward nine months, and — boom! — you bring the baby home. You're crazy excited. You're *forming* a family!

Soon, the reality of parenting sets in. The baby won't sleep through the night. He cries all the time. You and your partner are exhausted and increasingly irritated with each other. You haven't had an evening out together, just the two of you, in months. Welcome to the *storming* stage of your new family, or team.

Eventually, the baby starts to sleep. He figures out how to soothe himself, so there's not so much crying. You've found a few babysitters to step in so you and your partner can have some time alone. You settle into a routine. This is your team's *norming* stage.

Before you know it, your baby is 2 years old. Although some challenges remain (they don't call them the "terrible twos" for nothing), things have settled down. Your "team" is *performing* quite well! In fact, having forgotten how painful the storming stage was, you're even thinking of having another child. When you do, you'll be right back at the forming stage, and the cycle will start again.

Of course, growing families aren't the only "teams" that follow Tuckman's Stages. These stages also apply to work teams and to the lifecycle of companies. And although this example showcased what happens to a "team" when new people are added, the same cycle occurs any time a significant event occurs, such as an acquisition, starting a new project, converting to a new system, organizational changes, changes to company leadership, or the departure of team members. (Just ask any parent whose child goes off to college about how their "team" has changed!) These days, the one thing we can count on is that change is a constant. Understanding Tuckman's Stages can help leaders ensure that team members stay engaged amidst change.

All teams must go through the forming, storming, and norming stages to get to the performing stage. If you think you've skipped a stage, look a little more closely. Teams rarely skip stages. The speed at which a team progresses through these stages will depend on the size of the change, the experience of the team members, the experience of the leader, and how engaged the team is as a whole. Strong, engaged teams will find ways to accelerate through the stages.

This simple but powerful team-development model has stood the test of time, and continues to be used even today by academics and consultants in classrooms and workshops across the world. The key points to keep in mind about Tuckman's Stages is that they're a natural aspect of team development, they should be anticipated, and in many ways they're part of a virtuous cycle.

The forming stage

Teams, whether at work or at home, always begin in this stage, and will return to this stage whenever a significant change occurs — for example, when people are added to the team, when members of the team leave, or when a new project starts.

In the forming stage, particularly on new teams, team members tend to exhibit the following behaviors:

- **They're fired up to be part of the team, and they're eager for work ahead.**

- **They have some anxiety and uncertainty.** They're wondering things like, "What's expected of me?", "How will I fit in?", or "How will my performance measure up to others?"

- **They may be reticent to ask questions and share ideas.** During this stage, politeness often prevails. On the surface, team members will appear cooperative, and there will be lots of face-to-face agreement. Often, however, there are unspoken opinions and silent disagreements.

- **They may test the situation and each other.**

- **Their commitment and motivation levels are high.** Productivity levels, however, are merely moderate, as people are still learning the goals, the roles, and what's expected.

To expedite the forming stage, the team leader must focus on providing direction and structure and building relationships and trust. This kickoff process involves the following:

- Defining and clarifying team and individual goals, roles, expectations, and practices.

- Discussing past practices to determine what worked and what didn't.

- Building relationships and rapport by ensuring that the team spends time together and engaging in team-building activities. (You'll learn more about team-building activities that foster rapport and engagement later in this chapter.)

- Establishing team norms (that is, the "rules of the tavern" and best practices for communicating, making decisions, and so on).

- Assessing strengths and weaknesses of team members and identifying ways they can help each other improve.

- Articulating your management philosophy, your strengths, and your weaknesses, and asking the team to provide ongoing feedback.

For maximum engagement, team leaders must help team members understand and manage transition and change. That includes familiarizing team members with the four stages of team development (forming, storming, norming, and performing). This will help team members prepare for what's coming and deal with the inevitable highs and lows. Team leaders must also teach and model the skills and behaviors they want to see on their teams, and recognize those skills and behaviors when they see them.

Whether you're the leader of a new group, your existing team has "inherited" new members due to an organizational restructuring, or you've just joined the company in a supervisory position, the members of your team are depending on you to provide direction, structure, and support. They'll be watching you closely and taking their cues from your leadership. Certainly, you want your new group to become a cohesive team — to perform at high levels and be highly engaged from the start. The trick to achieving this is to take charge with a strong kickoff process early on.

The storming stage

Over time, teams will move from the forming stage to the storming stage. Why? Because as team members become more familiar with each other, they become comfortable enough to state their true feelings and beliefs, which inevitably leads to disagreements.

During this stage, conflict is the watchword. Think: *Hell's Kitchen* with Gordon Ramsay. Team members may experience some of the following:

- ✔ They may discover that the team doesn't live up to early expectations.
- ✔ They may feel frustrated, confused, or angry about the team's progress or process (or lack thereof).
- ✔ They may react negatively to the team leader and to other members of the team. Power struggles may ensue.
- ✔ They may have conflicts and disagreements about goals, roles, and responsibilities, expressed openly or behind the scenes.
- ✔ Commitment, morale, and productivity may take a downturn.

As frustrating as this stage may be for team members and leaders alike, remember: It's okay to storm. In fact, it's healthy! What's *not* healthy is to remain in this stage indefinitely. To accelerate movement from the storming stage to the norming stage, leaders should legitimize the conflict to ensure that it's constructive. That means doing the following:

- ✔ Bringing conflict out into the open
- ✔ Acknowledging with the team that storming is natural, inevitable, and essential to the growth of the team
- ✔ Creating forums and encouraging open discussion of issues, even if it's directed at you as the leader
- ✔ Establishing norms for constructive discussion and debate
- ✔ Reinforcing positive conflict-resolution efforts
- ✔ Balancing individual needs with team needs

For more on resolving conflict, see Chapter 5.

In addition, team leaders should revisit and clarify goals, roles, and expectations. (Note that teams may move more quickly through storming if the tasks in the forming stage were done well.)

The norming stage

In the norming stage, things begin to smooth out. Turbulence subsides, a sense of calm prevails, and commitment and productivity take a turn for the better.

For team members, this stage is characterized by the following:

- ✔ They begin to resolve the discrepancies between their expectations and the reality of the team experience.
- ✔ They have an increased understanding of accountabilities and expectations.
- ✔ They develop self-esteem, as well as trust and confidence in the team.
- ✔ They become more comfortable expressing their "real" ideas and feelings.
- ✔ They start using "team language" — that is, saying "we" rather than "I."

The danger inherent in this stage is complacency. Teams become so comfortable that they just stay here. To nudge team members to the next stage (performing), leaders must focus on encouraging participation, the development of norms, and continuous improvement. That means doing the following:

✔ Being less directive and more participatory

✔ Collectively reviewing team norms, processes, and practices and adjusting them based on what's working and what isn't working

✔ Encouraging and giving recognition for taking initiative, taking risks, creative problem solving, and seeking and acting on feedback

In addition, the team leader should continue to build trust and relationships through personal interactions and team building.

The performing stage

Ah, the performing stage . . . the sweet spot of group development. In this stage, life is good. Members feel excited to be part of the engaged, high-performing team, which functions as smoothly as Barry White at a singles bar. That's not to say there's no conflict or disruption, just that the team has set rules for handling it.

During this stage, team members

✔ Are focused on team versus individual results

✔ Understand and take advantage of team members' strengths, valuing their differences

✔ Exhibit high levels of confidence

✔ Demonstrate a sense of true collaboration and shared team leadership

✔ Demonstrate high levels of commitment, morale, and productivity

✔ Can function at a high level, even absent of the team leader

Not surprisingly, people on teams in this stage are hesitant to introduce change, thereby reverting to the forming stage. After all, if it ain't broke, don't fix it, right? Besides, moving through all those stages can be painful! But introducing change is a must. Otherwise, the team risks becoming complacent, stale, or overconfident.

It's far better to spur change voluntarily than to be put in the position of having to react to an unplanned alteration in course. If you don't believe me, take a moment to ponder successful sports franchises. These organizations recognize that they must continually cycle back to the forming stage by bringing in new players, coaches, and/or systems, even when they're winning. The same goes for companies. Kodak and Polaroid may have owned the print film business while in the performing stage, but they were ultimately toppled by competitors who smartly re-formed around digital photography.

This is the end: What to do when a team ends

Some teams will dissolve after a period of time — for example, when their work is completed (such as a project team or task team, which is typically temporary) or when the organization's needs change (such as in the case of a reorganization or integration). When this happens, you may find that team members have various feelings about the team's impending dissolution. They may also exhibit varied emotions and behaviors, such as anxiety (due to uncertainty about their new role or future responsibilities), sadness or a sense of loss, or satisfaction about the team's accomplishments. Some may lose focus, causing productivity to drop. Others may find focusing on tasks at hand to be an effective response to their sadness or sense of loss.

To help usher team members through the termination of a team, team leaders should

✔ Acknowledge team members' feelings and address their concerns ("What's going to happen to me?") in a straightforward and caring way.

✔ Complete any deliverables and achieve closure on remaining team work.

✔ Capture "lessons learned" as a team and pass them on to a new team leader or sponsor for future use.

✔ Have some kind of closing activity or event that acknowledges and celebrates the contributions and accomplishments of individuals on the team, as well as the team as a whole.

Clearly, a key task for team leaders in this stage is to be on the lookout for new challenges, and to guard against complacency and groupthink. At the same time, they must work to enhance the skills of team members, and inspire more interdependence, shared ownership, and accountability for results. That means doing the following:

✔ Giving people more responsibility and delegating some of your tasks to develop team members' technical, business, and leadership skills

✔ Providing more feedback and additional "big picture" information to help team members make links to the larger organization

✔ Injecting new perspectives into the team via transfers in or out, promotions, new hires, external expertise, market intelligence, and benchmarking

✔ Continuing to celebrate individual and team successes

Putting it all together

Need a little assistance assimilating all that information about Tuckman's Stages? Table 9-1 should help.

Table 9-1	Characteristics of Tuckman's Stages			
	Forming	**Storming**	**Norming**	**Performing**
Member Behavior	Anxiety Search for structure Silence Being reactive to the leader Superficiality Being overly polite	Increased testing of norms Fight-or-flight behavior Attacks on the leader Polarization of the team Power struggles Hostility or silence Failure to commit to action plans	Effort to get along Constructive conflict Realistic norms and guidelines Functional relationships Acceptance of each other and of the leader Caring, trust, and enjoyment	Cohesiveness Conflict management Active listening Shared leadership Creative problem solving A focus on the here and now
Attitude about Leadership	Being accepted or tested by members Tentativeness	Power struggles Jockeying for position or control	General support Acknowledgment of differences	Distribution of leader- ship among members by expertise
Decision Making	Domination by active members	Fragmentation Deadlocks Team leader or the most power- ful or loudest team member making decisions	Decisions being made based on individual expertise Decisions often being made by the leader in consultation with team members	Decisions being made by consensus Teams doing whatever it takes col- lectively or individually to make decisions
Climate	Caution Feelings of suppression Low conflict Few out- bursts	Subgrouping Overt or covert criticism Disagreements between sub- groups	Teams dealing with differences Members open- ing up and shar- ing true feelings Straight con- frontation	Shared responsibility Open expression Prompt reso- lution of dis- agreements

	Forming	Storming	Norming	Performing
Task Functions and Major Issues	Getting the team started, establishing identity Developing common purpose Orientation Providing structure Building trust Managing transitions	Questioning identity Managing increased conflict Openly confronting issues Increased participation Testing of group norms Increased independence from leader	Establishing realistic guidelines and standards Team responsibility Cooperation and participation Decision making Confronting problems Shared leadership Quality and excellence Team assessments	Progress toward goal True collaboration Monitoring of accomplishments Critiquing of process Assessment of interactions Avoidance of "groupthink" Satisfaction of members' personal needs
Leadership Roles	Reduction of uncertainty Setting of goals Clarification of purpose Drawing out questions Letting members get to know each other Modeling expected behavior	Legitimization of conflict Examination of own response to conflict Reinforcement of positive conflict-resolution efforts Acknowledgment of conflict as essential for change Not becoming more authoritarian	Encouragement of norm development Development of goals Use of consensus Redirection of questions Development of positive listening skills	Maintenance of team skills Maintenance of technical and interpersonal skills Providing feedback on group's effectiveness Assisting in gaining more meaning from meetings

From a Distance: Leading Teams from Afar

If you're charged with leading a team from afar, you'll need some special competencies. Most notably, you'll need the ability to manage boundaries and barriers. Staff in remote locations face significant obstacles — logistical and otherwise — which impede and even prevent success. You have to be prepared to help your team navigate those obstacles. In addition, you'll need to master technology for communication and collaboration, such as Microsoft SharePoint, Skype, extranets, and of course, e-mail. (Note that this includes understanding e-mail etiquette.) Finally, particularly if your staff are located in other regions or countries, you'll need a strong dose of cultural awareness.

Here are a few tricks to keep up your sleeve:

- ✔ **Focus on relationships first, and cultural and language differences second.** Get to know your employees. Do you know their family situation? Do you know the names of each employee's spouse and kids? Do your remote employees feel you care about them as people? *Remember:* You can't be an empathetic boss without knowing your employees personally.

- ✔ **Develop a way to share information.** When managing remote or virtual employees, technology is the great equalizer. Make sure remote employees have an opportunity to share their information with the team via SharePoint, Skype, webinars, and so on. The idea is that they should feel like they're in the room with you.

- ✔ **Consider time zones and share the associated sacrifices equally.** If you're leading people in a different region or country, be sensitive to their time zone. Shift calls so they aren't always the one whose phone rings at 11 p.m. Rotating time-zone hardships is a simple way to reinforce that you're sensitive to the work–life balance.

- ✔ **Identify communication preferences for team and individuals.** Some individuals and/or teams may be more visual by nature, so using tools to share documents may be better than describing them over a conference call.

- ✔ **Create a team-level communication protocol and stick to it.** This protocol might outline how communication will be handled, when team members can expect communications, and what to expect on an ongoing basis.

- ✔ **Be accessible.** Although you do need to set some boundaries if there are time-zone differences, you have to make yourself more available than you might if you were right down the hall. Remote employees are prone to feeling isolated. If, when they reach out, they get the "I'm too busy right now" treatment, their sense of isolation will increase exponentially.

✔ **Develop ways for your remote employees to virtually "stop by."** Have a virtual open-door policy and encourage your remote employees to "swing by" when they need to chat, have a question, want to check in, and so on. Confirming that it's okay to text or instant-message you whenever and wherever will minimize their loneliness. Texting is often a great "check-in" communication tool because it's quick and informal and happens in real-time.

✔ **Make sure remote employees have the opportunity to participate in company initiatives.** These include surveys, task teams, meetings, socials, holiday parties, and so on. Be aware of the "out of sight, out of mind" phenomenon that exists with remote employees. Camaraderie is a significant engagement driver — and even more so with remote employees, who don't get the benefit of the "water cooler" companionship that in-house workers experience. Effective remote managers go out of their way to include their remote employees on intradepartmental initiatives and special projects.

✔ **Communicate more often, and in different modes.** Send frequent informational e-mails, and regularly keep in touch with remote team members with phone calls or other forms of communication.

Team Player: Exploring Team-Building Activities

One of the most important things a successful leader does to foster engagement, particularly in the early stages of a team's development, is to build trust and relationships. In this case, *trust* is the confidence among team members that their peers' intentions are good and, consequently, that it's unnecessary to be defensive or wary within the group.

Building trust doesn't just happen. It requires shared experiences over time, evidence of credibility and follow through, and an in-depth understanding of the unique attributes of each team member. Ultimately, the team leader and team members must become comfortable with each other, and get to know each other beyond a purely work-related context.

Fortunately, team leaders can accelerate this process, building trust in a relatively short period of time, by taking a few specific actions, or team-building activities. These activities enable leaders to build relationships and trust through personal and professional self-disclosure, and to increase self-awareness and awareness of each other's strengths, blind spots, and unique contributions to the team.

Before getting into the specific activities team leaders can do to build trust, this section discusses the ins and outs of running a successful team-building activity and common challenges you'll face.

Running a successful team-building activity

In an ideal world, you'll have the budget to hire team-building consultants, or perhaps have qualified organizational development (OD), training, or HR folks to lend you a hand. If not, this section has tools to help you lead the team-building activity yourself.

Before the team activity, you'll want to be sure you truly understand the ins and outs of the activity. You want to be crystal clear about what will happen, when, why, and how. Also, make sure you have all the necessary materials, and test them to make sure they work with the activity. Next, set up the room as needed, making sure all tables, chairs, flip charts, and whatnot are in place. Finally, anticipate any potential problems, and take steps to prevent them.

At the beginning of the activity, welcome your team. Give them a brief overview of the activity — why you're doing it, the steps or rules, and so on. Show some enthusiasm! You want to fire up the group, so they become interested and excited. Before moving on, make sure the team understands the activity. Set clear expectations, and give team members the opportunity to ask questions.

When everyone's up to speed, distribute the necessary materials and get started. As team members work, be encouraging and supportive. Be sure to thank whoever goes first — that takes courage! Watch for opportunities to clarify instructions. If the activity is timed, keep team members abreast of how much time remains.

When the activity is over, conduct a debriefing session. Ask questions — either the ones provided with the activity or your own. Here are a few examples of questions you may ask during the debrief:

- ✔ Why is it important for us to get to know each other outside a purely work-related context?

- ✔ How difficult (or easy) was it for you to share information about yourself with others?

- ✔ How can we learn more about each other back on the job?

For most questions, there is no right or wrong answer. Try not to critique. Instead, provide positive nonverbal feedback and/or summarize any responses offered. If you can, avoid singling out anyone by name to answer your question. Be comfortable with the silence. Ask your question and then count to ten. The silence may feel like an eternity to you, but I promise, it feels even longer to the group! Eventually, someone will break and answer your question.

Later, when you're on the job, remind team members about the activity to reinforce learning. This may include bringing up something positive or personal that someone shared during the activity. Plan follow-up "get to know you" activities to reinforce, emphasize, and build upon what was learned.

Tackling common challenges

Sometimes, conducting a team-building activity is a little like herding cats. In other words, it can be challenging. Here are a few challenges you may face in your team-building efforts and some steps you can take to overcome them:

- ✔ **People don't want to participate.** Unfortunately, not everyone is thrilled by the prospect of a team-building activity, particularly if they're shy. To get them onboard, clearly articulate the purpose of the activity. Remind them that in order for it to be team building, everyone must participate. Reassure them that everyone *will* participate, and that no one will be singled out or otherwise embarrassed. If the activity allows, have your more outgoing team members go first (or go first yourself).

- ✔ **People are unclear about directions.** Fortunately, this one's easy to address. Just be sure to speak slowly when explaining the activity. Pause after each direction to let it sink in. When you're finished, start over and repeat the directions. Ensure that any difficult or confusing steps are put in context.

- ✔ **There aren't enough materials.** This challenge also has an easy fix: Make sure you bring more than enough materials for all participants.

- ✔ **People don't contribute during the debrief.** As I mention earlier, after asking a question, pause and silently count to ten. This gives people time to think. Reword questions only if someone says he didn't understand. If no one answers, offer your own observation, and then ask what others saw or felt that was similar or different from what you shared. As a last resort, call on someone by name to respond. Start with a more outgoing team member, who won't feel embarrassed by the attention.

Looking at effective team-building activities

This section contains several team-building activities that you can use to strengthen your own team.

Hello, My N.A.M.E. Is . . .

In this exercise, members introduce themselves by presenting their first names as acronyms. This allows them to learn interesting things about each other.

Materials

None

Instructions

1. **Give the group five minutes to think of interesting facts about themselves that correspond to the letters of their first names.**

2. **Share your acronym as an example.**

3. **Have each person share his or her acronym.**

Example

"Hi. I'm Logan. L is for Led Zeppelin, one of my favorite rock groups. O is for Ohio, which is where I live. G is for German, the only foreign language I know. A is for Aunt Wendy, my favorite relative. And N is for No Fish because I don't eat seafood."

What Makes Us Tick?

Provide members with a way to share things about themselves that aren't observable to others, but have an impact on others. This gives team members an opportunity to look for ways to support each other.

Materials

- Flip chart paper/whiteboard (or "web meeting" equivalent)
- Blank sheets of note paper

Instructions

1. **List sentence starters on a flip chart or whiteboard.**

   Include a few or all from this list, as time allows:

   - What is important to me in the next six months is . . .

- I feel very confident that . . .
- I'm not as confident that . . .
- The team can help me by . . .
- If you see me doing something that you think is a mistake, please . . .
- The best way to communicate with me is . . .

2. **Allow five to ten minutes for team members to write down their answers.**

3. **Go around the group one question at a time, allowing each person to share his or her response to the question.**

   Allow time for clarification and some reaction and discussion to make it interactive and animated.

Debrief

During the debrief, ask the following questions:

- ✔ What did you hear in common with particular team members?
- ✔ Reflect on the differences expressed during this exercise. How can those differences become an asset for the team?
- ✔ What suggestions do you have for how we can honor each member's needs?

Option

Give team members a worksheet with the sentence starters listed as pre-work so they have more time to think through their answers.

A Penny for Your Thoughts

This lighthearted activity reveals a quick, personal fact about each person.

Materials

One penny for each participant. (Ideally, these should be shiny, easy to read, and less than 20 years old.)

Instructions

1. **Give a penny to each person.**

   As you do this, try jokingly asking whether they realized they were going to get a cash bonus today.

2. **Ask each team member to share something significant or interesting about himself or herself from the year on the penny.**

3. **Go first to set the example.**

4. **As people share, let the other members ask questions.**

Examples

"My penny is from 1999. That was the year that I let my husband talk me into going skydiving with him."

Variations

Have team members explain what they would do differently if they could relive that year. Alternatively, have them say what their favorite song, book, movie, or TV show was from that year. Allow participants to use their smartphones if they need a little help jogging their memories!

Personal Histories

This activity enables you to foster trust by giving members an opportunity to demonstrate vulnerability in a low-risk way.

Materials

None

Instructions

Go around the group and have everyone answer four questions about themselves:

- Where did you grow up?
- How many siblings do you have and where do you fall in the birth order?
- What was the most difficult or important challenge of your childhood?
- What is your best memory from childhood?

Set the tone to focus on positive outcomes from difficult situations. Otherwise, this exercise could devolve into a series of "how my childhood was worse than yours" stories. It could also bring out some very negative emotions if not handled well by the leader.

Debrief

During the debrief, ask the following question:

What did you learn about others that you didn't know?

Variations

Other questions could be used here, as long as they call for moderate vulnerability. For instance, "What is your favorite food?" wouldn't work because it involves virtually no vulnerability. Likewise, "How do you feel about your mother?" also doesn't work — in this case, because it could be too invasive.

Inquiring Minds Want to Know

This exercise gives team members the chance to uncover something unusual or intriguing about each other.

Materials

Flip chart paper/whiteboard (or "web meeting" equivalent)

Instructions

1. **Ask each person in the room to pick two questions from the following list (displayed on a flip chart) that they would like to ask someone:**

    - If you could do anything, what profession (other than your own) would you like to do? Why?

    - What profession would you definitely *not* like to do? Why?

    - What is your favorite word? What is your least favorite word? Why?

    - What is a funny memory that you have from your childhood?

    - What are four words that your best friend or partner would use to describe you?

    - What do you think is one of the first things that people (at work) notice about you?

    - If you could be a rock star, an actor, or a celebrity, who would you be? Why?

2. **Ask each person to pair up with someone he or she doesn't know very well.**

3. **Have each person "interview" his or her partner using the two questions previously selected.**

4. **Ask each person to introduce his or her partner and share that person's answers to the interview questions.**

Variation

Instead of providing a list of questions in Step 1, ask team members to write down two creative or interesting questions they'd like to ask someone. Use one or two of the questions in the list as an example.

What I Bring to the Team

This exercise is an opportunity for team members to recognize and disclose their own strengths and areas for improvement. It can also be an opportunity for the team leader or other team members to give each other positive feedback.

Materials

None

Instructions

1. **Ask each person to reflect on why he or she was chosen for his or her position on the team (strengths, experience, and so on).**

   Specifically, ask each person to list the following:

   - One or two things that he or she is really good at

   - One or two things that he or she needs to work on or that can be a blind spot

2. **Ask each person to reveal his or her answers.**

Variations

- ✔ **Have the team leader provide feedback to each person in front of the group, commenting on strengths only.** The team leader should share one or two specific things that he or she thinks makes the person a good fit for the position or a unique, important quality that he or she brings to the team.

- ✔ **If appropriate, and if time allows, encourage others in the room to comment on what they see as the strengths of each person.**

- ✔ **Give each person a sheet of flip chart paper and ask him or her to draw a symbol that represents his or her answers.** For instance, an employee who views her strength as being able to multitask might draw an octopus. Someone who views his strength as having global experience might draw a picture of planet Earth.

Scramble

In this frantic activity, team members simultaneously strategize, gather, and summarize information about each other. Afterward, they present their findings to the team. (Note that this activity isn't suitable for virtual teams.) Be sure to let team members know this activity will be chaotic, and to watch the time carefully.

<u>*Materials*</u>

None

<u>*Instructions*</u>

1. **Divide the team into groups of three to nine participants.**

2. **Give each group a topic. (Make sure you have enough topics for all groups.)**

   Topics may be work related (for example, pertaining to college degrees earned, languages spoken, or previous employers) or non–work related (for example, pertaining to pets, birthplace, last vacation destination, hobbies, and so on).

3. **Give the groups three minutes to determine how they'll gather the information for their topic from all the people in the room.**

4. **Give the groups three minutes to gather all the information for their topics.**

   This happens simultaneously for all groups.

5. **Give the groups three minutes to summarize the data they collected.**

6. **Give each group one minute to present their findings to the whole team.**

<u>*Debrief*</u>

During the debrief session, try asking the following questions:

✔ How did you accomplish your goals during each phase?

✔ Did you adjust your strategy during the activity? How?

✔ During which phase did you feel most rushed? Why?

✔ How does that relate to how you approach work? In other words, when do you feel most rushed or under pressure?

<u>*Variation*</u>

Give the teams an extra minute or two in the summarizing phase to record their findings on a flip chart. Then, instead of making a presentation, have them post their findings on the wall. Encourage folks to walk around the "gallery" to view the findings.

Heads or Tails

In this icebreaker activity, members tell an anecdote about themselves. The anecdote can be true or untrue. This activity gives members an opportunity to learn some interesting facts about each other.

Materials

- ✔ A coin
- ✔ A paper cup

Instructions

1. **Have the team sit around a table so everyone can see each other.**

2. **The first participant starts by placing the coin face up or face down under the cup so no one can see it.**

3. **If the participant placed the coin face up, he or she must tell a true story about himself or herself; if the participant placed it face down, he or she must tell a story that is untrue.**

4. **The group tries to guess whether the story is true or untrue.**

5. **The participant lifts the cup to reveal the answer.**

6. **Repeat until all members have had the chance to tell their stories.**

Debrief

During the debrief session, try asking the following questions:

- ✔ How did you decide whether the story was true or untrue?
- ✔ If you made up a story, where did it come from?
- ✔ What's the value of getting to know each other outside of a purely work-related setting?

Variations

- ✔ Limit stories to work situations.
- ✔ Have participants make a statement about themselves rather than tell a story — for example, "I've been to every continent at least once."
- ✔ Make it a bit competitive. Break the team into two groups. Have a member from each team share his or her story or statement, and have the other team confer to guess if it was true or untrue. Take turns sharing stories and guessing whether they're true. The team with the most correct answers after everyone shares their story wins a small prize.
- ✔ For virtual teams on the phone, have the member reveal his or her correct answer without using the coin and cup.

Rainbow of Diversity

This exercise helps members recognize and appreciate what's going right among them.

Materials

A different-colored crayon for each participant. (A large box of 48 works well.)

Instructions

1. **Give a crayon to each person.**

2. **Have each person pair up with someone whose crayon is close to his or her own color.**

   Don't let team members get too worried about the "correct" or closest color.

3. **Give everyone two minutes to discover what strengths they have in common that contribute to the success of the group.**

4. **Have them pair up again, this time with someone whose crayon is very different from their own color.**

   Again, don't let them get too hung up on finding the exact opposite.

5. **Give them four minutes to identify what each others' strengths are and how they can learn from and appreciate those different skills or abilities.**

6. **Have all the participants get together in a circle, standing next to colors that are most like their own; ask the debriefing questions (see the next section) while in the circle.**

Debrief

During the debrief session, ask the following questions:

✔ What did you learn about the person with a color similar to yours?

✔ What did you learn about the person with a color different from yours?

✔ What does this circle say about our team?

Hit Me with Your Best Shot: Conducting a High-Impact Team Workshop

Picture this: You've just been asked to lead a major, high-profile, long-term project that requires your staff to work closely with employees from other departments and outside consultants. Of course, you could try to engage these myriad dynamic forces via e-mail and teleconferences, but there's a better way: a high-impact team (HIT) workshop.

A HIT workshop is designed to align and engage your employees to work toward a common goal. It involves bringing together all the key players, face-to-face if possible, for a one-and-a-half-day gathering. This highly interactive and engaging workshop mixes team dynamics analysis, process improvement, communication networks, group problem solving, action planning, and of course, fun!

To conduct a HIT workshop, follow these steps:

1. **Clarify the current state of the business and/or project (that is, "Where we are now?").**

   This step involves a thorough discussion of the key metrics of the business and/or project.

2. **Have breakout discussions on where the business or project should go (that is, "Where are we going?").**

   This phase should weave in discussion of current impediments and strengths.

3. **Construct a high-performing action plan (that is, "How we will get there?").**

   This action plan, along with an implementation strategy, should be created and agreed to by participants in the workshop.

Experience shows that an individual or team that develops its own action plan is overwhelmingly more likely to follow through on the actions than when the action plan is assigned.

A great tool to assist with prioritization is the idea priority matrix (see Chapter 2).

Throughout the workshop, apply team-building activities liberally. Opt for activities that are focused on building the competencies required of engaged teams.

A well-structured process like the one in a HIT workshop pays countless dividends, including the following:

- ✔ Improved communications, which expedites work and work processes
- ✔ A common sense of direction, established through mutual goals and expectations
- ✔ The ability to hit the ground running and avoid costly startup mistakes
- ✔ Practice working together in a controlled setting
- ✔ Group interaction, and getting to know one another
- ✔ A level of comfort and joint ownership of solving a common problem

Chapter 10

Brandy, You're a Fine Girl: Driving Engagement through Branding

A few years back, I was retained as a consultant for a retail chain (let's call it "Company X") that was struggling to engage its employees. To kick off the gig, we held a three-day meeting with Company X's leadership team — the first two days focused on operations, and the last day on engagement.

During the first two days of the meeting, I was deeply impressed by Company X's diligence in and approach to understanding its customers' demographics and buying patterns. The company used external research consultants, video-camera focus groups, internal research, customer interviews, and more to better understand who its customers were and what and why they were buying. They analyzed *everything* — from the size of the shopping cart to what happens when you move coffee or produce from one aisle to another. They understood when customers bought, what they bought, and when they stopped buying. They even understood these buying patterns relative to where product was placed in the store. "Wow!" I thought. "This company really gets it!"

Then came day three. That morning, the leadership team presented its engagement challenges. It turned out, their employees — or "associates," as they called them — were disengaged. Retention was a real issue. In fact, Company X had much higher voluntary turnover than its competitors.

To get to the bottom of things, I asked the leadership team why they themselves work for Company X. They stumbled through their answers. Next, I asked them why any associates might stay. Again, they didn't know. Finally, I asked them about their employment brand. They admitted they didn't really have one. See, this firm, like so many others, invested all its time communicating its product brand — "what we do." But it had invested virtually no time communicating its employment brand — "who we are."

Ideally, "what we do" and "who we are" will be like two sides of the same coin. In other words, the product brand will be linked to the employment brand. Take Apple. Apple hires the most creative people to make the most creative products. Similarly, BMW hires people who are driving enthusiasts to build the "ultimate driving machine." And Southwest Airlines, which has positioned its product brand as being all about fun, hires people who have fun in their DNA. All these companies are great at linking their product brand with their employment brand. Not surprisingly, they also enjoy excellent employee engagement, not to mention business success!

In this chapter, I explain how branding and engagement are connected, walk you through writing an employee value proposition (which basically says who you are and why people should work for you), explain how to communicate your brand internally and externally, and introduce you to the power of tri-branding.

Better Relate than Never: Understanding How Branding and Engagement Relate

So, what does branding have to do with employee engagement? Well, a few things:

✔ Identifying and communicating your brand is vital to ensuring that you hire the types of people who can succeed and be engaged at your firm. (For more on hiring for engagement, see Chapter 12.)

✔ Generation Y, soon to be the largest segment of the workforce (if it isn't already), is all about branding (see Chapter 8 for more info). That attitude informs what they wear, where they shop, what device they play, and what company, or brand, they work for. Understanding and crystallizing your brand will position you to find, retain, and engage this key workforce group.

✔ Building and branding a culture that is unique to your firm will enable you to leverage social media to engage customers, employees, future employees, and other key stakeholders with your brand.

In the past, companies sought out good employees. These days, thanks to the emergence of social media, the tables have turned. If you want your firm to win the "war for talent," you'll need to make sure employees (and customers) are able to seek *you* out.

Hello, My Name Is _____: Defining Who You Are

Odds are, your employees — excuse me, your "associates" (or, if you're Disney, your "cast members") — can articulate what you do, the services you offer, and the products you sell. But can they speak to who you are, and why you're a great employer? For many companies, this is an area of real struggle — and this struggle can lead to a lack of engagement.

To rectify this, you must identify your company's employee value proposition (EVP) — that is, who you are and why people should work for you. Think of this as your "employment brand." An EVP consists of a clear and compelling story that describes, among other things, why people want to work for your firm, key points that differentiate your firm from its competitors, and a message that resonates with and engages staff. If your firm has an engaging, healthy culture, developing an enticing EVP is a breeze.

Every firm should crystallize and document its EVP. An effective EVP includes the following:

✔ A clear and compelling story that describes why people want to work for you

✔ Key points that differentiate your firm from its competitors

✔ A theme that prompts candidates to self-select in or out (A strong EVP helps to ensure the "right" people seek out your firm and helps to discourage those who simply aren't a fit from applying. Let's face it, the Marines aren't for everyone — which is why their EVP is all about being one of "the few.")

✔ A message that resonates with and engages existing staff

That last point is key. It's how you know your EVP is accurate. That said, the EVP doesn't have to be based strictly in reality. It can be equal parts reality, aspiration, and inspiration.

So, how do you define your firm's EVP? Follow these steps:

1. **Create a committee of key employees.**

   This committee should be a diverse group of people, representing marketing, HR, operations, and leadership. If you're a small organization, start with you and two or three of your key people.

2. **Make a list of high-performing employees who have excelled within your culture.**

3. **Identify the behaviors and traits that are shared among these high-performing employees.**

   For help, read the section "Trait Up: Pinpointing Key Behaviors and Traits," later in this chapter.

4. **Conduct a series of interviews with these high-performing employees.**

   Ask them such questions as the following:

   - Why do you work here?

   - Why do you stay here?

   - What are the best things about working here?

   - Why do people leave competitors to join us?

   - What makes this firm unique? (For more info on this point, see the upcoming sidebar.)

   Don't get too caught up in what your firm does. The idea is to pinpoint what makes you unique, what defines your culture, and why people jump out of bed to come to work in the morning.

5. **If you're feeling ambitious, conduct an employee engagement survey and/or pulse survey to help identify your EVP.**

   For more info on employee engagement surveys and pulse surveys, see Chapter 3.

6. **Using information gathered in the previous steps, develop a draft EVP.**

   Your EVP should also align with your firm's mission or purpose, vision, values, and strategy (see Chapter 5).

7. **Share your draft EVP with your leadership team, and work together with them to finalize the EVP.**

Here are a few examples of memorable EVPs:

- ✔ **Apple:** Think Different

- ✔ **Southwest Airlines:** Freedom to Travel Around the Country

- ✔ **Disney:** The Happiest Place on Earth

REAL WORLD EXAMPLE

If your firm has an engaging, healthy culture — think Google, Apple, Nordstrom, Whirlpool, and so on — you'll find developing an enticing EVP quite easy. But what if your work is challenging or stressful? In that case, honesty is probably the best policy. Take this HELP WANTED ad, posted in 1914 by British explorer Sir Ernest Shackleton, who sought men for an expedition to Antarctica:

> Men Wanted for Hazardous Journey. Small wages, bitter cold, long months of complete darkness, constant danger. Safe return doubtful. Honour and recognition in case of success.

To say Shackleton's EVP was "not attractive" to many people is an understatement. But by being honest about the challenges — and about the possible rewards — Shackleton attracted 5,000 inquiries for the 27 positions on his vessel. Perhaps more important, Shackleton was able to use his HELP WANTED ad to frighten off those who were not fit for the journey and to attract those who truly identified with the role. Shackleton recognized that hiring the right kinds of people, with the right behaviors and traits (more on that in a moment), was critical to engaging a group of explorers to achieve success.

Discovering what makes you unique

Although every company is unique in some way, most companies fail to identify their unique characteristics. Part of developing your EVP is pinpointing what makes your firm unique. One way to do this is to poll employees via surveys, exit interviews, and stay interviews. (For more on these, see Chapter 3.)

As you uncover what makes your firm unique, try to link your EVP to your firm's vision and purpose. If your EVP appears to be disconnected from your vision and purpose, you have a problem. Either you haven't captured the right characteristics or, well, you have the wrong vision and purpose. Figuring out the connection between your EVP and your firm's vision and purpose is important to establishing a line of sight to connect and engage your employees to your brand.

Remember: Sometimes, merely identifying your uniqueness is not enough. Successful firms proactively *create* uniqueness. In the early days of Southwest Airlines, founder Herb Kelleher (no relation) created an EVP that was fun, and built his hiring and branding efforts around it. Even today, you will continue to see remnants of Herb's EVP on Southwest Airlines promotional materials, including the following passage:

> Fun-LUVing Attitude: Don't take yourself too seriously, maintain perspective (balance), celebrate successes, enjoy your work, and be a passionate team player.

Talking It Up: Communicating Your Employment Brand

Of course, it's not enough to develop your EVP, which you may think of as your employment brand. You must also communicate that employment brand, both internally and externally. If you commit to broadcasting to your employees and to the rest of the world why you're a swell place to work, in time, they'll come to believe it (assuming, of course, that it's true)! In this way, you can engage existing employees and entice the very best recruits, not to mention making the best possible impression on potential new clients!

Essentially, by communicating your employment brand, you foster pride in your company among your workforce. And trust me: That's no small thing. Indeed, according to a 2012 report by researchers at Dale Carnegie, "What Drives Employee Engagement," pride in one's organization is one of the top three drivers of engagement. (The other two, in case you're wondering, are satisfaction with one's immediate manager and trust and belief in senior leadership.)

Unfortunately, as discussed in the introduction to this chapter, most employers spend the majority of their time crystallizing, branding, and communicating what they *sell,* not who they *are.*

Your organization's marketing team should be working hand in hand with your staffing and HR teams to publicize messages about your employment brand, both internally and externally.

Branding internally

Early in my career, I came across a survey that ranked employers by "Best Employee Benefits." Surprisingly, the companies that boasted the best employee benefit programs were not the companies with the best employee benefits. Instead, the companies with the best programs were the ones that did the best job of communicating the benefits they *did* offer.

This study made a lasting impression on me about the power and impact of effectively branding a benefit (or message, initiative, idea, and so on). This is why I make a big deal about companies who conduct an employee engagement survey taking time to communicate to their employees their plans for revealing the results. Essentially, these companies are "branding" their efforts to disseminate the information. (Sadly, if employees don't hear updates, they tend to become a tad bit cynical and assume nothing is happening — which can lead to a lack of engagement.)

Repetition is key. There is a reason we connect Clydesdale horses with Budweiser, or talking geckos with Geico. We've seen these brands advertise so often that the animals have become synonymous with their products. The same goes for other types of branding as well — including your employment brand.

Sadly, many organizations spend countless hours on their external product branding efforts that they fail to communicate their employment brand on the inside. They underbrand their culture and EVP, while perhaps overbranding their services and products to the outside world. But the fact is, you must continually remind your employees of your firm's employment brand, or EVP. Engaged companies will practically scream "We're great!" over and over to their employees (even if that message is more aspirational than reality based). They know that employees and leaders both want the same thing: to work for a company whose culture rocks.

Branding externally

You've identified who you are. You've effectively communicated that message internally. Now it's time for that message to reach the outside world.

This can happen in any number of ways. One is the traditional route — using mainstream marketing and advertising tools to publicize your employment brand. For example, a recent Walmart commercial focuses on a young employee, named Nathaniel, who views his job with the firm as an opportunity to move up in the world, noting that at Walmart, 75 percent of store management started as hourly associates. He goes on to say that he can use Walmart's education benefits to obtain a college degree. The ad ends with the tagline, "Opportunity. That's the *real* Walmart." Whatever your feelings about this corporate behemoth, there's little doubt that the ad effectively communicates an important aspect of the company's employment brand!

Other avenues for external branding include leveraging "Best Place to Work" surveys and awards and using social media. For more on these tactics, read on.

Leveraging "Best Place to Work" surveys and awards

I know what you're thinking. "Best Place to Work" awards are akin to popularity contests. And you're not the only one who believes that. I once heard an executive announce at an employee meeting, "We don't want to win a 'Best Place to Work' award. We want to *be* a 'best place to work.'"

Although I admire this executive's thirst for authenticity, I also think he was missing the point. The fact is, companies that pursue "Best Place to Work" status receive many tangible rewards . . . even if they don't win.

Here's one: The simple act of filling out a "Best Place to Work" survey provides companies with a quick snapshot of what's working and what isn't. Essentially, this acts as a benchmark for the firm's engagement efforts, and helps illuminate where you should be focusing your energy.

Here's another: Even if you know you have a lot of work to do before you reach top-50 or top-100 status, just the application process itself can become the push that the leadership team needs to embrace your engagement efforts. Indeed, "Best Place to Work" surveys, which are usually brief and inexpensive, often prompt a full companywide survey to gauge the pulse of your employees.

And if you win? What a branding opportunity! It's a well-known fact that companies that receive "Best Place to Work" status receive more résumés from qualified candidates than other firms in their peer group. Indeed, firms that make *Fortune* magazine's "100 Best Companies to Work For" list receive *twice* as many applications as firms that are not on the list. And how about this statistic: Edward Jones — which earned the top spot on *Fortune*'s list in 2002 and 2003 and, as of this writing, has been on Fortune's list for 14 years running — now receives ten times more applications than it did before being named to the list! Moreover, according to Wayne Cascio and John Boudreau, authors of *Investing in People* (FT Press), these companies' employee turnover levels are less than half those of their competitors.

Being named a "Best Place to Work" also offers irrefutable evidence of your claim that you are, indeed, an elite employer. With "Best Place to Work" status in your back pocket, you can prove to employees and to the outside world that you're something special.

Bain & Company, a management consulting firm, has won several "top employer" awards. How do I know? Because Bain has rather intelligently featured this accomplishment on the main page of its website (www.bain.com). It's literally *the first thing you see.* Clicking the link leads to a separate page (www.bain.com/about/what-we-do/awards) that lists the awards Bain has won — including, as of this writing, #1 "Best Firm to Work For" by *Consulting* magazine, #4 "Best Places to Work" by Glassdoor, #1 "Best Firm to Work For" and "Vault Consulting 50" by Vault, "Best Companies 2012" by *Working Mother* magazine, and "Best Places to Work for LGBT Equality" by Human Rights Campaign for Equality. What's particularly interesting about Bain is that its focus on "who we are" even takes precedent over "what we do."

Accelerating your employment brand using social media

Companies that can articulate their employment brand can take advantage of a great branding accelerator: social media. Enlightened organizations use this new technology to tweet, post, and blog about job openings, new hires, internal thought leaders, company news, and how swell the company is to work for. Yesterday, a company could get away with telling the world what it does. Today and tomorrow, companies will be able to accelerate their branding by telling the world not only what they do, but also who they are . . . in 140 characters or less!

Of course, the use of social media isn't just limited to companies. Rank-and-file employees use it, too. For more on galvanizing your employees to use social media for the good of the firm, read on.

Tri-Angle: Understanding Tri-Branding

One summer Saturday, I became irked with my kids. They were too busy with friends and other activities to hang out with their mother and me! In a huff, I headed to our local camping goods store, and $3,000 later, I returned home with two new kayaks, oars, life jackets, and a roof rack for the car, with the goal of paddling the waterways every weekend with my wife. So, what if the kids no longer wanted to spend time with dear old Dad? I had a new hobby. Their loss!

Naturally, this decision was made with my heart — but not so much with my head. I failed to factor in my wife's level of interest . . . or lack thereof ("You bought what?"), New England's short kayak season, the difficulty of getting the kayaks on and off the roof of the car, and so on. But I was engaged with the idea of kayaking. Ultimately, I taught my wife to kayak and worked through the logistic and seasonal issues, and today, we consider kayaking one of our favorite pastimes.

This example illustrates what happens when we make decisions from our hearts. Clearly, decisions made in this way aren't entirely rational or logical. So, what does this have to do with branding? Simply put, branding is a lot about capturing someone's heart. Consider Apple. Although Apple's star shines brightly today, it wasn't so long ago that Apple was on the brink of collapse as PCs were killing Macs in the marketplace. But Mac users had such a strong emotional tie to the Apple brand that they essentially kept the brand alive until Steve Jobs could launch iTunes, the iPod, the iPhone, and the iPad. Apple truly succeeded when its products captured both the hearts *and* the heads of consumers.

Employee engagement occurs when an organization is able to capture its employees' heads *and* their hearts. And how do they do this? By branding their EVP and effectively linking the firm's purpose, vision, values, and strategy to the firm's brand. This emotional connection is why an employee becomes a brand advocate for his or her employer.

In recent years, our society has become very brand conscious, thanks in part to the proliferation of social media on such sites as Facebook, Twitter, and LinkedIn. Indeed, social media is an extremely effective tool for driving brand engagement internally, externally, and via your external stakeholders. This is at the foundation of what I call *tri-branding*. With tri-branding, companies link their product or service and employment brands, and then leverage employees, customers, and other key stakeholders to sing their praises (often via social media) or "live" their brand (see Figure 10-1).

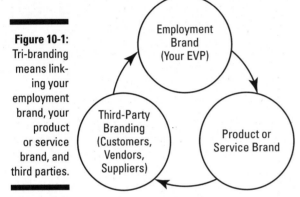

Figure 10-1:
Tri-branding means linking your employment brand, your product or service brand, and third parties.

Take my favorite case study, Apple. As mentioned, Apple excels at linking its product brand with its employment brand, and hiring the most creative people to make the most creative products. But that's not all. Apple also excels at getting employees, stakeholders, and particularly customers to sing its praises and live its brand. Me? I'm a Droid user. But I'm consistently amazed by how many of my friends swear by their iPhones, and take particular delight when some feature on their phone trumps the same feature on mine. These people actually *live* the Apple brand. They're both logically and emotionally attached to Apple.

Still don't understand? Try asking your teenager if working at Burger King is cool. Odds are, she'll say no. Then ask if it's cool to work at Starbucks; I'm guessing you'll get a different answer. Not to pick on the Burger Kings of the world, but why is Starbucks considered "cool" when other fast-food places, which pay similar hourly rates, aren't? Simple: because of branding. This brand connectedness helps firms find and retain talent, while also boosting engagement levels. Whole Foods, Rackspace, Zappos, Southwest Airlines, Virgin Atlantic, Salesforce.com, HubSpot, Warby Parker — all these firms ooze coolness in their respective markets. They're not just cool to their consumers; they're also cool to their employees and to other key stakeholders. This linkage is what defines tri-branding.

The growing importance of Klout scores

Not sure who your connectors are? Fortunately, there's an easy way to find out: checking your employees' Klout scores. A Klout score is a statistical score from 1 to 100 that ranks people on such variables as how many people they reach through social media, how trusted they are, and on what topics.

As noted by Klout CEO Joe Fernandez, "Influence has really become the currency of the social web, and Klout is the standard measurement for that." Don't believe him? Consider this: Recently, when advertising for a community manager position, Salesforce.com listed "a Klout score of 35 or over" as one of the desired skills. Clearly, there is a shift underway. *Fast Company* put it this way: "The line is quickly blurring between the value of what we know and who we know."

Enlisting your employees as brand ambassadors

Sure, it's great when your company uses social media to broadcast its employment brand. But what's *really* great is when a company's employees use these technologies for the same aim — particularly when those employees are what author Malcolm Gladwell calls "connectors" (see Chapter 2).

According to Gladwell, connectors are people "with an extraordinary knack of making friends and acquaintances." If the whole "six degrees of separation" thing is true — that is, the notion that everyone on the planet is connected to everyone else by six degrees — it's in part because of connectors. These people often have very large social and professional circles. And when they tweet or post good things about your company, a lot of people will see it. In effect, an engaged connector becomes a brand ambassador of sorts.

Think about it: Including nieces and nephews, there are about 30 Kellehers in my family. Counting them, my neighbors, and my friends, my inner circle reaches approximately 100 people. Back in 1995, if I liked (or didn't like) my employer, my boss, the restaurant where I just ate, the movie I just saw, or the store I just visited, my reach to communicate those feelings was limited to this 100-person circle. Today, my reach — and your reach, and the reach of your employees (as well as your customers and key stakeholders) can be in the thousands or tens of thousands. And if someone is a connector, that person's reach might be in the hundreds of thousands or even in the millions!

Of course, in order for your firm to leverage your connector employees' networks, those employees must know your employer brand, or EVP, inside and out. That's another reason your internal branding efforts are important: They enable you to clearly communicate this information. The internal piece is necessary to ensure consistency and accuracy when tackling external branding.

Incredibly, many companies fail to see how valuable their own employees are when it comes to social media. Some even go so far as to prohibit its use. Why? Because they're afraid of employees saying the wrong thing, badmouthing the employer, inadvertently sharing information that should remain private, and so on. These concerns are legitimate — after all, employees can and sometimes do say negative things about the company they work for, especially if they work in a toxic culture — but the fact is, social media is not going away. Particularly if you want to engage Gen Y employees, you'll need to put on your big-kid pants and deal with it.

If you're over 50, you may remember when companies locked employees' rotary telephones so they wouldn't "steal" company resources by calling their friends and relatives. Those over 35 probably recall restrictions on e-mail use, the concern being that employees might steal the company's intellectual property. Nowadays, these concerns seem silly. Odds are, in time, the same will be true of concerns over the use of social media.

Even if you don't embrace and leverage social media, your departing employees probably do — and they may well rake your organization over the coals when they leave!

Your employees can either be brand ambassadors or brand naysayers. As the war for talent continues to heat up, it will be increasingly difficult to find good people. Those select firms that have a sea of employees singing their praises will be in a far better position to hire and retain the best. Employees who are engaged are more likely to "brand" you as a great employer. And employees who aren't engaged? Well, you get the picture.

One more thing: Employees don't just communicate with people outside your company. They also communicate with each other. In the mini-society that is the workplace, attitudes, be they good or bad, are infectious. If your brand has negative connotations internally, you are facing an uphill battle in engaging employees. Your employees are the first-line consumers of your message, and their perceptions and emotional responses are profoundly important!

Making sure your customers sing your praises

Earlier, I mention that Apple is great at getting customers to live their brand. But it's not the only one. BMW, Southwest Airlines, Harley-Davidson — these are all companies whose customers live their brand.

What's their secret? In a word, it's *engagement* — but in this case, customer engagement. Just as employee engagement is more important than employee satisfaction, so, too, does customer engagement trump customer satisfaction. A satisfied customer will supply a positive review of your company if asked, but an engaged customer will go out of her way to "brand" her satisfaction with your product. As an extreme example, a person who owns a Harley-Davidson motorcycle may be satisfied. But a person who has a Harley-Davidson tattoo on his forearm? That guy's *engaged.*

Here's an example of the power of an engaged customer. A few years back, a passenger on a Southwest Airlines flight made a video recording of an airline flight attendant singing a country song as part of her "buckle up" spiel. The passenger then uploaded the video to YouTube. Since then, millions of people have watched the video. Think of the marketing benefits, not just from a product branding standpoint but from an employment branding perspective. In addition to showing how fun it is to fly on Southwest, the video demonstrated that working for the company is so great, people sing on the job! And it didn't cost Southwest a dime.

Of course, disengaged customers are equally powerful. Take Dave Carroll, who spotted a United Airlines bag handler mishandling his guitar, causing it to break. Carroll sought reimbursement from United, but he received only denials and, ultimately, a rejection. Frustrated, Carroll wrote a song titled "United Breaks Guitars," created a video for it, and uploaded it to YouTube. Soon, close to 13 million people had watched it. Carroll subsequently appeared on several major media outlets, released follow-up videos, and even published a book. United, on the other hand, faced a PR nightmare. In the end, United was forced to offer an apology and reimburse Carroll for his loss. Oh, and the company now includes "United Breaks Guitars" as a customer-service training video.

The point? Social media is not going away . . . and if you don't take control of it, it can take control of you!

Leveraging other stakeholders in your tri-branding efforts

In addition to leveraging engaged employees and customers in your branding efforts, you should also leverage your organizational stakeholders. These include vendors, applicants, the media, contractors, former employees, the government, colleges and universities, local civic organizations, and the community as a whole.

For example, if you want to rehire a former star employee, are you making an effort to stay in touch with that person, perhaps via an "alumni newsletter"? Are you showing your best face to applicants who don't get hired but may someday be customers? Are you a good corporate citizen and neighbor? Do you engage your vendors and consultants and treat them like true partners?

If you answered "yes" to these questions, then you may well be the beneficiary of effective tri-branding. If not, you may never know how your brand is being tarnished — and how that affects your employees' levels of engagement.

Chapter 11

Game On! Driving Engagement with Gamification

*G*amification. Say the word, and chances are, the response will be, "Gesundheit!" The fact is, the term just hasn't made it to the mainstream vernacular — although I'm confident it will soon. Before August 2010, almost no one searched for the term *gamification* on Google. Since January 2011, however, searches for that term have spiked.

If the results of a 2012 survey by the Pew Research Center's Internet & American Life Project in conjunction with Elon University's Imagining the Internet Center is any indication, interest in gamification will continue to grow. According to the ensuing report, titled "The Future of Gamification," 53 percent of respondents agreed that by 2020, there would be significant advances in the adoption and use of gamification. Their reasoning? As one respondent so aptly put it, "Playing beats working. So, if the enjoyment and challenge of playing can be embedded in learning, work, and commerce, then gamification will take off."

They weren't the only ones. Gartner, the famous technology consultancy, predicts that by 2014, more than 70 percent of Global 2000 organizations will have at least one gamified application, and that by 2015, 50 percent of corporate innovation will be gamified. And Deloitte, another major consulting firm, included gamification as one of its Top 10 Technology Trends of 2012.

This chapter serves as a brief primer for gamification. If you're interested in finding out more, crack open *Business Gamification For Dummies* by Kris Duggan and Kate Shoup (Wiley).

Paging Mr. Webster: Defining Gamification

So, what is gamification? Simply put, *gamification* is the use of game mechanics and rewards in a non-game setting to increase user engagement and drive desired user behaviors. In part, the idea behind gamification is to tap into people's innate desire to play games to influence how they behave and what they do.

Sound creepy? Fair point. Yes, gamification can certainly be used to promote behaviors in which people may not otherwise engage. But the best gamification programs operate by rewarding people for behaviors they are already inclined to perform or are required to perform, increasing their engagement and enjoyment. In other words, gamification makes the things you have to do more fun. And by now, you should know that injecting fun in the workplace goes a long way toward increasing employee engagement.

To be clear, gamification isn't about creating a game. Instead, with gamification, you use game mechanics to enliven an existing experience — say, an employee training program, a company intranet, or a database application — making it more engaging. Note that the "experiences" listed here are digital in nature. These types of experiences are the focus of this chapter. That's not to say, however, that some principles of gamification can't be applied in a real-world setting. In fact, my fellow organizational development, facilitators, and training professionals and I have used a non-digital form of gamification for years when facilitating experiential exercises into our workshops. We learned years ago that that there are real benefits to injecting fun into our agendas. Engagement — and energy — always goes up!

But What Does It Do? Understanding What Gamification Does

Does your organization have low retention rates? Is your onboarding process a drag? Do you have trouble getting employees to collaborate, share knowledge, or keep records the way they should? All these problems stem from — you guessed it — a lack of engagement.

Enter gamification.

Gamification enables you to drive, measure, and reward high-value behaviors by employees. Game mechanics leverage design and behavioral psychology principles inherent in today's social games to drive and reward specific user behaviors in business environments. Smart gamification elements — such as points, achievements, levels, leaderboards, missions, and contests — can be employed to drive desired behaviors on virtually any enterprise application.

Your employees, like anyone, crave attention, recognition, approval, and rewards. With gamification, you feed this craving — and in the process convert employees into highly engaged collaborators and advocates.

Get with the Program! Developing a Gamification Program

Interested in applying gamification to *your* business? If so, the first thing you need to recognize is that gamification, like engagement, requires an investment of time to develop a multistep process to ensure success. Gamification is a program, not just a project. You can't just apply gamification for three months and call it a day — you need to invest in the strategy for the long term.

Developing a gamification program involves these broad steps:

- ✔ Pinpointing your business objectives
- ✔ Identifying the user behaviors that will drive your business objectives
- ✔ Choosing rewards
- ✔ Selecting game mechanics

Pinpointing your business objectives

For your gamification efforts to be successful, first you have to pinpoint your business objectives — what, exactly, you want to achieve. For example, maybe you want to speed up business processes. Or maybe your goal is to drive sales. Encouraging collaboration is another common aim, as is improving employee education and training and developing an effective onboarding process.

Whatever your objective, gamification can help you meet it — while at the same time fostering engagement! For details, read on.

Speeding up business processes

Most business software, though designed to automate business processes, still relies on human participation. For example, companies such as Oracle, Microsoft, Salesforce.com, and others offer sales, financial, and communications technology to help businesses run more efficiently. Quite frequently, though, actual humans must input and manage the data. Often, they don't do so well, resulting in lost productivity and diminishing the value of the extremely expensive software.

For example, consider a support organization in which a key business process is the opening and closing of support tickets in a service desk application. Using gamification, you could recognize key behaviors such as opening a support ticket and closing one. After the behavior tracking is in place, the system could reward high-performing employees. In the end, the result would almost certainly be an increase in the rate of closing those tickets, and in engagement in general.

Driving sales

Gamification can reward people for performing key business processes in sales applications and, in doing so, speed them up. For example, in a sales application, sales teams must manage their leads and opportunities by inputting critical data points. By measuring and tracking desired behaviors, you can set milestones and showcase success on a leaderboard. The social pressure to succeed can help drive adherence to company processes. They'll naturally fill out more lead forms, creating more opportunities for the business.

Encouraging knowledge sharing and collaboration

As companies have observed the power of social sites like Facebook, Twitter, and even Wikipedia, they've tried to apply similar principles in their own organizations by providing internal social networks, blogs, *wikis* (websites that allow for the collaborative edit of content by users), and other technologies to promote knowledge sharing across the workforce. But more often than not, the workforce tends not to use them. According to Forrester Research, such tools are adopted by only 12 percent of the workforce.

Why not? One reason is that people are resistant to change. They're used to e-mail and their other creature comforts. They also believe knowledge is power, and they aren't terribly inclined to surrender that power to others. Using gamification, companies can champion employees who leverage these types of collaborative applications. As people share valuable knowledge, other employees can benefit. Improving knowledge sharing and collaboration can also speed up productivity — another common business objective.

Improving training and education

At many companies, people must complete various training courses online. The problem is, no one wants to actually complete these courses. In fact, sometimes it seems as if the age-old instinct to play hooky becomes more powerful than ever when you're faced with the prospect of completing online training. By leveraging gamification programs, companies can acknowledge and champion employees who complete important training.

Aiding with onboarding

These days, to get started at a new company, employees must move through a mountain of paper or digital paperwork (see Chapter 14). By gamifying certain processes along the way — for example, filling out forms, completing compliance training, and learning about key company policies — companies can improve the rate at which these tasks are completed.

Identifying desired behaviors

Next you have to determine which user behaviors will drive the objectives you identified. Put simply, behaviors are the foundation of all gamification programs. Once key behaviors are identified, you can determine which game mechanics are most likely to drive those behaviors and reward users for performing those behaviors — that's what gamification is all about.

Here's a list of the aforementioned business objectives, along with behaviors that may drive them:

- **Speeding up business processes:** The specific behaviors associated with speeding up business processes will vary depending on the business and the process. For the sake of example, suppose you run a service department that responds to customer complaints. The key behaviors associated with speeding up business processes may include responding to an issue, resolving the issue, and updating records associated with the issue. For even better results, you could upgrade these behaviors from simple ones to more complex ones by being more specific, with time as your qualifier: responding to an issue within 30 minutes, resolving the issue within 24 hours, and updating records associated with the issue within three days.

- **Driving sales:** Key behaviors in sales include calling, e-mailing, or meeting with a customer; responding to a lead; following up on a lead; converting a lead into an opportunity; and closing a deal (with extra credit for larger deals). As with speeding up business processes, you may see even better results by upgrading some of these behaviors from simple ones to complex ones — again, with time as your qualifier: responding to a lead within 30 minutes, following up on a lead within three days, and converting a lead to an opportunity within three weeks.

- **Encouraging knowledge sharing and collaboration:** Behaviors associated with knowledge sharing and collaboration include asking questions on the company intranet, answering questions, voting on answers, and receiving votes for your answers.

- **Improving training and education:** Relevant behaviors in this area include starting a training course, advancing to the next module of a course, answering questions correctly, and completing the course.

Arguably, that last behavior — completing the course — is the most important one. For that, you could offer an extra-special reward or broadcast that the employee has earned some type of certification. By leveraging gamification programs, companies can acknowledge and champion employees who complete training.

✔ **Aiding with onboarding:** With regard to onboarding, these behaviors are likely the ones that count: reading about company policies; completing compliance training; filling out HR forms; setting up health insurance, 401(k), and retirement benefits; and exploring the company's culture.

Gamifying these behaviors — or, really, just about any behaviors — can be even more effective if you make the results visible to other employees in the company. When everyone across the company can see who is being recognized for a behavior, more employees tend to adopt the behavior. This is thanks to a little thing middle-school counselors call "peer pressure."

Choosing rewards

Even the mere *hope* of receiving a reward — even a really lousy one — can motivate a person to perform a desired behavior. Why? Oddly, it's not the reward itself that's motivating; instead, it's the achievement tied to the reward. That is, the reward acts to validate the achievement. It makes sense, then, that successful gamification hinges on the use of rewards (preferably good ones).

In a gamification program, rewards can be divided into three categories:

✔ Recognition

✔ Privileges

✔ Monetary rewards

Conferring recognition

Pretty much everyone wants to be recognized for their achievements. Indeed, recognition is part of just about every type of competition on the planet. (You'll learn much more about recognition in Chapter 17.) Recognition for completing a task or accomplishing a goal not only feeds this basic human need, it also encourages engagement and increases repetition — both of which are probably in your list of business objectives. In a gamified environment, you can recognize your users in a couple different ways:

✔ **Reputation:** For some users, it's all about reputation. These employees are intrinsically motivated by esteem. They want to be *respected*. Rewarding these users for their expertise is key — assuming, of course, that their expertise relates to your area of business. By rewarding employees for expertise, you enable them to develop a reputation.

✔ **Status:** Whereas reputation is tied to expertise and a body of work, status refers to the relative position of one individual compared to another, with those having a higher position or rank being conferred greater status. In a gamified environment, status is often tied to valuable behaviors that support a company's business objectives.

A great way to confer status (and, for that matter, reputation) is through the use of badges. If you were ever a Boy Scout or a Girl Scout, then you're already familiar with the idea behind badges, such as the Stamp Collecting, Bugling, and ever-useful Nuclear Science merit badges available to scouts nationwide. To quote Merriam-Webster, a *badge* is "an emblem awarded for a particular accomplishment." Badges can be physical (like the aforementioned merit badges, which are sewn onto scout uniforms) or virtual (like the badges earned on various websites). As you can guess, the latter is more common in gamification programs — even the most loyal employees typically don't want to sew badges on their clothes.

Giving privileges

Although some users prefer to be rewarded with reputation or status, others will be more motivated by receiving privileges. These may include the following:

✔ **VIP access:** Giving your top employees access to key personnel is a great way to reward, engage, and motivate them. For example, you may offer lunch with the chairman of the board, general manager, or district VP to employees who reach a certain score in your gamification program.

✔ **Moderation powers:** One way to reward users is to empower them. For example, on an intranet forum, you may endow your top thread starters with the power to moderate the site. This is doubly excellent, because the user is typically thrilled to take on this responsibility, and you essentially receive free labor. As Wikipedia has taught us, people will work for nothing if they're intrinsically motivated to do so. Giving users powers over the general riffraff is also a way of conferring status.

✔ **Stronger votes:** To quote George Orwell: "All animals are equal, but some animals are more equal than others." Which is why you may decide to give some of your users stronger votes — on an intranet site in which content is voted up or down, for example.

Giving monetary rewards

Some users will certainly be satisfied with recognition and privileges, but others may hold out for more tangible benefits. These benefits are typically monetary in nature but could also involve free stuff.

These are not bonus programs, and the monetary rewards should always be nominal in value. As the Enrons of the world have proven, if you inject too much value in rewards, you'll encourage cheating.

Here are a couple examples of monetary rewards:

- ✔ **Discounts:** If you're in the business of manufacturing or selling a consumer product, you may give top performers a special price break on items in your catalog.

- ✔ **Prizes:** Prizes can be literally anything, from a wee food item to an American Express gift certificate. But the easiest type of prize to give is whatever you have on hand. Are you an electronics retailer? Then electronics are the logical choice as prizes. Another good type of prize is one that broadcasts your brand — say, a coffee mug or baseball cap with your logo. This is a form of tri-branding (see Chapter 10), where you'll be encouraging key stakeholders to brand on your firm's behalf.

Although prizes generate buzz and excitement, offering even humble amounts can be expensive in the aggregate, and may not result in a lasting engagement or even positive feelings on the part of employees. This is especially true if the prize is stuff rather than an experience. That is, if someone wins a TV, that TV will likely decrease in value (emotionally speaking) over time. In contrast, if someone wins a weekend away, the trip will increase in value due to the happy memories that result.

Selecting game mechanics

Game mechanics are the components of a game — the tools employed by game designers to generate and reward activity among players (or, in the case of a gamification program, employees, customers, or other users). Most gamification programs leverage game mechanics in one way or another.

When it comes to game mechanics, various tools are available to you, each designed to elicit a specific reaction from players. These tools, which can be combined in infinite ways to create a broad spectrum of responses and experiences, include the following:

- ✔ Points
- ✔ Leaderboards
- ✔ Levels
- ✔ Missions, challenges, and quests
- ✔ Feedback

In addition, you'll want to consider anti-gaming mechanisms. We cover all these subjects in this section.

Points

Points help users know they're in a gamified environment and that many of the small behaviors they take along the way are being recognized at a system level. Companies running gamification programs use points to spur desired behaviors. These points can then be compiled into a score. To really drive desired behaviors, game designers can weight points. *Weighting points* means awarding more points for those behaviors deemed more valuable or that require more effort.

Leaderboards

Winning is great. But you know what's even better? When everyone else knows you won. That's the power of the leaderboard. A *leaderboard* is a board that displays the names and scores of current "competitors" in a gamified system. Companies with robust gamification cultures may even consider adding these scores to their balanced scorecard! Alternatively, a leaderboard may simply indicate a person's ranking in the system without noting the scores of others.

Recognizing that achievement is super important, the purpose of a leaderboard is to show people where they rank. Those at the top enjoy the notoriety it brings; as for everyone else, the leaderboard shows them where they stand relative to their peers. Building friendly competition is a key cog in a high-performing culture.

Often, the very presence of a leaderboard can elicit the desire to play. The simple goal of rising up the rankings serves as a powerful motivator to continue. People like to keep score. Understanding this and providing easy ways to do it is a great way to foster engagement. For some, the mere sight of their rank on the leaderboard is all the reward they seek.

Levels

Anyone who has ever played Donkey Kong, Pac-Man, or Angry Birds (or, for that matter, pretty much any electronic game ever) is familiar with the concept of levels. After you conquer one level, you move on to the next one. Each level constitutes a sub-game of sorts, often with different types of obstacles and tools at the player's disposal, and typically more and more difficult.

A gamified experience doesn't employ levels in quite the same way as arcade games do. If your goal is to gamify your company intranet, users won't, for example, suddenly see their whole screen change to offer a new set of challenges the moment they "level up." Instead, gamified systems more closely mirror role-playing games such as Dungeons & Dragons, where a level is effectively a rank that corresponds to the player. It's earned through accomplishments and represents additional privileges or abilities.

So, if players don't level up by rescuing a princess from a giant gorilla, how *do* they level up in a gamification system? In a gamified system, the change in level occurs when the user reaches a set point threshold, often indicated by the reward of a new badge.

Levels serve two important roles in gamification systems:

- ✔ **They indicate progress.** Proceeding from one level to the next gives players a sense of satisfaction.

- ✔ **They convey status.** A player who has reached level 42 of your system can reasonably be considered more expert than someone who has failed to advance beyond level 7.

It's a good idea to make the first few levels easier to attain because that encourages users to participate more often. The highest levels may require extended usage over a longer period.

Missions, challenges, and quests

Mission, challenge, and *quest* are essentially different words for the same thing. They require users to perform a prescribed set of actions, following a guided path of your design. A mission, challenge, or quest may involve a single step (for example, completing necessary paperwork during the onboarding process) or several steps — even as many as 20. Often, missions are about discovery or education.

Sometimes, the actions in a mission must occur in a certain order; these missions are called *progression missions.* Other times, actions can occur in any order; these are called *random missions.* The tasks in a mission may revolve around the same behavior (reading five posts, for example), or could be an around-the-world variety, where different behaviors are performed (for example, reading a post, commenting on a post, and adding your own post).

As each action is completed, the player is generally given a reward. The player is also given a reward — usually status based — when the mission is complete. At the same time, the next mission is unlocked. Successive missions contain harder-to-earn rewards. From the player's point of view, completing missions is a lot like leveling up in a particular topic. As the player completes each mission, her perceived status will likely increase.

A *track* is a collection of missions. Like missions, tracks can be ordered or unordered, although if the track centers around expertise, ordered tracks are the way to go. Why? Because the ordered progression of missions represents increasing mastery or advancement in a particular topic or specialization. In other words, the user must complete the first mission before progressing to the second mission, and so on.

Feedback

One way to encourage engagement in your gamification program is to broadcast well-written, helpful, engaging onscreen feedback in the form of real-time notifications within the game system and/or via e-mail when users perform a desired behavior, level up, unlock a reward, or need to complete an additional behavior in order to earn their *next* reward.

Notifications may appear in the user's activity feed or as a small pop-up on the screen and can become increasingly sophisticated, triggered by any behavior or series of behaviors. Often — especially in gamification systems that involve daunting goals — feedback can keep players from feeling paralyzed, as if no progress is being made.

Don't go crazy with feedback, or you'll likely overwhelm your user.

Anti-gaming mechanics

Sadly, people can be jerks. (Not you, obviously.) Which is why you can rest assured that at least one bozo out there will try to *game* your system — that is, attempt to cheat or to earn points by exploiting loopholes. If it could happen throughout the banking system, as it did in 2008 and 2009, it can happen with your gamification program.

For example, suppose you offer a free T-shirt to all employees who earn 10,000 points. Suppose further that users receive 10 points for each page view on your company intranet. Users may attempt to game your system by simply clicking page after page after page. They're not really doing what you want them to do — reading the content and interacting with it — they're just clicking to increase their points.

Fortunately, you can apply various anti-gaming mechanisms to thwart them. Don't worry — unlike with matter and anti-matter, applying game mechanics alongside anti-gaming mechanics won't cause an explosion. But it will enable you to prevent users from gaming your system.

Here are a few anti-gaming mechanics to consider:

- ✔ **Cool-downs:** If you follow IndyCar racing, you may be familiar with the *push-to-pass* feature. When a driver presses the push-to-pass button on his steering wheel, the car receives extra horsepower for a few seconds, enabling the driver to pass the car ahead (or defend against one creeping up from behind). So, what's stopping the driver from pressing that button all the time? Simple. IndyCar officials implemented a cool-down mechanism. After the button has been pressed, drivers must wait a certain period of time before pressing it again.

A similar approach is used as an anti-gaming measure. With cool-downs, you wait a certain period of time before rewarding a behavior. For example, if you reward users for visiting a page, you might require a 30-second gap between each page view. This increases the likelihood that users are actually doing what you want them to do — in this case, reading the content on the page.

✔ **Rate limiting:** Using that same push-to-pass example, IndyCar officials took further steps to ensure that drivers didn't spend all their time with their fingers on the push-to-pass button by limiting the number of times they could press it per race (or, in some cases, limiting the total amount of time per race the button could be depressed).

Similarly, to prevent users from gaming your system, you might limit the number of times you reward a behavior over a certain period of time. For example, you might decide to reward players 10 points for each view — but you might limit the number of points rewarding that behavior to 50 per day, 20 per hour, 10 per minute, or what have you.

This approach does have a negative aspect: It could discourage users for accessing additional content. So, just be sure to strike a balance.

✔ **Count limiting:** Another option is to limit the total number of times a user is rewarded for performing a certain behavior, ever. For example, you could set things up such that users receive a reward for visiting a particular page just once.

In addition to these approaches, you can also manually remove points from problem players' totals and remove problem players from your leaderboards. (That'll learn 'em!) You can also set up your system to measure behaviors that are harder to fake — for example, receiving votes from other users.

Part III

Selecting the Right Employees to Increase Engagement

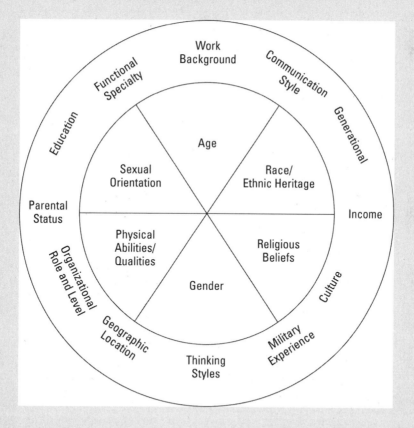

In this part...

- ✔ Explore the BEST approach to select engaged employees with the right **b**ehaviors, **e**ducation, **s**kills, and **t**raits.

- ✔ Develop effective interview questions to select engaged candidates.

- ✔ Prepare new hires for immediate success and engagement.

- ✔ Establish performance expectations to ensure a high-performing, highly engaged organization.

Chapter 12

You're Hired! Hiring for Engagement

Suppose you're a basketball coach, and your team, well, your team just sucks. Sure, they have ball-handling skills, and they can shoot. But as a unit, they just don't gel. They're not cohesive. They're selfish. They communicate poorly, if at all. It's almost as if they don't care whether they win or lose!

Obviously, the team suffers from a lack of engagement. But you may not be dealing with an engagement issue, per se. That is, your problem may not be that you haven't developed a system by which to engage your players. Instead, it may be that you just picked the wrong people to be on your team. In other words, you have a *selection* issue. If you select the right players for your team, engagement will naturally occur.

Often, when faced with selecting employees (read: hiring), employers focus on candidates' education and skills. After all, those are easy to quantify. But really, it's a candidate's traits and behaviors that will be key to her success in an organization. That's not to say that education and skills aren't important — after all, you probably can't win a basketball game if you can't dribble and shoot — but they're only part of the equation. In this chapter, you find out how to pinpoint success characteristics — those traits and behaviors that yield superior performance and engagement — and to hire people who display them.

Be proactive and not reactive in your hiring practices. Successful organizations are always interviewing potential candidates, even if there are no current openings. Don't wait for someone to quit to begin the recruitment process.

Trait Up: Pinpointing Key Behaviors and Traits

Back in the dark ages (1985), while working for an engineering firm, I was sent to recruit at MIT. Not surprisingly, in terms of education and skills, all 15 of the candidates I met were off the charts. It was MIT, after all! How on earth was I supposed to determine which ones to invite back to our office for meetings with senior executives? Fortunately, a great mentor of mine, Ed Burns, told me, "Pick the one person you would love to have over to your house for a cold beer." Yes, we had to hire people who were technically brilliant, but we also needed people who would interface well with our clients. Of the 15 brilliant individuals I interviewed, all had the necessary education and skills to perform as an entry-level staff engineer. But Ed's filter enabled me to narrow things down. In the end, it came down to the behaviors and traits necessary for the job we needed done.

Since then, I've often been amazed at the misguided focus of hiring managers, who place too much emphasis on education and skills and not nearly enough on behaviors and traits. The fact is, the most engaged employees are engaged because of behaviors and traits they exhibit, not because of their skill set or the educational degrees they hold. Indeed, if my nearly 30 years in HR taught me anything, it's that employees are promoted for displaying specific behaviors and traits — namely, those that define high performance and high engagement.

Sure, education and skills are important. Having the necessary education and skills is similar to having Jacks or better — you need them just to stay in the poker game! But often, it's the intangibles, like behaviors and traits, that get people promoted in the workplace. In fact, if you were to ask a leadership team to define the common attributes of the top 10 percent of their workforce, or to define their most engaged employees, they would most likely outline a common set of behaviors and traits — rather than education or skills — that all these individuals possess.

To determine what behaviors and traits are most important for your organization, gather a cross-sectional group of leaders and list the employees who consistently embody excellence at your company. (The actual number of names will depend on the company's size; target the top 10 percent.) It doesn't matter how junior or senior the employees are, or whether they're from research and development (R&D), retail, finance, or HR. Then start listing the behaviors and traits that make these individuals shine, making sure to limit your list to personal qualities rather than achievements.

For example, let's say an employee on your list, John, an architect, always comes up with the best numbers. Why? Is it because he's a great architect, which you could attribute to education and skills? No. It's because he's tenacious, creative, and resourceful. These are traits. In addition, John surrounds himself with the best people, chases clients the company never would have pursued otherwise, modifies his business development plan to incorporate new findings based on proposal wins and losses and subsequent contact with clients, and is dogged in following up and following through. These are behaviors.

If the people on your list all possess the same 15 behaviors or traits, you can assume these are the distinguishing characteristics you should be looking for in new hires and candidates for promotion. Of course, education and skills are important. But those are what's needed merely to get a candidate's foot in the door or to suggest adequate performance. You don't want adequate — you want *excellent.*

Here are several behaviors and traits commonly associated with high performance and high engagement (your requirements may differ):

- ✔ Is enthusiastic
- ✔ Is solution oriented
- ✔ Is team oriented
- ✔ Is selfless
- ✔ Is optimistic
- ✔ Shows a passion for learning
- ✔ Asks "Why not?" instead of simply saying, "That won't work"
- ✔ Passes along credit but accepts blame
- ✔ Goes above and beyond

Behaviors and traits also have an effect on the opposite end of the employment spectrum: getting fired or laid off. Often, the first employees to be let go exhibit certain behaviors and traits — in this case, those that define low performance and low engagement. If you were to ask a group of HR executives if they've ever fired an accountant because she couldn't add or fired a designer because he couldn't design, their answers would likely be a resounding no. But if you were to ask that same audience if they had ever fired an accountant or designer because of a certain behavior or trait, the heads would nod in a definitive yes.

Following are several behaviors and traits commonly associated with low performance and low engagement. Naturally, these are behaviors and traits you want to avoid:

- ✔ Is negative
- ✔ Is pessimistic
- ✔ Has a history of absenteeism
- ✔ Shows a "me first" attitude
- ✔ Is egocentric
- ✔ Accepts credit but passes along blame
- ✔ Focuses on monetary worth ("I'm not being paid to do that")

Based on my experience, people who model the aforementioned high-performing traits will accelerate their careers, while those who model the low-performing behaviors and traits . . . well, they won't.

The good news is, just as employees can add to their education and improve their skills, they can, with effort, modify their behaviors — when they know which behaviors your organization considers valuable. You can help them along by recognizing and rewarding the behaviors you want to promote (and punishing the ones you want to discourage). Note, however, that traits are a little more difficult to modify. For example, say you work in hospitality, and your organization values extroverted personality types. Odds are, any introverts in your midst will have a hard time becoming extroverts. In that case, the correct response may be to counsel introverted employees to shift their careers toward a less extroverted career path within the business — say, switching from the front desk to the finance department.

List the traits that you'd like to see in an employee. Then list the behavior you think demonstrates each trait.

Good, Better, Best: Using the BEST Approach for Job Selection and Advancement

Most static organizations — that is, organizations that are change-averse or that refuse to embrace new technologies, workforce trends, or market changes — evaluate the skills and education of candidates when determining whether they're suitable for hire or promotion. In these environments, job descriptions focus on what experience, education, and skills a candidate will need to have to be considered for a job.

In contrast, dynamic organizations — that is, organizations that are nimble and innovative, that embrace new technologies and approaches, and that are their market change leaders — couple this evaluation with defining behaviors and traits that correspond to success in a job and incorporate these behaviors and traits in their selection process. Job descriptions in these environments include requirements for experience, education, and skills, but also outline the traits and behaviors a candidate must exhibit in order to be considered. Emphasis is on the things a candidate *does* — her accomplishments.

I use the acronym BEST to describe the process that managers should use to weave behaviors, education, skills, and traits into their employee selection and hiring process. BEST stands for the following:

- **Behavior:** How a person acts or reacts to specific circumstances. Behavior is demonstrated through performance, actions, and conduct. It's seen by our clients, our co-workers, and ourselves. Examples of behavior include expressing oneself clearly, meeting project deadlines, and remaining calm under pressure. Behaviors are often dictated by traits.

- **Education:** The information and knowledge a person carries with him. In other words, education is what people know, usually indicated by diplomas and certificates, but also through conversations. Examples of education include a master's degree in science and certification as a database administrator. Education is one of the primary reasons people are hired, but it ultimately plays a relatively small role in their success or failure (assuming, of course, that their education is adequate for the position in question).

- **Skills:** What a person can do. In other words, skills pertain to a person's ability to function in a job and perform the duties assigned. A skill, which can be taught more easily than a behavior or a trait, becomes evident through activities or demonstrations. Examples of skills include technical writing, accurately interpreting lab results, and proficiency in Microsoft Excel.

- **Traits:** Characteristics that define someone's personal nature. These may include integrity, honesty, accountability, enthusiasm, optimism, and so on. Traits are demonstrated through actions and behaviors.

Often, people get hired because of their education and/or skills. Based on exit interviews, however, the vast majority of employees who leave an organization or fail in a job do so not because of their education or skills, but because of their traits and behaviors, or their attitude.

In the following sections, I walk you through writing a job description based on the BEST approach. Then I give you examples of BEST characteristics found in high-performing employees.

Assembling the BEST job description

Many organizations kick off the hiring/selection process by filling out the dreaded new-hire requisition form — a form that, in most organizations, was originally written by Adam or Eve. Generally, these forms are all about education and skills, with little focus on behaviors and traits. The focus of these static documents is a *job* description; they request information on experience, academics, industry, responsibilities, competencies, blah, blah, blah.

The trick to hiring the person with the right combination of behaviors, education, skills, and traits is knowing what behaviors, education, skills, and traits will yield superior performance for the job you seek to fill, and developing a job description that takes these into account. This will involve some thinking on your part.

No pressure, but doing a really good job on this task is very important. Your efforts here will direct all subsequent activities involved with hiring a high-performance candidate who is ready to be engaged.

First, define six to eight performance objectives for the position. Here are some examples of performance objectives (these will vary based on the position and your needs):

- ✔ Improve the organization of the department by creating and maintaining an accurate filing system for both hard-copy and electronic versions of material.
- ✔ Successfully manage at least four projects to conclusion, within 10 percent of budget and 10 percent of deadline.
- ✔ Lead the social media advertising campaign for the company's six divisions, working within the desired budget and timeline.
- ✔ Open eight new branch locations within the next six months.
- ✔ Hire two new field technicians within the next two months, and have them fully trained in all product lines within the first nine months of their hire date.
- ✔ Evaluate and create a plan to improve the intranet site for ease of use, aesthetics, and navigation.
- ✔ Build a succession plan for the firm's top 100 positions by the end of the calendar year.

With these performance objectives in hand, consider what behaviors, education, skills, and traits a candidate will need in order to meet your performance objectives. For example, if you've established a performance objective of leading the social media advertising campaign for the company's six divisions, working within the desired budget and timeline, the applicable behaviors, education, skills, and traits may include the following:

- ✔ **Behaviors:** Shows initiative, is a self-starter, collaborates, exhibits autonomy, exhibits self-discipline
- ✔ **Education:** Bachelor's degree in communication, master's degree in digital media preferred
- ✔ **Skills:** Outstanding written and oral communication skills, knowledge of current social media and search optimization trends, expertise in mobile technology applications
- ✔ **Traits:** Creative, tenacious, competitive, high achiever

This information will serve as the foundation for the position's job description.

Naturally, some behaviors, education, skills, and traits will be more important than others. For this reason, you may opt to weight them.

If you wind up with several behaviors, education credentials, skills, and traits in your list, consider dividing them into two categories: absolute and desirable. Behaviors, education credentials, skills, and traits in the "absolute" category *must* be present or the candidate is not eligible for the position. Desirable behaviors, educational credentials, skills, and traits are "nice to haves." In other words, they would add value to a candidate. For example, you might say that an associate's degree is required (as a "must have," it's in the "absolute" category), and a bachelor's degree is preferred (it's a "nice to have," in the "desirable" category). You might even go so far as to weight behaviors, educational credentials, skills, and traits to aid in your decision making. For example, you might weight having a general bachelor's degree as a 5, a bachelor's degree in a subject directly related to the role as an 8, and a bachelor's degree in a related subject from a top-tier school in that discipline as a 10.

Not sure what behaviors, education credentials, skills, and traits will best serve a performance objective? Think about the employees you currently have who are excelling in a position like the one you seek to fill and pinpoint their BEST characteristics. For example, if you're looking to hire a sales/account executive, take an inventory of your current high-performing sales/account executives and determine what behaviors, education credentials, skills, and traits they possess. This will give you an idea of the BEST requirements for that position.

You'll also want to devise a series of questions designed to suss out whether a candidate has the requisite behaviors, education credentials, skills, and traits. (For more information, see Chapter 13.)

Figure 12-1 shows a worksheet I've designed to help you develop a job description that factors in the BEST model — what I call a "BEST profile." Feel free to modify or copy it and use it in your own organization.

B.E.S.T. Profile
Requisition/Position Description

Req. #: _____
Date Posted: _____

Requisitioner _____   Date Requested _____   Desired Start Date _____

Complete the Appropriate Information about the Position

Replacement for: _____   Full -Time   (36 – 40 hours)   _____
New Position: _____   Part -Time   (number of hours) _____
Budgeted (salary): _____   On -Call   (number of hours)   _____
                                          Temporary   (length of service) _____

Position Description

Title: _____   Grade: _____   Reports To: _____
Location of Position: _____   Service Line: _____   Dept. #: _____   Section #: _____

Describe at least 6 performance objectives expected (long and short term) :

1 _____
2 _____
3 _____
4 _____
5 _____
6 _____

Behaviors, Education, Skills, Traits (B.E.S.T.) Requirements

Competencies required for this position

Behaviors and traits required: _____

Degree or education level: _____   Focus of study or discipline: _____   Professional certifications or registrations: _____

Years experience in similar position: _____   Years total experience: _____

Skills needed (including language skills) _____

Prospects

Any internal candidates? Name(s): _____   External candidates? Name(s): _____

Candidate Sourcing Options

For advertising purposes, describe what the employee will be doing in the position, primary responsibilities, selling points, etc.

All positions will be posted on [list sites]. Please list other potential sourcing opportunities (e.g, specific organization/association websites, journal ads, newspaper ads, etc.)

Approvals

Requisitioner: _____   HR Manager: _____
Supervisor: _____   VP or CSCM: _____

Two additional pages of instructions and samples included with full version.

Figure 12-1:
Use this sheet to hire the BEST candidates.

Illustration by Wiley, Composition Services Graphics

Looking at a sample BEST characteristics matrix

Table 12-1 shows an example of a BEST characteristics matrix, which contains characteristics of high-performing employees in the four pillars of the BEST profile (behaviors, education, skills, and traits). Shown are examples of characteristics found in high-performing employees. (Notice the emphasis on behaviors and traits over education and skills.) This matrix is meant to serve as a guide for you as you develop your organization's own BEST profile.

Table 12-1	A Sample BEST Characteristics Matrix		
Position	**Behaviors and Traits**	**Education**	**Skills**
Any employee	Demonstrates integrity, optimism, confidence, and extra-mile mentality	Specific to job function (see below)	Specific to job function (see below)
	Is open to feedback and willing to learn		
	Expresses himself or herself clearly		
	Is proactive and innovative		
	Follows health and safety guidelines		
	Treats others with respect		
	Responds appropriately to adversity and change		
	Promotes the company		
	Works well with others		
	Sets and achieves realistic goals		
	Focuses on results and is accountable for outcomes		

(continued)

Table 12-1 *(continued)*

Position	Behaviors and Traits	Education	Skills
Admin	Takes initiative in looking for additional work Communicates amicably with other admin personnel	Coursework in Microsoft Office (or equivalent experience)	Able to perform minor maintenance on office equipment Proficient in Microsoft Office programs Some administrative experience
Project manager	Changes communication style for technical and nontechnical conversations Anticipates potential problems and plans contingencies with teams and clients Maintains self-control Provides clear, specific direction and feedback Is efficient in time, cost, and safety management	Degree in technical field Certificate in project management Professional certifications	Able to do technical writing Able to write proposals Able to use time-management tool(s) effectively Prior experience as project manager in a similar industry
Line manager	Hires high-performance employees Provides clear, specific direction and feedback Maintains open communication Creates an environment that motivates and inspires	Degree in technical field Certificate or classes in supervisory skills In-house: attended company's leadership training	Able to do technical writing Able to write proposals Able to use time-management tool(s) effectively Able to facilitate team meetings

Position	Behaviors and Traits	Education	Skills
	Creates and facilitates a productive team		Able to follow a problem-solving process
	Coaches and counsels employee development		Experience in industry
	Analyzes situations and responds appropriately		Some experience in management preferred
	Is efficient in time, cost, and budget management		
	Exemplifies and is accountable for compliance with safety guidelines		
Sales	Creates and builds relationships with clients/prospects, as well as within company	Degree in technical field	Able to do technical writing
	Demonstrates an indomitable must-win approach	Certificate in sales training program	Able to write proposals
	Handles rejection objectively	In-house: completed company's sales training	Able to use time-management tool(s) effectively
	Attends networking functions to proactively build contacts		Able to build long-lasting relationship with clients and potential clients
	Addresses customer concerns		Able to use appropriate sales software
	Looks for opportunity		
	Recognizes sales maturity and process		
	Is efficient in time and cost management		
	Represents the company with passion and enthusiasm		

(continued)

Table 12-1 *(continued)*

Position	Behaviors and Traits	Education	Skills
Technical	Completes tasks in a logical manner	Degree in technical field	Able to use appropriate computer software
	Documents time and effort accurately	Certifications a plus	Able to use applicable measurement tools
	Works productively in a collaborative environment	40-hour OSHA health and safety training	Eight years of experience in the field
	Listens for potential business opportunities	Professional certifications	
	Demonstrates growth potential and is eager to learn		
	Accountable for safety compliance		
Staff specialist	Completes tasks in a logical manner	Degree in technical field	Able to use appropriate computer software
	Documents time and effort accurately	Certifications a plus	Able to use applicable measurement tools
	Works productively in a collaborative environment	40-hour OSHA health and safety training	Four years of experience in the field
	Listens for potential business opportunities	Professional certifications	
	Demonstrates growth potential and is eager to learn		
	Is accountable for safety compliance		

Your hiring process should be dynamic, focusing on one's role rather than on the job. Success characteristics are defined by the key behaviors and traits in your culture and by high performance.

The BEST profile is fluid. Modifications are made to fit the candidate instead of attempting to squeeze a person into a dated job description. The idea is to hire engaged employees who have the behaviors and traits it takes to be successful — even if their skills and education aren't quite perfect.

Mix and Match: The Importance of Diversity

Back in the day, fostering diversity in the workplace was mostly about complying with various laws that guarantee equal opportunity regardless of age, gender, race, physical ability, religious beliefs, and in some areas, sexual orientation. Now, however, smart companies grasp that diversity — or, as I prefer to think of it, inclusion — is both broader and more subtle. Inclusion allows for more comprehensive solutions to the problems facing your organization. Perhaps even more important, inclusion garners more comprehensive support for a solution . . . *if* the various constituencies within your organization feel they've been given a seat at the table. The end result? You guessed it: higher levels of engagement.

As you assess the level of diversity in your organization, ask yourself: Do the heads of your teams and divisions look like your company? Does your company look like your clients?

Diversity isn't just about age, gender, race, physical ability, religious beliefs, and sexual orientation, however. It's also about such things as communication style, thinking style, parental status, and education. Look at Figure 12-2. In this image, the inner ring represents the traditional areas of diversity and inclusion (age, gender, race, and so on) with which most businesses are already quite familiar. In contrast, the outer ring represents considerations that businesses often overlook. But often, these outer considerations are the unseen contributors to an individual's motivation and behavior on the job. Now, I'm not suggesting that the items in the inner ring are insignificant — I'm just saying that in order to create a successful, engaged, inclusive culture, these considerations need to be broadened to include those in the outer ring.

Diversity is the future of business. Companies that focus on inclusion will have a distinct advantage. Today as never before, you can leverage diversity of all kinds to make sure your future has the broadest foundation . . . and the highest potential.

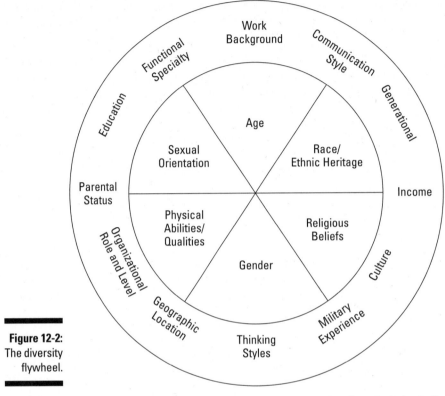

Figure 12-2: The diversity flywheel.

Heads or Tails: Hiring from the Outside or Promoting from Within

When a position opens in an organization, the inevitable question — the one Hamlet himself would ask, if he worked in HR — is: Should you hire from outside or promote from within? The answer is simple: Before you ever look to hire externally, you must advertise openings internally and evaluate in-house talent for promotional and or lateral opportunities. If you don't, I promise you: Your existing employees *will* disengage.

Understanding your existing talent is the key to developing that talent effectively. To that end, you can categorize employees in one of four ways:

- Investment employees
- Performers

   ✔ Potentials

   ✔ Transition employees

Figure 12-3 shows the relationship between these four types of employees, providing managers with a clear picture of how to move employees from one type to the next.

Knowing how to categorize your employees can help you determine how best to engage and develop them.

Identifying investment employees

So-called *investment employees* are the 10 percent to 20 percent of employees who really matter. They define the standard for exceptional performance, functioning above and beyond the norm. They're your go-to people — the ones you trust the most and who display the highest level of competency. Your star performers, these employees solve problems, generate growth, are innovative and creative, and inspire others. They actively pursue goals, and inevitably give more than you ask of them. Their potential as employees has largely been reached.

Odds are, you, as a manager, spend the least amount of time with these employees because they're on autopilot. They simply don't need your input. Managers may also "reward" these employees by piling more and more work on them (after all, they're dependable) or, worse, may limit their career progression ("I don't want to nominate Mary for this position because I don't

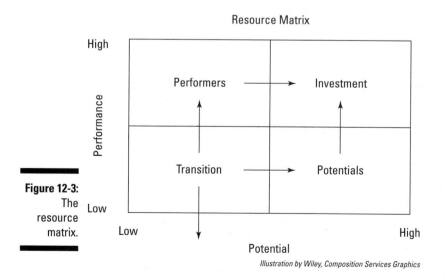

Figure 12-3:
The resource matrix.

Resource Matrix

Illustration by Wiley, Composition Services Graphics

want to lose her"). But be warned: If these employees are not challenged, recognized, and rewarded, they pose your highest flight risk — which is bad, because they're the employees you can least afford to lose. As such, they're the ones in whom you want to invest — hence their name, *investment employees.*

To engage investment employees, you need to continue to offer challenges (and rewards), work to maintain their interest, and develop the employees further — for example, coaching them toward promotions. Oh, and don't ignore this group. Just because they don't *need* your attention doesn't mean they don't *want* it!

Spotting performers

Performers, which typically comprise between 30 percent and 35 percent of your employees, are a little like investment employees. They solve problems and manage themselves without requiring much in the way of your attention. They're your solid, steady workers. They do what's expected of them, without causing problems for the business or its clients. The difference? They haven't yet reached their full potential — although they may, with encouragement and support. In addition, some performers have limited upward mobility, sometimes by choice. Perhaps their potential to grow is limited by skills, or by something personal such as family obligations or an unwillingness to travel.

To engage performers, you must provide opportunities for growth while ensuring that they maintain high levels of performance. The trick is to encourage them to take on other duties and responsibilities, push them to stretch and grow, and provide opportunities for them to get involved with other areas either inside the company or externally. Or, if the employee's growth is self-limited, that person can continue to perform at a comfortable level, freeing the manager to focus staff-development resources on employees with the potential to move to the next level.

Recognizing potentials

Like performers, *potentials,* which comprise between 30 percent and 35 percent of your talent pool, are employees who haven't yet reached their full potential or performance capabilities. Why? Because they haven't had time to develop. Maybe they're junior employees, or perhaps they've only recently been promoted to a new level of responsibility. These employees exhibit the behaviors and traits of high performance, but because of a lack of tenure, maturity, skill, or knowledge, they aren't yet producing at optimum levels. Potentials represent your future, but they require additional skill development and tenure.

Engage this group of employees by cross-training and providing growth opportunities. Indeed, these are precisely the employees in whom you should invest substantial training dollars. The objective is to improve performance while maximizing potential. To that end, try setting and monitoring specific production goals, evaluating their workload (with an eye toward determining whether they're taking on too much), and checking whether more training is needed or wanted. In addition, make it a point to challenge these employees with new tasks and ask them to shoulder work when times are busy. Why? Because potentials will gain much-needed experience from these challenges, and because this strategy helps you to prevent burnout among your organization's top performers, causing them to disengage.

Identifying transition employees

Transition employees are the 10 percent to 20 percent of employees who aren't quite making the grade. They simply don't deliver the type of results or performance you expect, or they exhibit major deficiencies. Maybe the employee is a new hire and just isn't up to speed. Or maybe the employee is technically sound, but has been forced into a job that isn't a good match. It could be that the employee's supervisor has failed to set adequate goals and objectives. Or maybe the employee is simply satisfied doing the bare minimum. Regardless of the reason, transition employees require constant follow-up. This is okay for the short term, but for the long term? Not so much.

No employees should remain transition employees for the long term. Your goal is to move these employees into functioning roles or move them out of the position. To achieve this, evaluate their performance, offer candid and straightforward feedback, and set incremental goals. In addition, identify and discuss other potential positions in the company, or *lateral moves*. A transitional employee can move in any direction — including right out the door.

If you want to disengage your workforce, ignore your transition employees. You'll soon see erosion in the engagement levels of your investment, performer, and potential employee groups. Why? Because these higher-performing employees will know who your transition employees are — maybe even before you do. Allowing a disengaged, underperforming employee to remain employed, without taking any kind of corrective action, is sure to demoralize those employees who do pull their weight.

Refer madness: Getting referrals from engaged employees

Increasingly, employers understand the importance of employee referrals as a source of engaged employees. Who better to understand a firm's culture than the employees of the firm? And engaged employees are more likely to find and promote yet more engaged employees. In fact, a 2012 study by the Temkin Group revealed that engaged employees are 370 percent more likely to refer their company to friends than disengaged employees are. And new employees who are referred by a friend are more likely to be high performing and engaged.

Social media provides every employee with a large referral network to broadcast just how wonderful their employer is. Odds are, that referral network contains at least a few excellent candidates for the position you need to fill. If, for example, one of your engaged employees tweets about your organization's charitable contributions, or shares a photo of your company's recent volunteer efforts, it increases the likelihood that potential job seekers in her network will have a positive impression of your organization. Be sure *your* employees are taking advantage of this wonderful tool!

Here are a few other ways to bolster your employee referral program:

✔ **Connect to your EVP.** Your employee referral program should resonate with your brand. For instance, if your culture values corporate social responsibility, why not reward the employee who refers the most new hires in a calendar year with a week off, with pay, to work with a charity such as Habitat for Humanity?

✔ **Make it visible.** Use posters, social media, paycheck postcard inserts, and other reminders to promote your program.

✔ **Make it fresh.** Update your employee referral program every year with a new look and feel, and new prizes for employees who generate the most referrals.

✔ **Link your employee referral program to your onboarding program.** New hires are a great source of referrals. In fact, they often can be like Pied Pipers for other equally engaged recruits. Create an automatic system to ping new hires multiple times during their first year (for example, on day 30, day 60, day 90, and so on) with information about your employee referral program and a list of current job openings.

✔ **Promote, promote, promote.** Promote your employee referral program on LinkedIn and Facebook, in company newsletters, in CEO communications, at company socials, and so on.

What Newspaper Ad? Leveraging Social Media

Back in the olden days — you know, 15 or 20 years ago — anyone seeking employment would look first to the local newspaper's Help Wanted section. These days, you'd be hard-pressed to find a job this way. What was once a major section of every daily newspaper, particularly on Sundays, is now a scant few pages (if any).

These days, the lion's share of job searches take place online, either on dedicated job-search sites such as Monster (www.monster.com) and CareerBuilder (www.careerbuilder.com) or, perhaps more commonly, on social media sites such as LinkedIn, Twitter, Facebook, and even YouTube.

If you're looking to find engaged employees, this is great news! Social media enables employers to post employment opportunities while at the same time positioning their overall brand. Some companies have even begun eschewing the former for the latter, focusing their hiring-related social media campaigns more on the company's brand and culture — what they do and who they are — than on highlighting individual jobs. Why? Because these employers understand that the key to hiring engaged employees is finding people who are a good fit for the firm's culture, more so than for a particular post.

Exploring LinkedIn

If you're looking for new hires, a great first stop is LinkedIn (www.linkedin.com). With more than 200 million users in more than 200 countries and territories around the world, LinkedIn is far and away the largest professional networking site.

Many corporate recruiters, both internal and external, use LinkedIn to identify *passive job candidates* (people who aren't searching for a job per se, but who may be open to changing positions given the right set of circumstances). For their part, job seekers use LinkedIn to identify firms that may be hiring, and to keep their own profiles and résumés up to date in case an employer finds them. Indeed, for many on LinkedIn and other forms of social media, the focus has shifted from applicants finding new employers to employers discovering potential recruits!

Using Facebook for recruitment

The world's largest social networking site, Facebook (www.facebook.com) boasts more than 1 billion (that's *billion,* with a *b*) users. Although originally a social networking site for people to stay connected with family and friends, Facebook is increasingly becoming a tool for job seekers and employers alike.

What can you do to leverage Facebook as a recruiting tool? Here are a few ideas:

✔ Establish a company Facebook page and use it to post job openings.

✔ Encourage existing employees to share job postings on their personal Facebook pages, and reward those who bring in new talent — not just with recognition and thanks, but with an employee referral bonus. (For more on employee referrals, see the nearby sidebar, "Refer madness: Getting referrals from engaged employees.")

✔ To increase the number of eyes on your job postings, use Facebook's promotional tools. For a fee, you can target those Facebook connections whose profiles match keywords you identify.

✔ Link your company's website to your company's Facebook page. Several apps are available that enable you to update your Facebook page automatically when new job postings are added to your company's site.

Ironically, many companies maintain a Facebook page but ban the use of Facebook in the workplace. If you want your company to leverage social media, you need to encourage its use as a "connector tool." Employees need to feel comfortable using Facebook and other forms of social media as professional tools to make professional connections. Simply put, firms that disallow Facebook at the office are out of touch. You have to trust your employees to use social media properly in the workplace. Besides, if an employee spends three hours a day goofing around with his friends on Facebook, you have a performance issue, not a social media issue!

Connecting with potential recruits on Twitter

Twitter (www.twitter.com) is the world's fastest-growing social media site, with close to 600 million users and 11 accounts added every second. Not surprisingly, it has also become a popular site for employers looking to post job openings as well as to communicate other unique aspects of their companies, not to mention find prospective recruits.

Here are just a few reasons to use Twitter for hiring:

✔ Twitter enables you to directly connect with current and potential employees.

✔ If you follow the right people and organizations, Twitter is a great source of business information, 24 hours a day.

- ✔ With Twitter, you can broadcast important company or industry messages and share links to press releases, blogs, or news.

- ✔ Twitter enables you to post pictures and videos about your firm, exponentially increasing your ability to convey your EVP.

- ✔ With Twitter, you can confidentially connect with potential employees, and they with you (via direct messages).

- ✔ Twitter enables you to recruit globally . . . for *free*.

- ✔ Using Twitter, you can build relationships with passive job candidates.

- ✔ People with whom you establish relationships on Twitter will remember your brand, may help you share your message (through retweets), and may even recommend you to potential candidates.

- ✔ Loyal followers may go beyond Twitter, spreading information about your brand and your job openings outside the Twitterverse.

- ✔ Twitter will almost certainly continue to grow. The sooner you discover its advantages, the better able you'll be to use it as part of your portfolio of recruitment tools and branding efforts!

Brand McNally: Positioning your brand to attract top recruits

Chapter 10 discusses how branding can drive engagement among employees. Not surprisingly, however, branding can also play a part in helping you to attract engaged recruits. That's why your organization's marketing team should be working cheek and jowl with your staffing and resource teams to co-brand and co-publicize messages both internally *and* externally. This way, you'll entice the best recruits while at the same time making the strongest and best impression on potential new clients.

People want to work for a winner. Even during peak years of staff shortages in the early 2000s, General Electric, Google, Southwest Airlines, Microsoft, and other employers of choice in their respective industries had ample candidates from which to choose. Why? Because as brands, they were "winning." Is *your* brand able to attract the best?

What are you doing to promote your business as a winning proposition? As with other areas of engagement, you need to set goals, measure and communicate them, and pursue them in a highly visible way. Are you seeking to enter the Top 100 Places to Work? If so, then you need to apply to the organizations and news outlets responsible for making that designation. Even if you don't succeed the first time around, be committed to telling your employees and the rest of the world that you're a great place to work. With repetition and follow-up, your employees, customer base, and applicant pool will begin to believe it.

Using YouTube to find prospective employees

Looking to communicate about job openings and about your culture at the same time? Then YouTube (www.youtube.com), which boasts more than 1 billion unique users each month, may be the way to go. On YouTube, an employer can post videos describing what the organization is, preferably from the eyes of actual employees. Think about it: If a picture is worth a thousand words, and a three-minute video contains thousands of pictures . . . well, you do the math.

YouTube is unique in that it's a branding, communication, alignment, and entertainment tool, all wrapped in one. The days of CEOs sending out boring mass e-mails to communicate company messages are gone. (Well, CEOs may still do that, but the results won't be thrilling.) These days, enlightened CEOs send quick company updates via video to the masses via YouTube. This allows leaders to quickly and inexpensively broadcast their messages to a large population, both inside and outside the company. (This assumes the information in the video isn't confidential. If it is, the video should probably live on your company's internal server instead of on YouTube.)

YouTube is also a great way to communicate your EVP, which can boost your recruitment efforts. Videos are a great way to show your company culture to potential employees (while at the same time enabling you to convey your brand to potential customers). As an added bonus, YouTube videos often go viral because they can be easily shared by employees or others via e-mail or social media sites such as LinkedIn, Facebook, and Twitter. This can increase your reach considerably.

You don't need to spend a fortune to produce YouTube videos. In fact, my company recently produced a YouTube video, "Who's Sinking Your Boat," done by a wonderfully talented intern from a local college, which received thousands of views in its first few weeks. And if you're producing a video for internal use only, your employees might even prefer an "amateur"-style video over one that's professionally produced. Often, these videos are shot with nothing more than a smartphone by employees themselves. To engage your employees, seek volunteers to help with their production. You'll find that Millennials in particular will enjoy taking ownership of the creation of these videos. You can even make a contest out of it, with a prize for the employee who submits the best, most entertaining video.

Of course, if you're producing a YouTube video for external use, partnering with a professional can help you create a terrific promotional and recruitment tool. For an example of a terrific recruitment video for Twitter, visit `http://youtu.be/vccZkELgEsU`.

Making the Sale: Selling Yourself to Prospective Employees

In a typical hiring scenario, candidates attempt to "sell" themselves to a potential employer. But the truth is, it should be the other way around. Companies should view the hiring and selection process as a sales opportunity of sorts.

Think of the preparation that goes into the sales process: Companies spend thousands if not millions of dollars hiring experts to help crystallize their brands and messages. But people generally don't think of the hiring process in the same way. This needs to change. Because of the growing popularity of social media — in particular, of work-oriented sites like Glassdoor.com — companies must better sell their employee value proposition (EVP) to leverage their brand potential. In the future, firms will need to steal a page from their marketing departments to "sell" potential employees on why they should work for them. That's where having defined your EVP will really come in handy. Your most engaged candidates have choices; armed with your EVP, you can convince them to choose you.

I'd go so far as to suggest that your HR department create a "sales sheet" for candidates in order to communicate your EVP (see Figure 12-4). Make it pop! Your sales sheet should include the following:

- ✔ **What you do:** Describe what you do, share your company's history, and provide an overview of your company — for example, its sales, financials, and clients. Also, list any relevant rankings (for example, "We're the second largest engineering firm in the U.S., according to *Engineering News Record*"), highlight unique selling features of your product or service, and discuss your brand.

- ✔ **Your purpose:** State your values (that is, your guiding principles) and your core purpose, or reason for existing.

- ✔ **Who you are:** Talk about why you're unique. For example, maybe you've earned "Miami's Best Employer" awards for six years running. Maybe you were honored by *Women's Magazine* as "Top Employer of

Company ABC

Company Overview

- Since 1968, one of the pioneer firms in the environmental industry
- Financially and strategically stable company with worldwide brand recognition
- Top 20 all-environmental firms (Engineering News Record 1995-2005)
- 1,700 employees in 70 offices around the world
- Operating as a seamless organization
  - Cross-border work sharing is strongly encouraged and a competitive differentiator
- Expertise in 60 different technical and management disciplines
- Strong, stable, and experienced senior management leadership

Our Culture

- Industry-leading employee retention – annual turnover in single digits
- Employee-centric business model
- Strong emphasis on learning/professional development (project management, leadership, sales workshops, on-the-job training, tuition reimbursement, external technical training, conferences/seminars) documented in annual Employee Development Plan, and reviewed every 6 months.
- Conduct Employee Satisfaction Survey every 2 years – resulting in dynamic employee feedback to help focus driving issues. Each location creates employee-generated responsive action plan implemented by employees.
- Innovation Committee over 1,000 ideas regarding new markets and business operations submitted to our "idea website" with one-third of them implemented. All ideas are rewarded.
- Technical Paper Cash Bonus awarded to employees who publish in a book or technical journal, or present published paper at a conference.
- Employee recognition program ensures all employees are appropriately recognized for outstanding efforts.

Career Opportunities

- Diverse service lines provide cross-training opportunities.
- National and international locations offer opportunities in over 70 worldwide locations.
- Philosophy of promoting from within; about 15% of employee base promoted annually.
- Prestigious client list – some of the largest and most successful companies worldwide.
- Key account strategy enables employees to work nationally and internationally.

We're a company with 24,000 employees operating in 60 countries worldwide, providing design and management services in the transportation, facilities, and environmental markets through a family of operating companies.

Figure 12-4:
Developing a sales sheet is a great way to communicate your EVP.

Illustration by Wiley, Composition Services Graphics

Minorities." Or maybe you have expertise in 16 different technical and management disciplines. You can also discuss the size of your organization, your operating principles, your employee retention rate, and the results of your latest employee engagement survey.

Don't sell something you can't deliver. In other words, your sales sheet shouldn't make exaggerated claims about your firm. There's no better way to turn an exciting prospect into an embittered, resentful employee than to over-promise and underdeliver!

Chapter 13

Why Do You Want to Work Here? Interviewing Job Candidates

In This Chapter

▶ Considering a candidate's behaviors, education, skills, and traits

▶ Developing effective interview questions

▶ Knowing what to do with the candidate's responses

*Y*ou've pinpointed your employee value proposition (EVP) and created your "sales sheet," outlining why you rock as an employer (see Chapter 10). You've built your BEST profile (see Chapter 12). You've leveraged social media as a branding and staffing tool (see Chapter 12). Now it's time to interview the bevy of candidates who are sure to come your way. This chapter discusses the interviewing process and how you can tweak it to hire only the most engaged employees.

Best in Show: Interviewing the BEST Way

In the preceding chapter, I introduce you to the BEST approach to hiring candidates. This approach goes beyond evaluating a candidate's skills and education to also consider his behaviors and traits (hence, the acronym BEST). If you opt to use the BEST approach to hiring, you'll need to adapt your interview process accordingly. In this section, I show you how.

Step 1: Develop your BEST profile

In Chapter 12, you develop a job description that factors in the BEST model. You need that job description — what I call a "BEST profile" — on hand as you embark on the interviewing process. This profile guides you in developing questions for candidates, so if you haven't developed your BEST profile yet, turn back to Chapter 12.

Step 2: Develop your interview questions

Using the BEST profile for the job you want to fill, develop your interview questions. These questions should be designed to tease out each candidate's behaviors, education, skills, and traits. Note that you'll want two sets of questions: a shorter one for the phone interview (discussed in the next section) and a more detailed one for the face-to-face interview (see the upcoming section "Step 5: Hold face-to-face interviews").

As you develop your questions, you may realize that some of them are more important than others. For more information on developing questions, see the section "Kick Ask: Asking the Right Questions."

Step 3: Conduct preliminary phone interviews

In the interest of saving time, you'll want to conduct preliminary phone interviews, or, more precisely, phone screenings. Telephone interviews should be short, highly structured conversations aimed at identifying unsuitable applicants. They also give you an opportunity to be objective. Physical appearance and age are inconsequential when you can't see the candidate; in a phone interview, you'll be able to concentrate more on what the candidate is actually saying.

Here are some tips to ensure you get the most out of the phone-screening process:

✔ **Review your BEST profile to develop a set of standard questions that you'll ask each candidate during the phone-interview phase.** These questions should cover personal/professional details, education, career history, experience, and so on. Also, ask for the desired salary range if the candidate didn't provide this information on her résumé or in her cover letter. As you interview the candidate, be sure to stick to the pre-planned questions. That way, you'll get the most out of the interview, as well as demonstrate your preparation, commitment, and focus. (For more information on crafting effective questions, see the section "Kick Ask: Asking the Right Questions.")

Developing questions is critical. Unstructured interviews almost always result in the wrong people getting hired because interviewers tend to ask questions that are directly related to what's on the candidate's résumé, which generally focuses on education and skills rather than behaviors and traits. You have to identify the behaviors and traits you're looking for in a particular position and then ask specific questions designed to ferret out whether the candidate possesses those behaviors and traits. Hiring right takes time, due diligence, and planning — which includes deciding ahead of time which questions you're going to ask each candidate. Don't forget the old adage "Hire easy, live hard; hire hard, live easy!"

✔ **When you call the candidate (or leave a message), explain who you are and ask when would be a good time to have a brief discussion about the job opportunity.** If now is a good time, continue. If later is better, schedule accordingly.

✔ **Keep a glass of water handy.** This will help you stave off mid-call coughing fits.

✔ **Smile.** Your interviewee will be able to "hear" your smile. It projects a positive image of you and your company.

✔ **Ask the candidate whether he minds if you take notes during the call.** For example, say, "Do you mind if I take notes? I want to be sure that I understand and remember what you're telling me." Just be sure note taking doesn't occur at the expense of a natural dialogue. Plan to write more detailed notes after you hang up.

Be sure any written notes are legal and job related. Document only those details that are specific to the job interview. Avoid including personal opinions or observations that are *not* specific to the position, because any personal reference could be construed as discriminatory in nature. For example, writing down a description of the candidate to jog your memory could cause a problem down the road, particularly if you inadvertently note a candidate's inclusion in a protected group (such as gender, race, or age). Also, interviewers should understand the legal ramifications of taking notes during the interview process, because notes are discoverable in the case of a discrimination lawsuit.

Organizations should train anyone who is going to be interviewing candidates on the basics — what they can and can't ask, and what they can and can't write down. Seek help from an employment attorney when designing this training.

✔ **Follow the 80/20 rule: Spend 80 percent of your time listening and 20 percent explaining the job and the benefits of working at your company.** (For best results, you should do the selling part at the end of the conversation.) Also, remember to keep silent when appropriate. Give the candidate plenty of time to fully answer your questions and to ask any of her own.

Some people express their anxiety by talking a lot. Don't assume this is a sign of inexperience or incompetence. In fact, this mannerism may hide real ability. Just be aware when interviewing these talkative types that you may need to frequently interrupt them to ask specific questions.

✔ **Regardless of whether you think the candidate is a "go" or a "no go," be sure to thank the person for his time.** Let the candidate know when and how he can expect to hear from you — for example, "I'll be in touch by e-mail within one week, so be on the lookout for that message."

By the end of the phone screening, you'll have a good sense of the candidate's level of knowledge about your organization, how closely the candidate fits the BEST profile for the position, and how well the candidate communicates verbally. You'll also have determined how well the candidate was able to "sell" herself to you by phone and whether you and the candidate have any "chemistry." All this information will help you decide whether it makes sense to invest more time in this candidate with a face-to-face interview.

Within the timeframe you outlined, contact the candidate. If the candidate is a potential fit for the job, outline the next steps in the review process, along with the approximate timeframes, set up a time for a face-to-face interview, and ask how best to reach the candidate in the interim. If the candidate isn't a good fit, let him know. If you know of another opportunity at your company that *may* be a good fit, mention that as well.

Adopt the "rule of threes" and interview at least three candidates for every opening. Most of the time, companies hire in crisis mode, seeking to replace an outgoing employee. ("The work has to get done. Hire anyone with a pulse — now!") This is a sure-fire way to make a hiring mistake. Speed is great if you're in the Indy 500, but it's a handicap in the hiring process. By interviewing at least three candidates for every opening, you ensure a more thorough evaluation of candidates. Crummy employers often have no choice but to interview just one candidate; often, that's all they can find. But firms with engaged cultures that have built a strong EVP will have an applicant flow that allows for more candidates.

Step 4: Prepare for the face-to-face interview

You wouldn't go out on a customer call without being prepared, right? Along those same lines, you should never interview a candidate without preparing beforehand. After all, when the candidate comes in for a face-to-face interview, your goal is to sell him on your company and the position.

Review the BEST profile to develop a set of questions to ask during the face-to-face interview in order to tease out each candidate's behaviors, education, skills, and traits. (For more information on developing effective questions, see the section "Kick Ask: Asking the Right Questions," later in this chapter.) For best results (no pun intended), write down your questions in a customized candidate evaluation form. Figure 13-1 shows a blank version of this form, which you can copy or use as the basis for your own. (Note that this form includes fields for "Rating" and "Weight." I fill you in on these items later in the chapter.)

Candidate Evaluation Form

Candidate: _____   Position: _____
Interviewed By: _____   Date Interviewed: _____

Summary Notes:

Rating Scale:	Weighting Factors:
3 = Expert/excellent match	3 = Critical
2 = High/good match	2 = Important
1 = Satisfactory/acceptable	1 = Helpful
0 = Unsatisfactory	

Education /Skills	Rating	Weight	Score
1. Educational Background:	×	=	
2. Technical Skills:	×	=	
3. Related Experience:	×	=	

Behaviors/Traits	Rating	Weight	Score
4.	×	=	
5.	×	=	
6.	×	=	
7	×	=	
8.	×	=	
9.	×	=	
10	×	=	
11.	×	=	
12.	×	=	
13.	×	=	
14.	×	=	
15.	×	=	
16.	×	=	
17.	×	=	
OVERALL SCORE			

Closing Questions and Information

1. What aspects of the job sound particularly appealing? _____
2. What aspects of the job are of concern to you? _____
3. References requested? Y N References provided/date? _____
4. Thank applicant for their time commitment.
5. Follow-up time-frame given _____ Follow-up action _____

Figure 13-1: A candidate evaluation form.

Illustration by Wiley, Composition Services Graphics

Staying focused during interviews

Experienced interviewers know that listening for extended periods of time takes effort. The first clue that your mind is beginning to wander is when you begin to hear sounds rather than ideas coming from the speaker. Learning to recognize loss of attention early is an important part of becoming a good interviewer. One way to stay focused during an interview is to concentrate on the applicant's facial expressions and other nonverbal behavior.

In addition to developing your questions, decide who else will participate in the interview process. Strive for diversity of thought. For example, if you're interviewing an accountant, consider including someone from marketing or procurement on the interview team. That said, avoid overwhelming the candidate with too many people. When scheduling interviews for a candidate, which generally occur one-on-one throughout the day, stick with five or fewer people (including HR) or risk interview fatigue. Also, decide who will ask which questions. For a candidate, nothing is worse than having to answer the same question five times! Make sure everyone knows what topics they'll be covering, and when.

Anyone involved in the hiring process should be armed not only with a precise understanding of the attributes a candidate needs to succeed, but also with the skills to discover those attributes during an interview. To aid with this, your organization should provide training and refresher courses on hiring for anyone who will be interviewing candidates.

Finally, before the candidate arrives, think about what questions that person is likely to ask, and be prepared to answer them. *Hint:* Most candidates will want to know more about the job and about opportunities for learning and promotion.

Step 5: Hold the face-to-face interview

Many of the points to remember during the face-to-face interview come down to simple good manners: starting on time; treating the candidate like a guest (for example, personally greeting the candidate when he or she arrives rather than sending a minion to do it); giving a warm smile and a firm handshake, and offering coffee, water, or juice; staying within your time constraints; and so on. Beyond that, the majority of the points for phone interviews apply here, such as sticking to the pre-planned questions, taking notes, following the 80/20 rule, and so on.

In addition, you'll want to keep the following in mind:

- ✔ **Start with small talk, and then take control by reviewing the agenda for the interview.** Also, provide a very brief overview of what you do and how your job relates to the position.

- ✔ **When you ask questions, concentrate on what the candidate's answers reveal about her honesty, values, beliefs, personality, and work ethic.** It goes without saying that these things are as important as — in some cases, even more important than — anything you could learn about a candidate's technical skills! If the candidate offers evasive or "canned" answers, keep probing until you feel comfortable with his response.

- ✔ **Close the interview by asking the candidate if she has any questions or additional information to share.**

- ✔ **Communicate your next steps.** For example, you may say, "We're just starting the interview process and plan to get back to all candidates within the next ten days."

Avoid expressing your delight in the candidate (for example, "You're the best candidate we've seen so far!"). Otherwise, you risk having to come up with a reason why the candidate wasn't selected if you decide to hire someone else. Likewise, never hint at a rejection or lack of interest during the face-to-face interview. If you do, you risk the candidate going into overdrive to sell himself — not a pretty sight! As a general rule, don't show your hand.

If you run across a great candidate, do what you can to accelerate the process. Otherwise, you risk losing her to another employer.

- ✔ **Provide the candidate with information about your company (ideally, in the form of a "sale sheet"; see Chapter 12).** Even if you don't end up hiring the candidate, you want that person's opinion of your company and your brand to be positive!

The people in charge of interviewing new recruits must be informed of the company's vision. Otherwise, they won't be able to convey the culture to a potential employee. If you're hiring employees who don't fit your culture, you'll have trouble persuading those people to become invested in your organization and to work alongside you to achieve your goals.

Step 6: Collect input from your selection team

After you interview at least three qualified candidates, take time to collect input from your selection team. For best results, have everyone fill in the details on the candidate evaluation form (refer to Figure 13-1), taking care to avoid subjective impressions. This form contains fields for rating candidates and weighting answers; you'll want to fill these in to determine each candidate's score, which you can use to determine who is the best fit. (For more on rating and weighting, see the section "Kick Ask: Asking the Right Questions," later in this chapter.) Remember, though, that hiring is not a democratic decision. Ultimately, the person who will be the employee's direct manager (the "boss") should be empowered to hire his "BEST fit" candidate.

At the risk of contradicting myself, be aware that there are times when you simply won't get three qualified candidates. For instance, suppose your BEST profile requires a multilingual chemical engineer with experience working in the biomedical field who is willing to relocate to Afghanistan for a two-year expatriate assignment. Odds are, you won't receive much in the way of résumés from candidates who meet all these criteria. In that case, you'll want to skip the whole "interview at least three qualified candidates" rule. (If you do find one candidate who fills the bill, trust me: You'll want to accelerate your offer!) You'll also want to skip this rule if you find yourself interviewing a superstar candidate who fits the BEST profile ideally, comes highly recommended by internal staff, and is also being wooed by your key competitors. That's another scenario where you'll want to extend an offer sooner rather than later!

Conduct a "post-mortem" of each interview — what you did well, what you'd like to do better, and so on. That way, you'll have the tools to improve your interviewing skills, which will almost certainly lead to better hiring practices.

Step 7: Check references

In a perfect world, you could just take every candidate's word as to her accomplishments and experience. But as is evident by the simple fact that hot dogs are typically sold in packages of ten, while buns are usually sold in packages of eight, we don't live in a perfect world. That means you'll need to check up on your applicants to make sure they're on the level.

Your first and most obvious step is to contact the references provided to you by the candidate. When you do, consider using the reference check form in Figure 13-2. This form will help guide you in asking the right questions — questions designed to elicit responses that give you a sense of the applicant's behaviors and traits in addition to his skills and education. Of course, if the candidate has been referred by an existing employee, that employee is the first person you should contact!

Don't stop with the references the candidate lists, however. Make it a point to leverage the web in general and social media in particular to learn more about your candidate. Start with the person's LinkedIn profile; then consider searching the web for the candidate's name. No doubt, you'll learn all kinds of things about the candidate — some related to the job at hand, some not.

B.E.S.T. Reference Check

Applicant's Name: ____________ Position Applied For: ____________

Reference Name and Title: ____________ ____________

Reference Place of Employment: ____________ Tel. # ____________

Experience/Education

Title/Position: ____________ Dates of Employment: ____________

How long and in what capacity have you known the applicant? What was your working relationship?

Position-specific "education/experience "question:

Skills

How would you describe/rate the applicant's technical ability?

How would you describe/rate the applicant's performance on the job?

How would you rate the applicant's organizational/writing/oral communication skills?

Position-specific "skills-related" question:

Behaviors and Traits

How does the applicant get along with other people? Is the applicant a team player? A loner?

What are the applicant's strong traits and weak? Are there any goals you feel the applicant should address?

Position-specific "behaviors/traits-related" question:

Closing

Would your organization rehire this person? Yes No

Any additional comments? ____________

Signature: ____________ Date: ____________

Illustration by Wiley, Composition Services Graphics

Figure 13-2: A reference check form.

Never settle for an employment agency's reference. Agencies are too vested in their candidates getting the job. Your own personnel should always check references.

Step 8: Extend an offer of employment

Did you find a candidate who matches your BEST profile, who interviewed well, and whose references check out? If so, you may well be prepared to make an offer. When you do, remember: You're not selling used cars. Make the highest final offer you can afford based on sound compensation practices, including the evaluation of external and internal market data. Repeat after me: "I will not enter into a negotiation with the candidate." After all, you're selling your company's culture. If the candidate is all about money, that in itself might tell you that she isn't a good fit culturally and likely won't fit your definition of an engaged employee.

Nothing — and I mean *nothing* — will disengage your current staff like paying incoming employees with like credentials and experience more money. I cannot emphasize this enough. You must maintain internal equity. Your offer should not exceed the compensation of your current employees if skills, traits, years of experience, and academic credentials are the same. Otherwise, the inevitable (and accurate) perception of unfairness will be a major demotivator for your current employees.

Interviewing internal candidates

Interviewing internal candidates is much like interviewing applicants from the outside, with one key exception: An internal candidate's interview should acknowledge the value of that individual's past contribution to the company and the knowledge that he possesses. This is important for several reasons:

✔ Promoting an internal candidate is often smarter (in terms of time and resources) than hiring a new one.

✔ The interview process must not disengage existing employees, regardless of whether they "win" the promotion.

✔ Hiring from within is a way of bolstering the line of sight between an individual's career path and the company's goals.

✔ Promotions are an optimal branding and communications opportunity. An internal success story is a powerful reminder of the investment your staff have in your company.

Kick Ask: Asking the Right Questions

A candidate's résumé says a lot about her education and skills — the E and S in the BEST profile. It also likely contains all you need to know about her experience and work history. But as I explain in Chapter 12, a candidate's behaviors and traits — the B and T in the BEST profile — are often at least as important as her education and skills. Indeed, a candidate's behaviors and traits are likely the truest barometer of her performance level and her ability to fit in at your organization. Odds are, however, you won't find *that* information in a résumé.

So, how do you find out about a candidate's behaviors and traits? After you've identified the behaviors and traits you're looking for, map these into your interviewing process. Most likely, your existing interview process stresses past assignments and accomplishments too heavily. Although these factors are necessary in evaluating candidates' experience and qualifications for the job, they don't necessarily speak to the deeper issues of how those candidates will perform according to your company's priorities or how well they'll work within your corporate culture. It's up to the interview team to ask the right questions in order to capture this information.

Based on the theory that past behavior is the best indicator of future responses, the "behavioral interview" has become popular in recent years — and with good reason. Behavioral interview questions require the interviewee to provide concrete, narrative examples of past situations. Often, these responses reveal the degree to which the candidate possesses the behaviors and traits identified as essential to top performance within your organization. Such questions avoid the typical hypotheticals ("Where do you see yourself in five years?") and instead focus on how an individual has responded to specific situations in the past. Obviously, you'll need to tailor your questions to the position's responsibilities and context, but here are a few examples of "typical" interview questions and their "behavioral interview" counterparts:

> **Typical interview question:** What was the biggest accomplishment in your last job?
>
> **Desired trait:** Creativity.
>
> **Behavioral interview question:** Describe the most creative work-related project you've carried out, and describe why you succeeded with this project.
>
> **Typical interview question:** Are you a team player?
>
> **Desired behavior:** Collaboration.

Behavioral interview question: Give an example of a time when you were able to successfully complete a project on a team where there were personality conflicts.

Typical interview question: What major challenges and problems did you face at your last job?

Desired trait: Resilience.

Behavioral interview question: Describe a difficult and tense situation in which some people were losing hope and you were able to influence them in a positive direction.

The idea is to craft questions that are targeted toward the *specific* behaviors and traits that are unique to your organization and to the position. Although traits like enthusiasm, patience, selflessness, and optimism may be desired in almost any company, there will be differences in positions' requirements that require tailored inquiry. Examples may include a job that requires travel, involves client or customer interaction, includes management of other staff, or requires working remotely.

Table 13-1 contains a list questions to suss out an individual's important qualities. Use these as a starting point as you tailor your own questions.

Table 13-1	Questions for Determining Behaviors and Traits
To Determine . . .	*Ask . . .*
Ability to learn	What kinds of things do you learn quickly? What kinds of things do you have a harder time picking up?
Adaptability, flexibility	Tell me about a situation in which you had to adjust quickly to changes over which you had no control. What was the impact of the change on you?
Analytic abilities, honesty	What do you know about our company and its services?
Character, values, commitment, goals	How would your close work associates describe you? What traits are you most proud of? What trait best suits you for this job?
Client focus	What experiences have you had that demonstrate your commitment to your client?

To Determine . . .	Ask . . .
Coaching, leadership	Tell me about a time when you took someone under your wing and what you tried to teach him or her.
Communication, accountability	Tell me about a time when your active listening skills really paid off for you — maybe a time when other people missed the key idea being expressed.
Communication, feedback	Tell me about a time when you had to be critical of someone else. What happened?
Communication, influence	Describe the most successful experience you've ever had in persuading someone to do something.
Communication, relationships	Give an example of a situation when you were able to communicate successfully with a person who didn't like you.
Communication, self-expression, listening skills, tact	Are you more skilled at written or verbal communication? Why?
Communication (written), innovation	What is the most challenging report you've ever written? What made it unique? To what audience was it written?
Customer service, analytic abilities, empathy, efficiency	What is your process for handling customer complaints?
Decision making, analytic abilities	Tell me about the most difficult customer-service experience you've ever had to handle — perhaps an angry or irate customer. Be specific. What did you do, and what was the outcome?
Decision making, integrity, realism, common sense	Everyone has to bend or break the rules once in a while. Can you give me an example of how you handled this kind of situation?
Decision making, problem solving, creativity	Give me an example of a problem, issue, or concern that you handled in a unique, creative way.
Decision making, realism, willingness to learn, accountability, confidence	Tell me about a time when you made the wrong decision. What went wrong? What would you do differently knowing what you know now?

Table 13-1 *(continued)*

To Determine . . .	Ask . . .
Efficiency, analytic abilities	How do you prioritize your work?
Energy, drive, initiative	What are some examples of your going beyond your job requirements? What are you currently doing to improve your overall performance?
Enthusiasm	What achievement are you most proud of?
Frugality	Describe a time in which you saved money for your company and/or client.
General	What special characteristics should I consider about you as a person?
General	Give me a quick overview of your current or prior position and describe the biggest impact or change you made.
General, analytic abilities, creativity	Describe your ideal job.
General, analytic abilities, detail oriented	Walk me through a typical day in your work life. What is your favorite part? What is your least favorite part?
General, confidence	What has been your greatest accomplishment? Why?
General, confidence, accountability	What did you do in your last job to contribute to a positive work environment?
General, confidence, risk taking, willingness to learn	What has been your greatest challenge? Why? How did you handle it? What did you learn from it?
General, initiative	Give me an example of how you did more than what was required in your job.
Innovation, creativity	What approaches could you take to the following problem? (Then describe the problem for the candidate.)
Management style, philosophy	Describe your management style. How would direct reports describe your philosophy? What's most important to overall business success?
Personality, cultural fit	Who was the best manager you ever had? Describe that person's traits. In which of your past work environments were you happiest? Why?

To Determine . . .	Ask . . .
Planning, organization	Describe how you go about planning and organizing your work and setting priorities. When can planning get in the way of results?
Planning, organization, analytic abilities, delegation, realism	If you left your company today, what would be left undone?
Planning, organization, confidence	What did you do in your last job to be effective at accountability, planning, and organizing?
Problem identification, analytic abilities, problem solving, relationships, feedback integrity	If you observed someone displaying inappropriate work behavior, what would you do?
Problem solving, analytic abilities	If you were to get this job, how would you go about solving this typical problem? (Then describe the problem for the candidate.)
Problem solving, collaboration	Give me an example of a problem you faced on the job and tell me how you solved it.
Problem solving, thinking skills	From a technical challenge standpoint, what past experience was most stimulating? What kinds of problems do you enjoy tackling?
Professional development, analytic abilities, initiative	Is there some technique or technology you want to learn but haven't yet? Describe it.
Professional development, confidence, accountability	In your last performance appraisal, what was detailed in the "employee strengths" section?
Professional development, willingness to learn	How many training courses have you attended over the last three years? What were they and what did you learn? What have you implemented as a result?
Professional development, willingness to learn	In your last performance appraisal, what was detailed in the "developmental needs" section?

Table 13-1 *(continued)*

To Determine . . .	Ask . . .
Relationships	Describe how you've collaborated with people outside your department in the past. What cross-sectional teams have you participated in during your career and what role did you play on those teams?
Relationships, communication, collaboration	Give an example of when you had to work with someone who was difficult to get along with. Why was this person difficult? How did you handle that person?
Results oriented, confidence, realism	Give me an example of a goal you didn't accomplish. What went wrong.
Results oriented, innovation, initiative	Tell me about the goals you set for yourself last year and whether you achieved those goals.
Results oriented, innovation, planning	Tell me about your goals for this coming year and your plans to achieve them.
Results oriented, confidence, self-respect, enthusiasm	Tell me about a project you're particularly proud of having been associated with and why.
Risk taking, accountability	Describe a time when you weighed the pros and cons of a risk and why you decided to take it.
Stress management, willingness to learn, innovation	Tell me about a situation in which you were under significant pressure. How did you handle it?
Team leadership, ability to persuade/ motivate others	What do you see as being the advantages and disadvantages of working as part of a team? What are the challenges of leading a team?
Teamwork, collaboration, facilitation	Describe your most recent group effort.
Technical abilities, confidence	This position requires a variety of skills. Describe your strengths that are applicable to the position.
Trend of performance over time	How has your job or level of contribution changed since you began working in this field? How would your current manager describe your performance?

As you develop your questions, also keep these points in mind:

- ✔ **Even when detailed information on specific areas is required, keep your questions open ended.** The descriptive response elicited by an open-ended question will include specific information. The candidate's response may even reveal information that you never thought to ask about. *Closed-ended questions* (those that require only a yes or no response) won't yield a broad, informative response. Plus, open-ended questions can be followed by more specific ones.

- ✔ **Don't ask leading questions.** A *leading question* is a rhetorical question that indicates to the applicant the answer that the interviewer wants to hear. For example, "Don't you think that getting along with subordinates is absolutely critical to good management?" is a leading question.

- ✔ **Don't ask any questions that are legally off limits.** For example, it's illegal to ask a candidate his or her age, sex, marital status, parental status, health status, race, height, weight, or religion. This is by no means an exhaustive list, however. For more information on questions you shouldn't ask during an interview, visit `http://hiring.monster.com/hr/hr-best-practices/small-business/conducting-an-interview/common-interview-questions.aspx` or check with an HR or legal representative. Bottom line: If you're worried a question may be inappropriate or unacceptable, don't ask it!

Assessing the Candidate's Responses

Of course, knowing what questions to ask is only half the battle. You must also assess the candidate's responses to these questions to determine whether he's the right fit for the job and for your organization as a whole. Fortunately, this section offers a few ideas to help you make the best choice!

Weighting questions

After your interview, think about which behaviors, education, skills, and traits are most important for the position in question, and then weight your questions accordingly. Here's how I do it:

- ✔ I assign questions designed to suss out helpful behaviors, education, skills, and traits a weight of 1.

- ✔ Questions meant to uncover important behaviors, education, skills, and traits receive a weight of 2.

✔ Questions designed to reveal critical behaviors, education, skills, and traits get a value of 3.

For example, suppose you're interviewing candidates for a position as a brain surgeon. In that case, you might assign questions designed to illuminate the candidate's skills and education a weight of 3, but assign questions that pertain to revealing a candidate's personality a weight of 1. Or, if you're interviewing candidates for a position that involves working from home or a remote office, you might weight questions that pertain to independence more highly than those related to cultural fit.

Rating answers

In addition to weighting the questions, you'll want to rate the candidate's answers. I generally assign a rating of 3 to answers that indicate an excellent match, a rating of 2 to answers that are a good match, a rating of 1 to answers that are satisfactory or acceptable, and a rating of 0 for answers that are unsatisfactory.

Scoring candidates

So, how do you use this info? If you refer to Figure 13-1, you'll notice that the candidate evaluation form includes a "Rating" column, a "Weight" column, and a "Score" column for each question. To score the candidate's answer to a question, you simply multiply its rating by its weight. For example, if a question is weighted a 3, and the candidate's response is a 2, you would enter 6 in the "Score" column. You can then add the scores for all the questions to determine an overall score for the candidate. This score can then be compared to the scores of other candidates to determine who's the best fit.

Chapter 14

All Aboard! Onboarding Techniques to Foster Engagement

. . . .

In This Chapter

▶ Recognizing the importance of onboarding

▶ Seeing things from the new hire's point of view

▶ Knowing what to do before a new hire starts, on the first day, and in the first week

▶ Establishing performance expectations

. . . .

*Y*ou're super excited to start your new job — so excited, in fact, that you arrive early on your first day. When you do, however, you're locked out of the building, because you don't yet have a key card or badge. That means you're stuck waiting in the snow until a "real" employee comes along and lets you in (after you convince her you're not an ax murderer, of course).

Then what? You stand awkwardly by the receptionist's desk, waiting for someone to greet you. After what feels like an interminable wait, that some-one finally arrives, and you're relegated to a back room, where you fill out what feels like hundreds of documents and review a staggering number of company policies. Hours later, your new boss ushers you to your workspace and tells you to get to work.

This would never happen, right? Well, actually, it happens more often than you might think. Indeed, for many companies, this constitutes the whole of their onboarding process. But this type of onboarding will do very little to foster engagement among new employees. Read on to find a better way!

What's the Big Deal, Anyway? The Importance of Onboarding

There is no impression like a first impression. Indeed, studies show that roughly 33 percent of employees decide to stay onboard with a firm or jump ship within their first 30 days of employment. Given this, you'd think companies would work to put their best foot forward with new hires through effective *onboarding* (new-hire orientation).

Surprisingly, however, many firms treat onboarding like a chore, sort of like laundry. To them, it's a necessary evil — something that just gets done before an employee becomes productive. For most organizations, onboarding is a matter of shutting the new recruit in a room by himself or with other lonely souls (read: additional new hires) in a conference room, reviewing and filling out mountains of paperwork.

The onboarding process is often even worse in smaller companies or satellite locations of a larger firm. These locations may not have an HR presence, so the onboarding role usually defaults to the receptionist, administrative assistant, or worse, whoever draws the short straw. ("Hey Mickey! It's your turn to greet the new hire and help her with her paperwork!")

The fact is, effective onboarding is key to engaging new hires. An effective onboarding enables new hires to grasp the firm's culture, history, customer base, performance expectations, job requirements, communication expectations, and more. The best onboarding programs are well planned out in advance, with special attention given to "what" (the mountains of paperwork that must be completed), the "how" (the environment and handling of the onboarding process), and the "who" (the team with whom the new hire will be working).

Onboarding is so critical that Zappos, the notable e-commerce firm, puts all new employees through three weeks of company orientation before they start their new job, even going so far as to pay these new hires $3,000 if they decide not to stick with the company afterward. In other words, Zappos understands that the company's culture is so important that they're willing to pay you to *leave* if you determine you aren't a cultural fit. (Of course, people rarely take Zappos up on its offer, because Zappos does an outstanding job of determining a person's cultural fit during the interviewing and selection stage.)

Brain Swap: Considering Things from the New Employee's Point of View

As you develop your onboarding program, it helps to consider things from a new hire's point of view. You can assume that most new employees will have several questions. Some questions will pertain to their first day at work:

- ✔ Where and what time should I report?
- ✔ What should I wear?
- ✔ Whom should I ask for?
- ✔ Where should I park?

To aid in onboarding, these questions should be addressed in the employee's offer letter, but it never hurts to reiterate them in a phone call with the new hire prior to his start date.

Then there are the questions about matters that affect the new employee personally:

- ✔ What are my work hours?
- ✔ Do I need to report to work at a specific time?
- ✔ Will I be expected to work overtime, evenings, or weekends?
- ✔ Will I need to travel? If so, how often?
- ✔ How flexible are my work hours if I need to take time off to attend a child's school event or handle some other personal issue?

Addressing these questions early — either before the employee starts or early in her tenure — in an open, honest manner will help your employee to feel at ease and move on to more critical areas.

Consider assigning a buddy to your new hire to help answer some of these more basic questions.

Other questions new hires may have include the following:

- ✔ Who will I be working with?
- ✔ Who do I need to get to know in my department and in other departments?

✔ How will my work be evaluated?

✔ How does my work relate to the goals of the department and the goals of the organization?

✔ What channels exist to share ideas, suggestions, or concerns?

✔ How do people prefer to communicate within the organization (face-to-face, e-mail, phone, texting)?

✔ Do I get a laptop? A smartphone? Internet access? (Don't laugh. Incredibly, many companies still restrict Internet access.)

Not all these questions need to be answered before the employee joins, but helping the new employee to feel like he's an important part of your department (and ultimately the organization) is a key step in helping him feel at home, which is important with respect to engagement.

Finally, new employees may have questions about the organization itself:

✔ What are the firm's mission, vision, and values? How does my department fit into these?

✔ What is the culture like?

✔ Do we have a strategic plan? What does it entail?

Depending upon the new hire's role, some of this information may be less relevant. However, the firm's mission, vision, and values should be discussed as part of the new hire's orientation, if not before.

The Final Countdown: Preparing for a New Employee

Alexander Graham Bell once said, "Before anything else, preparation is the key to success." Nowhere is this more true than when it comes to onboarding new employees. You can take several steps to prepare for a new employee's arrival, to prepare for the day she starts, and to prepare for her first week on the job. For details, read on!

What to do before day one

You don't need to wait for the employee's start date to begin the onboarding process. In fact, you shouldn't. Here are just a few things you can do to help engage new hires:

Welcoming new hires to your company with an e-mail

Need a little help with your "Welcome to the Company" e-mail? Try starting with something along these lines:

Hello [Name],

On behalf of [Company or Department Name], I would like to welcome you!

As you become more familiar with our company, you'll find that it's an exciting and vibrant place to work, with many talented people and diverse opportunities. We know that you'll be an integral part of our team, and hope that you'll take advantage of all that our company has to offer.

When starting a new job, there's a lot to do and learn. Please know that there are many people here to help you and to answer any questions you may have — notably your supervisor, regional human resources team, office administrator, and co-workers. We want you to get the direction, support, and resources you need to be successful here, so please don't hesitate to ask if you have questions.

Thank you for choosing us as the place where you can make a difference, learn, and grow. We're glad that you're here to contribute to, and share in, our success!

Sincerely,

[Name]

Don't stop there, however. Think of your "Welcome to the Company" e-mail as an opportunity to share all sorts of useful info with your new hire. For example, you may include links to pages on your company website that include information about health and retirement benefits. You could even go so far as to give the new hire access to your company intranet, where he can access such info as your company's purpose, core values, and policies (including general company policies, IT policies, and so on), as well as contacts in HR and other key departments.

For best results, consider having both your HR rep and the hiring manager or direct supervisor send a welcome e-mail to the new employee. The message from the hiring manager or direct supervisor can be similar to the more corporate HR missive, but with a more personal touch. This is a great way to engage new staff — an employee's connection with his immediate manager is one of the strongest contributors to engagement.

✔ **Send a "Welcome to the Company" e-mail.** This e-mail should include contact information for all key people and other important information, such as links to benefits information, company policies, and more. (For an example of a "Welcome to the Company" e-mail, see the nearby sidebar.)

✔ **Have a key executive — maybe even the CEO, if it's a smaller company — give the new hire a call to welcome her to the firm.**

✔ **Send a company coffee mug, sweatshirt, or other branded welcome gift.** Apple sends all new employees a welcome box stuffed with swag and an inspiring note. (If you think this sounds like orientation for college freshmen, you get the picture.)

✔ **Direct new hires to your company's Yammer, Facebook, or LinkedIn page for new hires, where new hires can post their experiences, "meet" other new hires, and share survival tips.** If you don't already have such a page, create one!

✔ **Send the new hire any paperwork you need him to fill out — tax forms, the company code of conduct, and so on.** Completing this paperwork in advance is less painful than doing it during his first day or week on the job.

✔ **Tell the new hire what day and time she should arrive for her first day at work and who to ask for.**

What to do on day one

It's the big day! Your new hire is thrilled to be here and is primed and ready to work. Your mission, should you choose to accept it (you do), is to ensure she stays that way. At the day's end, your new hire should feel energized, excited, hopeful, and positive.

As with most critical missions, you need a plan. Smart organizations have a checklist prepared in advance to ensure that all the steps of the plan are followed. Otherwise, you may leave your new hire with the impression that you're part of a slipshod organization. Make it a point to put together a day-one agenda or schedule. In addition to the various onboarding activities (see the next section for details), this agenda should include who's taking the new hire to lunch. Be sure everyone who has a role in the new hire's first day is aware of it.

What to do during week one

Here's a list of things you'll need to do during a new hire's first week. Some of these activities may occur on day one; others could happen later in the week. This will help to orient and engage the new hire.

✔ **Complete all paperwork.** This includes those documents required by law in the organization's country and/or state (I-9 form, tax forms, and so on), signed offer letter, signed code of conduct, and so on. You can expedite matters by sending the paperwork to the employee prior to his start date.

✔ **Share information about benefits.** Make sure the employee understands what benefits are available to her. These may include health insurance, dental insurance, a flexible spending account, a 401(k) plan, and other miscellaneous benefits. Also, mention what steps the employee needs to take to enroll in these various programs. If you offer a 401(k) plan, consider offering a *negative election* (meaning all new hires are automatically enrolled in the plan unless they voluntarily opt out). This will increase your company's 401(k) participation rate and ensure your employees are looking after their retirement needs. (It's never too early to start planning!)

✔ **Talk about the company culture.** Touch on who you are, what you do, and why you do it. While you're at it, discuss the company's commitment to values, health and safety, and goals. Some companies play a video that outlines the company's history, values, mission, and so on. Other companies have a key company representative give a presentation about the company's culture followed by a Q&A to a group of new hires.

✔ **Talk about company policies.** Ensuring that new employees understand your firm's policies, procedures, and guidelines right from the start is key to avoiding confusion down the road. These may include your company's policies with regard to working hours, attendance and time off, employee conduct (including dating of co-workers), use of social media or the Internet, dress code, charitable contributions and/or matching gift policies, employee referrals, and hiring of relatives. You'll also want to cover the company's code of ethics and corrective action procedures for poor performance, as well as various employment law policies, such as employment classifications, equal employment opportunity (EEO)/affirmative action, sexual harassment policies, and substance abuse policies.

✔ **Discuss security.** Security — both physical security and data security — is increasingly critical for many organizations. If your organization maintains a security policy, be sure to discuss it with new hires. Also, if employees require a key or security card to enter and/or move about the building, be sure to hand one over to your new hire.

✔ **Show off your intranet.** Your new hire will probably forget everything you just told him about benefits, company culture, policies, and security procedures. Fortunately, new hires can refresh their memories on your company intranet (assuming you have one). During your new hire's first week, take time to show him this digital domain.

✔ **Give a tour.** Show the employee around. Don't forget to point out important stuff, like where the bathrooms and lunch facilities are. Also, draw the new hire's attention to emergency exits; while you're at it, cover emergency procedures.

✔ **Put faces to names.** In addition to showing the new employee an organizational chart, bring her around for introductions to the leadership team, as well as to her department colleagues. If you've assigned this new hire a "buddy" to aid in the onboarding process, make that introduction, too.

✔ **Outline job responsibilities.** Make sure the new hire knows what is expected of him during his first week, first months, and first year of employment. Also, indicate when he can expect his first few performance appraisals. You can also use this opportunity to discuss how work is assigned and the workload schedule.

✔ **Review the title and salary/pay grade.** During this discussion, you'll also want to provide an overview of compensation, as well as talk bonus programs and market-based adjustments.

✔ **Get technological.** Get your new hire set up with any equipment she needs to do her job — an iPad, a smartphone, a laptop, a desktop computer, or what have you. While you're at it, be sure she knows how to get tech support.

Great Expectations: Performance Management and Onboarding

During the onboarding process, you'll want to make it a point to establish performance expectations, goals, standards for high performance, promotional opportunities, and whatnot. Doing so is key to engaging new employees. *Remember:* Achievement is a key engagement driver (see Chapter 4). Reinforcing achievement is a must, even for new hires.

As part of this discussion, you should indicate your expectations for the first week, first month, first quarter, and first year of the new hire's tenure. Be specific. The more specific and open you can be about your expectations, the more likely you are to set up your new hire for success. While you're at it, cover the key systems your new hire will need to use to be successful and discuss your plans for getting him up to speed. Also make any introductions — internal or external — to people who can help the new hire complete his first few assignments.

To keep things on track, conduct a formal 90-day performance appraisal for new hires. The purpose of this appraisal is to assess the quality and quantity of the new employee's work, as well as her understanding of the position requirements. This review should also clarify employee concerns and questions, as well as management expectations. Finally, it should set goals for the next nine months, including timelines and measurements.

Specifically, the review should cover the following points, with employees rated as "Unsatisfactory," "Below Standards," "Fully Satisfactory," "Exceeds Standards," and "Outstanding":

- ✔ **Adjustment to culture:** Does the employee like it here? Is there anything the organization can do to help acclimate him to the culture? What is working? What isn't? What does the employee like about the organization? What should we change?

- ✔ **Conformance to position requirements:** Is the employee meeting performance expectations? Does she have strengths or weaknesses that require a modification to the position description? Successful firms evolve the job to fit the employee's strengths instead of doing the whole "force the square peg into the round hole" bit.

- ✔ **Quality of work:** Is the new hire a "get it done quick" or a "get it done right" employee? Establishing your quality standards is a must during these critical early days.

- ✔ **Productivity:** Is the new hire so focused on quality that he's not completing assignments? New hires who want to impress often make the mistake of trying to build a BMW when the job requires a Ford.

- ✔ **Communication skills:** Does the new hire lack the necessary communication skills to be successful? Does she suffer from a lack of confidence due to her newness? Is there training to help the new hire overcome these problems?

- ✔ **Working relationships:** Is the new introverted employee being overwhelmed by his extroverted co-workers (or vice versa)? Did you partner the new hire with a compatible "buddy"? If the new hire is struggling to adapt, consider a department luncheon, an after-work social, or partnership with a colleague on a project (especially with one of the department's more popular or respected members) as a means to jumpstart a relationship.

- ✔ **Planning and organizing:** Is the organization following its 90-day onboarding plan? If not, you may find that things will go astray as the new hire focuses on things *she* thinks are important rather than what the actual goals are.

Of course, you shouldn't wait 90 days to review a new hire's performance (good or bad). You should let your new hire know he's doing an amazing job, or that there are some performance concerns, well before then. Regular, ongoing communication is key to sustaining engagement. When you do review goals on day 90, there should be no surprises.

There is no such thing as holding a new hire's hand too much. A new hire will never quit a new job because, darn it, you've given her too much attention. In fact, the opposite is usually true. If a new employee fails to engage with the culture, team, department, and so on during her first 90 days on the job, that person is more likely to be poached by her former employer — who, if smart, recognizes that a great time to re-recruit a former employee is during that person's first 90 days with the new company ("Come back home! We miss you! Your seat is still warm . . .").

Fostering innovation among new employees

Your company doesn't have a monopoly on great ideas, approaches and processes. In fact, the architects of the present systems (that is, you and your current colleagues) are often incapable of "building the better mousetrap," so to speak.

Fortunately, new hires are amazing sources of new ideas. Their experiences outside your company may have exposed them to superior ideas, approaches, and processes. Unfortunately, however, most new hires are not yet confident enough to challenge how things are done in your firm.

To combat this, why not build a process into your onboarding program for the sharing of these types of ideas? For example, one approach may be to have new hires fill out a survey after 60 days to answer the following questions:

✔ What can we do better?

✔ What's one thing you love about working here?

✔ What's one thing you wish you could change?

✔ What did your old firm do better than we do?

The idea is to make it safe for new hires to offer their ideas early in their tenure. To sweeten the deal, you may even offer a gift certificate, company coffee mug, or some other form of recognition to thank them for their suggestions.

Part IV
Measuring and Recognizing Engagement

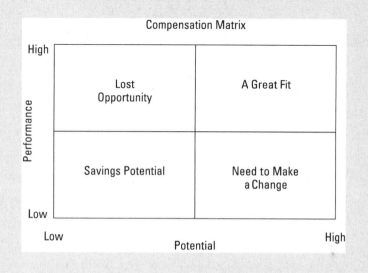

Compensation Matrix

	Low Potential	High Potential
High Performance	Lost Opportunity	A Great Fit
Low Performance	Savings Potential	Need to Make a Change

Find out how to establish an employee engagement committee, in a free article at www.dummies.com/extras/employeeengagement.

In this part...

- Build a balanced scorecard to measure and communicate your progress.

- Measure employee engagement because you get the behavior you measure.

- Establish SMART performance goals to drive engagement.

- Retool your performance appraisal process for today's changing organization.

- Recognize employees for a job well done to encourage desired behaviors.

- Help struggling employees become more productive and engaged.

Chapter 15

Measure Up: Measuring Performance and Engagement

. . . .

In This Chapter

▶ Building a balanced organizational-level scorecard

▶ Measuring individual performance

▶ Measuring team performance

▶ Measuring employee engagement

. . . .

*P*icture this: You're in the midst of a hotly contested game. Fans scream as both sides battle for the win. You glance up at the scoreboard . . . and it's blank. There's nothing — no score, no indication of how much time remains, nothing. "We're winning!" one coach screams. "No, *we're* winning!" screams the other.

If you're a player, what do you do? Do you continue to play? Is there a let-down? Can you sustain your momentum, not knowing if you're winning or losing? Do you even care anymore? If no one is keeping score and no one is keeping time, how will you know if and when you've won or lost?

This scenario might seem ridiculous. It could never happen, right? Wrong. Sadly, it happens all the time in business. Employees often don't know if they're winning or losing, if their business is succeeding or failing, or if they're high, average, or low performers. Employees are motivated to achieve — indeed, it's a key intrinsic motivator in just about everyone. Plus, it drives engagement. But if we don't know what the achievement metrics are — what constitutes "achievement" — how do we know if we've, well, achieved it?

This chapter is all about "keeping score" — that is, measuring performance on an organizational, individual, and team level. As you'll soon see, these measurements are a key component of employee engagement.

Score! Building a Balanced Scorecard to Measure an Organization's Performance

Business is not T-ball. Employees want and need to know the score. Yet, very few companies establish an organizational scorecard, often called a balanced scorecard, to aid in this. In layman's terms, a *balanced scorecard* is a set of quantitative metrics that a company can track and report on, hopefully to all employees. Simply put, a balanced scorecard provides a snapshot of the performance of a company (or individual, department, or business unit) compared to its objectives (see Figure 15-1).

Firms that select the right metrics to measure and effectively communicate those metrics reinforce their organizational line of sight (discussed in Chapter 6) between the organization's purpose, values, vision, and strategic plan. Under this system, daily operations are clearly connected to programs and services that themselves ultimately link to long-term goals.

Metric	Actual for Month	Plan for Month	YTD Actual	YTD Plan	Operations	Top 25%
Health and Safety						
OSHA Recordables	0	0	0	0	3	0
OSHA Recordables	0	0	0	0	3	0
Employee Engagement						
Training % of Payroll	1.8	2.9	1.9	2.8	2.5	2.8
Turnover %: Voluntary	1.5	8.0	4.7	8.0	9.4	5.2
Turnover %: Involuntary	0.0	0.0	0.0	0.0	1.6	3.0
Employee Engagement Survey Favorable Rating %	88	100	88	88	78	89
Profitability						
Total Utilization %	71.6	68.4	64.3	67.5	62.2	68.8
Contribution Margin ($000)	384	415	1,477	1,735	20,606	1,118
Contribution Margin (% of Net Sales)	51.7	54.3	51.9	54.3	55.0	57.4
Operating Profit ($000)	115	123	298	548	6,539	566
Operating Profit (% of Net Sales)	15.5	16.0	10.5	17.1	17.5	29.0
Revenue Growth						
Proposal Backlog ($000)	2,550	0	2,550	0	58,863	3,166
Booking ($000)	1,166	1,202	4,785	4,807	60,510	3,275
Project Backlog ($000)	4,509	4,000	4,509	4,000	87,111	5,281
Net Sales ($000)	744	765	2,844	3,199	37,454	2,112
Net Yield Multiplier x Total Utilization	2.01	2.03	1.81	2.00	1.87	2.20
Cost Management						
Total Facilities ($)	660	629	2,644	2,588	2,042	3,275
Total Discretionary ($)	442	447	1,671	1,764	2,123	3,275

Figure 15-1: An example of a balanced scorecard.

Illustration by Wiley, Composition Services Graphics

Such an approach can assist not only in bolstering a company's mission, but also in boosting employee engagement. After all, employee engagement is simply an outcome of a number of factors, not the least of which is the company's commitment to helping its employees reach their potential and the employees' commitment to helping the business reach its business goals. Measuring, tracking, and communicating performance goals on an organizational level, as well as the employee level, reinforces this mutual commitment.

Designing an effective balanced scorecard

An effective balanced scorecard is one that captures the right blend between profitability and other key organizational metrics. These would include both *hard metrics* (sometimes called "what metrics" or quantitative metrics) like profit, revenue, growth, and sales, along with *soft metrics* (often referred to as "how metrics" or qualitative metrics) like training and development, wellness, trust, purpose, recognition, and so forth. (Naturally, many of these soft metrics are more difficult to measure.)

There is no cookie-cutter approach to identifying which metrics to measure. They must flow from your company's strategic goals, and many are industry specific. For instance, in the retail industry, shrinkage metrics (that is, metrics pertaining to theft and damaged goods) are critically important. In the hotel industry, room occupancy is a key metric.

Pinpointing your metrics requires some thinking. Often, you have to drill down to smaller, more concrete goals and measurements to achieve the desired results. Suppose, for example, that you want to improve customer satisfaction. It's not enough to simply measure customer satisfaction; you must also measure the various aspects of your business that affect customer satisfaction. For example, one metric would obviously be customer service. But that's not the only one you need to measure. After all, you could have a whole team of Susie Sunshines providing extraordinary customer service, but if your product has defects, customer satisfaction will be compromised. This is why companies also include quality metrics when pursuing customer satisfaction goals. Likewise, if you have very high voluntary employee turnover or low employee engagement, there's a good chance your customers will be negatively affected. (This reinforces yet again the importance of employee engagement in key business metrics!)

Take time upfront to determine the metrics that make the best sense for the goals you're trying to achieve. This sort of advanced planning is essential to inculcating engagement and driving performance.

If this is your first attempt at building a balanced scorecard, the key is to keep things simple. Don't over-engineer the scorecard or make it overly complicated. Organizations that measure and communicate zillions of metrics cause their employees to lose focus, and blur that ever-important line of sight. The key is identifying which metrics deserve focus on your balanced scorecard in the upcoming year. This isn't to say that other key metrics that *don't* appear on the scorecard won't be tracked — it's just that they won't be as widely broadcast throughout the year.

Maintaining your balanced scorecard

After you build your scorecard, you must maintain and update your metrics. This includes an annual review of key metrics. Each year, preferably before the new fiscal year, your leadership team must decide which metrics to track over the next 12 months. Some metrics should always be included in your balanced scorecard — think metrics pertaining to profit and growth. In addition, the balanced scorecard provides an opportunity to highlight other key metrics to reinforce the organization's focus on needed changes and to get the attention of leaders and employees. Indeed, smart organizations, aware of the old adage "You get the behavior you measure," routinely tweak their scorecards to reinforce what's important in the coming year.

Once, a former employer of mine detected an increase in DSOs (short for "day sales outstanding"). When DSOs go up, that usually means customers aren't paying on time. High DSOs can significantly affect profits. By adding DSOs as a metric to our balanced scorecard, we were able to focus our entire staff on DSOs. Within a year, we significantly reduced this metric, greatly improving profitability.

In addition to an annual review of key metrics, you also need to perform a monthly update. (If you're a publicly traded company, it may need to happen quarterly.) The update involves communicating results for each metric to all employees. For more on communicating results, read on.

Communicating results

It's not enough to merely track metrics. You must also communicate the results to all employees. Failure to do so will result in their disengagement. When it comes to communicating these results, keep these best practices in mind:

> ✔ **Keep it simple and execute flawlessly.** It seems like more and more restaurants these days have, like, 82 pages of menu items. I don't know

about you, but this confuses the heck out of me. How am I supposed to choose, with so many options? The truth is, most people go glassy-eyed when faced with too many choices, and employees are no different. If you try to communicate a sea of metrics, you'll lose them. Focus on a few key metrics, and execute your communication of these key metrics flawlessly!

✔ **Take it from the top.** The president or CEO should communicate updates on performance on a monthly basis (or, if a publicly traded company, quarterly). This should be done in whatever venue works best for the CEO and in terms of organizational logistics (for example, single site versus multi-site and across time zones). Culture and style are also factors in terms of message delivery (that is, whether the results should be communicated via e-mail, video, town hall meeting, mobile application, blog, and so on).

✔ **Build in repetition via a cascading message.** Employ a "waterfall" messaging model, starting at the top, to ensure everyone receives the message (see Chapter 5). Also, ensure that the next level down communicates its own metrics in the same format, sequence, and time frame. For instance, the CEO of a large retail chain might communicate his or her organization-wide metrics on a Monday. That same week, the district manager should communicate district-wide results to his or her direct reports. Shortly thereafter, the local store managers should communicate their single-store results with all their employees. In an ideal world, individual department managers would then meet with their employees to discuss how their department results affected store-wide, division-wide, and company-wide results. This reinforces the line of site between what's important at the CEO level and what's important at the level of the individual employee. In addition, the repetition of messaging reinforces the key measureable metrics, which both drive and reinforce organization-wide behavior while building both alignment and engagement.

✔ **Make it interesting.** Keep your balanced scorecard vibrant and colorful. Metrics don't have to be boring. The look and feel of your scorecard will go a long way toward getting your employees to embrace it. Repeat after me: The accounting team should *not* design your balanced scorecard. Don't get me wrong: Accountants do a lot of things right, and heaven knows, you need their input. But your balanced scorecard has to really captivate your employees. The more you leverage various tools to communicate your metrics, the more you'll engage your employees in the metric process. Think *USA Today,* not *The Wall Street Journal.*

When you assemble your balanced scorecard task team, include your best IT, marketing, communications, HR, organizational development (OD), finance, *and* accounting brains.

✔ **Make it accessible.** Your balanced scorecard should reside somewhere, preferably on your intranet, Microsoft SharePoint, or other central repository of organization-wide information. That way, it's easily accessible to all employees. In addition, you might want to make the scorecard accessible to employees on the go, via smartphone. If you have the resources, you may even create a balanced scorecard mobile app for employees.

✔ **Take the good with the bad.** Use your scorecard to promote and highlight positive trends, as well as to highlight some negative trends that need attention (sort of an "early warning system").

To instill engagement at every level and to ensure that communication is not solely of the "top-down" variety, you might follow the example of one manager I encountered, who often asked his most junior staff to share scorecard results in meetings with the entire office. This small but powerful idea increased the junior staff's engagement levels and reinforced the importance of business metrics for all members of the office — not just the leadership team. It also was a great development opportunity for junior staff, tying them to the larger organizational goals.

Take It Personally: Measuring Individual Performance

Building a balanced scorecard to gauge your organization's success isn't enough. To increase the chances that your organization's goals will be met, you must connect the metrics in the balanced scorecard and other key organizational goals to each employee's job. This is critical in building that "line of sight" I keep mentioning, which is key to employee engagement. Typically, this is done through the dreaded performance appraisal process, which is generally despised by managers and employees alike. (For more on performance appraisals, turn to Chapter 16.)

Trust me: If there's one thing I've learned over the past 30 years, it's that employees don't want to be average — they want to win! To *really* get the most out of your people, you have to define and communicate what constitutes "high performance." If you don't, you can't expect improvement from your employees. The best scorecards build in "average" and "high-performance" norms to activate their employees' achievement gene. Your staff needs to have a clear picture of what's optimal, not just the minimum required to get by.

Most companies benchmark against competitors but shy away from benchmarking within their own organization, but this approach is foolish. You need to know who your top-performing employees are (or aren't) before you can determine why they perform highly (or don't). How do you define those individuals? What are their performance benchmarks?

A few years ago, I met with a manager to discuss his business metrics. Every single one was dead average: profitability, write-offs, business development, and so on. But this manager didn't want to share these stats with his staff. "Finding out they're average will demoralize them!" he insisted. "I hate to disappoint you," I told him, "but they *are* average. And they need to know that in order to improve." After all, why would an employee change her ways if she believes she's performing at a high level?

If you don't communicate average and high-performance norms, the best you can hope for is to sustain mediocrity. Case in point: After the aforementioned manager started sharing metrics with the members of that average business unit, the results were immediate. Stunned to discover that they were merely C students, team members immediately researched what high-performing units did differently. They met and collaborated, eventually developing dozens of ideas on how to improve. Over time, they reached top 25 percent performance!

So, what individual metrics should you measure? Not to be coy, but I can't really say. After all, there are probably dozens — if not hundreds — of different types of jobs at your company, let alone in the world, and there isn't one set of metrics that would apply to all of them.

I can say, however, that the best performance management and measurement systems include a blend of quantitative metrics (the "what") and qualitative metrics (the "how"). If an organization can capture and report on quantitative benchmarks for average and high-performing norms, employees will better understand what defines success. (Again, you're trying to leverage the natural achievement gene in us all!) For illustrative purposes, Table 15-1 provides examples of both quantitative and qualitative metrics.

Table 15-1   Examples of Quantitative and Qualitative Metrics

Quantitative Metrics	*Qualitative Metrics*
Number of defects	Teamwork
Number of calls per hour	Dependability
Number of customer calls	Initiative
Percentage complete	Planning and organization
Percentage of projects completed on time	Enthusiasm

(continued)

Table 15-1 *(continued)*

Quantitative Metrics	Qualitative Metrics
Number of projects completed on time and within budget	Mentoring and coaching
Number of projects completed within budget	Communication
Percentage of performance appraisals (of direct reports) complete	Empathy
Profit contribution	Cross-training
Sales	Customer orientation
Win rate	Cooperation
OSHA recordables (injuries reported to OSHA)	Quest for learning
Shrinkage	Project management
Number of patient re-admissions	Technological efficiency
Number of infections	Resourcefulness
On-time delivery rate	Inquisitiveness
Returns per employee	Creativity
Sales per employee	

Team Player: Measuring Team Performance

In addition to tracking performance on the organizational and individual level, you should also include metrics for teams — that is, internal business units and/or profit centers. For example, suppose you work for a national retail chain. If you include these types of measurements, employees who work at one of your retail stores can see how their store is performing compared to other stores in the chain. This can spark competition between the stores, which drives both engagement and results.

This process must be complementary, not destructive. Be sure you strike a balance between promoting internal competition and establishing a "We all work for one company" culture!

A great benchmarking tool for this process is the Team/Business Unit Performance Benchmark Matrix (shown in Figure 15-2). In this matrix, you can use any two measureable data points as your benchmarks (quality, employee turnover, customer satisfaction scores, shrinkage, and so on). Here, I used profit and growth in a comparison of five profit centers. (Each profit center is indicated by an icon, to preserve the anonymity of the other units — this helps you straddle that fine line between teamwork and competition.) In this matrix, the profit centers are assessed the same way employees are (see Chapter 12), as investment teams, performers, potentials, and transition teams. Using this matrix, teams and business units can quickly determine whether they're "losing" to other groups in the organization. Believe me, no team wants to find itself in that bottom-left quadrant. When they do, they'll become engaged and commit to moving out of the "transition" category!

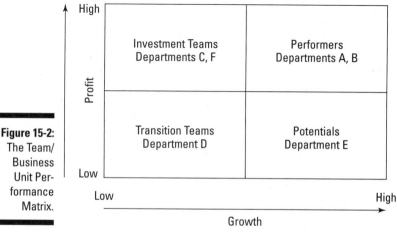

Figure 15-2: The Team/ Business Unit Per- formance Matrix.

Illustration by Wiley, Composition Services Graphics

Measuring whether a team is functional or dysfunctional is important. (For more about this, I recommend a great book by Patrick Lencioni called *The Five Dysfunctions of a Team* [Jossey-Bass].) To determine this, you can conduct a survey among team members, asking them to rate the following statements on a scale of 1 to 10 (with 1 being "not at all" and 10 being "excels at this"):

✔ Our leadership team makes decisions unselfishly, for the greater good of the company. They don't make decisions in their own self-interest.

✔ Our leadership team is seen by its employees as aligned on mission, strategy, goals, and priorities. They focus and align in one consistent direction and behave in a way that supports this focus.

✔ Our leadership team "walks the walk and talks the talk." They live the values the organization stands for. (Mutual commitments and values may include integrity, respect, balance, open communication, flexibility, safety, innovation, and so on.)

✔ Our leadership team automatically and consistently assumes the best intentions in one another. They don't assume that others have ulterior motives, especially when they disagree. All team members assume that teammates want what is best for the organization. It's okay to have different opinions, and the team can engage in an open and respectful discussion.

✔ Our leadership team openly discusses issues in meetings. We have open, respectful, yet challenging conversations in meetings. We don't have contrary discussions in the hallway, after meetings. Team members say what they want in the room, not after the meeting. We avoid "I won't comment on your sandbox if you don't comment on mine" behavior.

✔ When a decision is made in a meeting, our leadership owns the decision as ours and fully supports it outside the meeting. When decisions are made, our leadership supports them with employees. Employees hear a single voice.

✔ Our leadership is acutely aware of the impact of the shadow they cast on our organization. They recognize that employees notice everything they do — from their actions to their words to their moods. They act with the knowledge that others look up to them and emulate their behavior. They're seen by their employees as being aligned.

✔ Our leadership fully participates in initiatives instead of just "blessing" them. Because of the *shadow phenomenon,* which states that leaders have a tremendous influence on the company environment, leaders support company initiatives. They share in the responsibility, knowing that how we are led determines how we lead.

✔ All teams are managed and measured with the same level of accountability. Team members openly admit their weaknesses and mistakes. Team members willingly make sacrifices (such as budget, turf, and head count) in their areas of responsibility for the good of the team.

✔ We as individual team members are slow to seek credit for our own contributions but quick to point out those of others. Individual members focus on the needs of the team and not their individual or promotion needs.

Consider using a free survey tool, such as SurveyMonkey (www.survey monkey.com), to conduct this survey.

For best results, individual responses should be kept confidential. Results should be tabulated and used as a benchmark. After results are tabulated, the team should meet to discuss them and identify an action plan for improvement.

Measure by Measure: Measuring Employee Engagement

You need to measure employee engagement, just as you would any other business objective, regardless of whether employee engagement becomes part of your balanced scorecard.

Key metrics for measuring employee engagement

Historically, the gold standard for measuring employee engagement has been voluntary employee turnover. The problem? Voluntary turnover is a trailing indicator rather than a leading indicator. That is, you can't use this data until an employee has "left the building," so to speak. Also, not all voluntary turnover is created equal. That is, voluntary turnover among disengaged or low-performing staff is of far less concern than voluntary turnover among high-potential or high-performing employees. In fact, in this case, high voluntary turnover can be good!

Of course, if you *are* losing star employees in droves, that's clearly a problem, and you need to identify the underlying causes. Obviously, you can accomplish this only if you know who your high potentials and high performers are. If you're not capturing this data, you should. At the very least, you should be benchmarking your voluntary turnover against others in your industry. Yes, it's a trailing indicator, but it's still a revealing data point.

In addition to measuring voluntary employee turnover (flawed though that measurement may be), you should also measure the following at both the organizational level and the department or business-unit level:

- ✔ **Employee engagement survey results:** Unlike voluntary turnover statistics, employee engagement survey data are leading indicators. If you conduct a survey, you'll be able to benchmark your results against other firms in your industry. Even more important, you can benchmark your progress against your historical survey data and can compare business units with other business units — both of which are important benchmarks.

- ✔ **Recognition:** Recognition is a key — and free! — engagement driver, but few firms measure it. If you budget a nominal amount per department for recognition efforts, funded at the corporate level, you'll be able to track the amount spent on these efforts on a departmental basis. (For more on the importance of recognition to employee engagement, see Chapter 17.)

✔ **Employee referral percentage:** This is defined as the percentage of new hires who have joined your firm because of an internal employee referral. If none of your internal employees is referring your firm to others, that may indicate a serious lack of engagement.

✔ **Training and development investment:** Best-in-class organizations spend between 3 percent and 5 percent of payroll on training and development. Budgeting and measuring your investment as a percentage of payroll by department will enable you to track who is investing in their employees. There is usually a clear connection between engagement and investment in training and development.

Assessing your team's level of engagement

Need a quick, easy way to measure your team's level of engagement? The following questionnaire is designed to enable you to do just that:

1. **Which of the following statements most accurately reflects your team's sense of purpose?**

   A. Because not all members express their views, it's not clear that there's a sense of common purpose. Members are more focused on "How do I fit in?" than "How will we work together?"

   B. Members disagree about the purpose and goals of the group and individual responsibilities. There's a discrepancy between what people want and what's realistic.

   C. A sense of shared purpose is emerging. Goals for the team and individual roles are becoming clear, and the group is beginning to develop methods for achieving them.

   D. Each member can describe and is committed to the purpose of the team. Goals and individual roles are clear and relevant to the overall purpose. Strategies for achieving goals are clear and well accepted.

2. **Which of the following statements most accurately reflects your team's sense of empowerment?**

   A. There is low confidence in the team's ability to realize a shared vision. Members are frustrated with leadership, policies, and practices. There is a sense of competition rather than collaboration among team members.

   B. Members feel relatively enthusiastic about the future of the team but haven't yet acquired the necessary knowledge and skills to be productive. Policies, procedures, and practices are unclear.

   C. Members feel cautiously optimistic about the ability of the group to solve problems and to achieve desired results. There is a growing sense of power as skills continue to deepen. The group is learning to work together and to help each other.

D. Members feel a collective sense of power and have acquired the necessary skills and resources. Policies, procedures, and practices support the team's objectives. There is a sense of mutual respect and willingness to help each other.

3. **Which of the following statements most accurately reflects your team's relationships and communication style?**

A. Members often interrupt, withdraw, or express negative reactions to the formal leadership and/or to each other. Communication within the group reflects conflict and/or frustration. The group shows little evidence of listening or understanding.

B. Members act politely and cautiously toward each other, reflecting a lack of knowledge about one another. Members are often hesitant to express their feelings and opinions.

C. Team members are increasingly encouraging and supportive of one another. They tend to withhold negative feedback. Members are listening to each other more and more.

D. Team members express themselves openly and honestly without fear of rejection. Members listen to each other and express understanding and acceptance.

4. **Which of the following statements most accurately reflects your team's flexibility?**

A. Frustration and tension in the group limit team members' flexibility. Dissatisfaction is expressed by open aggression, withdrawal, and resistance.

B. The team depends entirely on the leader or formal organization structure for direction and approval. Members are cautious, formal, and stilted in their communication with the group.

C. Members are beginning to share responsibility for team functioning by using their strengths. There is an emphasis on maintaining harmony and good working relationships.

D. Members flexibly fulfill various roles to complete tasks and for team operation. Members freely express opinions and feelings, and are adaptable to changing demands.

5. **Which of the following statements most accurately reflects your team's performance?**

A. The team shows little evidence of completing tasks. The team's problem-solving and decision-making skills are underdeveloped.

B. The team shows some evidence of completing tasks. Members have difficulty with problem solving and decision making.

    C. The team shows definite evidence of completing tasks. Team members are fairly adept at solving problems and making decisions.

    D. The team completes work quickly and effectively. Members have highly developed problem-solving and decision-making skills and value each other's perspectives.

6. **Which of the following statements most accurately reflects your team's recognition and appreciation of each other?**

    A. Team members rarely recognize or express appreciation for each other. They tend to criticize each other or focus on negative aspects.

    B. Members look to the leader for approval more than to other team members.

    C. Team members increasingly recognize and express appreciation for each other, reflecting a developing sense of harmony and trust. Even so, team spirit remains somewhat tentative or fragile.

    D. There's a strong feeling of respect and appreciation among team members. Individual and team accomplishments are recognized by team members, as well as by the leader.

7. **Which of the following statements most accurately reflects your team's morale?**

    A. There are feelings of frustration, pessimism, and dissatisfaction among team members. The team is fractured, with members competing with each other or withdrawing from the group.

    B. Team members feel a sense of expectancy and hope, as well as some apprehension, as they develop ways to effectively work together.

    C. Team members feel a growing sense of team cohesion and confidence as they work better and better together. Positive feelings outweigh negative ones.

    D. Team members feel a sense of pride and excitement in being part of the team. Their confidence is strong, and they're very satisfied with the work being done.

When you're finished, give yourself 1 point for every A, 2 points for every B, 3 points for every C, and 4 points for every D. Here's what your score means:

  ✔ **24 to 28 points:** Way to go! You're part of an engaged team.

  ✔ **18 to 23 points:** You're on your way, but there's room to be great.

  ✔ **12 to 17 points:** You have a big opportunity for improvement.

  ✔ **7 to 11 points:** Buy this book for every member of your team — your team's engagement is low.

Chapter 16

Goal! Setting Performance Goals and Conducting Performance Appraisals

In This Chapter

▶ Establishing SMART performance goals

▶ Retooling your performance appraisal process

▶ Building succession into the performance appraisal process

Are goals important? In a word, yes. If you don't believe me, consider that a simple web search for the word *goals,* minus hits pertaining to soccer, yields nearly 700 *million* results.

We agree, then, that it's essential to set goals. (After all, if you aim at nothing, you'll hit every time!) What's also critical is to measure performance against said goals. In this way, you ensure that employees "know the score" on an organizational level (see Chapter 15), as well as individually. This chapter discusses the ins and outs of setting goals and outlines a new approach to performance appraisals — one that's meant to engage!

Get Smart: Establishing SMART Performance Goals

I once had a neighbor who was consistently the first guy on the block to get moving each Saturday. By 7 a.m., he'd be outside cleaning his garage, trimming the hedges, scraping the paint from his deck, or washing his car.

And yet, by late afternoon, he still wasn't finished. There would be ladders propped against the house, buckets of soapy water gone stagnant by his car, paint scrapers abandoned on the deck. The guy obviously had good intentions and lots of energy. What he appeared to lack was focus.

Goals without focus are merely ideas. Nowhere is this more true than in business. Perhaps entrepreneur and author Jim Rohn said it best: "Discipline is the bridge between goals and accomplishments." But often, we allow ourselves to be distracted and lack the discipline to complete what we start out to do. Other times, we jump into something in a reactionary way, without evaluating its impact on the overall goal.

Years ago, I supervised an HR manager who consistently struggled to meet his goals. Over time, I realized why: He allowed others to plan his day. That is, he spent every moment in reactive mode. A typical HR department is a very busy place. Often, you're balancing your priorities with real-time issues: An employee drops by to discuss a problem; a supervisor of another department calls to say an employee has just resigned; a candidate calls to request an exploratory interview. If a person in this environment has time-management issues, he'll spend all his time reacting to these real-time issues, thereby falling short of his proactive goals.

What does this have to do with employee engagement? I've come to realize that the accomplishment of proactive goals drives engagement. There is very little job satisfaction in reactive work because we don't receive the endorphin rush that comes from completing a goal. See, reactive work rarely is connected to goals, which is one reason people who are constantly in reactive mode rarely give above-and-beyond effort. That's where SMART goals come in. SMART goals are

- ✔ **Specific:** The more specific you make your goals, the better your results will be. Lack of specificity results in ambiguity — and ambiguity can't be measured. Goals should specify what you want to accomplish, why you want to accomplish it, when you will work toward the goal, and who is involved.

- ✔ **Measurable:** As mentioned in Chapter 15, you get the behavior you measure. That means you must set measurable goals. As you establish your goals, ask yourself, what are your metrics? Are they fair? If not, prepare for your employees to disengage.

- ✔ **Attainable:** Nothing is more demoralizing than pursuing a goal that you simply can't attain. Although you should always set stretch goals to drive employees to achieve, remember that there is a fine line between stretch goals and impossible ones.

✔ **Relevant:** Individual goals should jibe with overall company goals to reinforce that ever-important line of sight, discussed in Chapter 6. This is even more important if your company uses a balanced scorecard to communicate company-wide performance. For instance, if you're focusing on health and safety as a key organizational goal, you also need to establish specific measurable health and safety goals at the individual level.

✔ **Time-bound:** You must establish deliverable dates and deadlines. Goals that lack completion dates are not goals; they're suggestions.

So, how do you go about setting SMART goals? Here's a step-by-step guide:

1. **Define your specific goal, focusing on the what and the why.**

2. **Outline the steps that must be taken for the goal to be met.**

3. **Define the time frame required to meet the goal.**

4. **Select a *goal manager* (someone to manage the process of meeting the goal).**

5. **Consider the expected outcomes.**

   Ask yourself:

   • What will be different?

   • How will the business benefit?

   • What will we gain by achieving this goal?

6. **Consider the tradeoffs and obstacles.**

   Ask yourself:

   • What will we have to give up to achieve this goal?

   • What obstacles or difficulties exist or potentially exist? How will we manage them?

Setting SMART goals isn't just critical to performance. It's also key to engagement. One Gallup study determined that only half the people surveyed had clarity on what's expected of them, which caused enormous frustration (read: disengagement).

One more thing: When you set SMART goals for your employees, you must give them the equipment, resources, and support they need to attain them. Failing to do so will lead employees to conclude that you're not paying attention to them or that their work isn't important — another disengagement driver.

Don't Be a Tool: Retooling the Performance Appraisal Process

If you're like me, there are plenty of aspects of your job that you really like. Maybe you like your company. Maybe you adore your boss. Perhaps you enjoy the tasks associated with your work. But I'd be willing to gamble a fair share of my income that you *don't* like your organization's annual performance appraisal process. Even the term is scary. "We're going to *appraise your performance.*" Heck, I'm spooked just typing it!

You're not alone. I speak at a lot of conferences, and I often ask attendees to raise their hands if they like their companies' annual performance appraisal process. About 99 percent of the time, not a single hand is raised. Zero. Nada. Zilch. This crude and unofficial survey confirms it: *Nobody* likes performance appraisals.

The question is: Why? For one thing, there are the forms. The documents used for performance appraisals inevitably grow over time, especially as companies add more bureaucratic and legal "stuff" designed to protect the company's interests in the case of employment litigation. The result? Managers must essentially write a full-length thesis on each employee under their watch. No wonder these managers balk at the mere mention of quarterly or semiannual performance appraisals! It's more than enough to undergo this torture once a year. (Sure, there are some technology solutions on the market, but often, these solutions are just too complicated for your average manager.)

Plus, performance appraisals tend to focus on *trailing* feedback rather than *leading* feedback. Giving trailing feedback is a little like looking in the rearview mirror. It involves telling an employee how he has performed against goals in the past. Don't get me wrong: Trailing feedback is an important thing — but it isn't the only thing! Leading feedback involves projecting forward. It's like looking through the windshield. It has to do with future goals and objectives, with a focus on the employee's ongoing development. Truth be told, most employees are far more interested in the future — in learning how they can grow — than they are in the past.

Offering both trailing and leading feedback during performance appraisals is important because both help drive engagement. Trailing feedback (accomplishment against goals) reinforces achievement, which is a key engagement driver. And leading feedback tends to be more developmental in nature and, thus, reinforces the line of site between an employee's current job and where that person is going. Helping employees reach their potential through development is essential for engagement to take root.

Decoupling compensation from the performance appraisal process

If at all possible, remove all discussion of compensation, salary included, from the performance review process. Performance reviews should focus more on an employee development plan. Otherwise, during the review, the employee will be sitting there wondering what his pay increase is going to be — which is not conducive to long-term planning!

My recommendation is to schedule regular performance reviews during the off-season rather than when salary increases typically occur. For example, if salary increases are announced at the beginning of the year (which is often the case), performance reviews should occur during the summer. That way, you have months of performance data to support your decision about the salary increase (or lack thereof). Plus, managers will now meet with employees two times a year to discuss performance and goals!

Clearly, something is wrong with the performance appraisal process. In this section, I fill you in on three tools — employee development plans, 360 assessments, and "more of, same as, less of" feedback sessions — that are oh so right.

Building an employee development plan

Performance appraisals represent a significant opportunity for supervisors to build a mutual commitment with employees — which is a key engagement driver — but more often than not, this opportunity is wasted. That's because, as I mention earlier, performance appraisals tend to focus on trailing feedback rather than leading feedback. In other words, managers don't spend nearly enough time on the developmental side of the meeting.

A simple way to trigger this shift is to change your terminology. In other words, don't call them "performance appraisals"; call them "employee development plans" (EDPs for short). The purpose of an EDP is to motivate and guide employees to perform at the highest levels and to focus on employees' professional growth. Yes, EDPs should include a summary of accomplishments against prior goals, but the idea is to move away from a report card, instead supplying a road map for continuous development. By explicitly linking the employee goals to the company's strategic priorities, the plan reinforces the line of sight and acts as a natural extension of the firm's balanced scorecard.

A successful EDP fosters an open yet formal discussion of successes and shortfalls, as well as the factors that should be taken into consideration when cultivating a particular individual — that is, the individual's passions, training and development, family situation, immediate and long-term career goals, and so on. When done well, EDPs enable managers to spend as much (if not more) time discussing future goals and developmental action as reviewing performance. The result? Improved engagement!

The bottom line? The importance of input, coaching, and development is critical to an employee's level of engagement. Indeed, in their research on engagement, Dale Carnegie found that engagement levels are higher among employees whose managers give them feedback and encouragement to do their jobs better, who learn a lot from their managers, and who have opportunities to grow the skills in the organization. The EDP is a key part of that.

Dissecting the employee development plan

An EDP includes both an assessment of the employees' past performance and the development of a road map for the future. At the very least, this should be a 50/50 split, although managers can choose to place even more attention on the road-map portion of the EDP. To complete the EDP, managers should conduct a 360-degree assessment of the employee, as discussed in the next section.

Assessing past performance

In general terms, when it comes to assessing past performance, managers should summarize performance and progress made on goals and metrics established in the previous year's EDP or performance assessment. This includes noting actions taken toward professional and career development goals, such as completion of internal and/or external training, degrees, certificate programs, and so on. It also includes an assessment of the employee's strengths and areas for improvement. Areas to consider include (but are not limited to) customer satisfaction, technical competence and knowledge, quality, productivity, initiative, communication, planning and organization, dependability, teamwork, and so on. A sample form you can use to fill out this portion of the EDP is shown in Figure 16-1. Feel free to copy it and use it in your business!

Developing a road map for the future

Developing a road map for the future involves the following:

- ✔ **Establishing performance goals for the upcoming year:** This should be a list of five or six high-impact SMART goals to be achieved in the upcoming year. These goals should be linked to one or more of the company's strategic priorities (think environmental health and safety, employee engagement, innovation, quality, efficiency, and so on). Ways to measure progress should be included.

EDP

Employee Name _____   Review Period _____
Position Title _____   Office/Department _____
Salary Grade _____   Supervisor Name _____

Goal Accomplishment/Feedback on Skills and Competencies

Goals: What Was Accomplished
Summarize performance and progress made on goals/metrics established in the last annual EDP/performance review

Metrics					Comments
	Actual		Expected		
	Actual		Expected		
	Actual		Expected		
	Actual		Expected		
	Actual		Expected		

Comment here on progress achieving professional and career development goals

Feedback on Performance: How Results Were Achieved
Describe the employee's strengths and improvement areas

Strengths	Improvement Areas

Figure 16-1: A sample performance assessment form for an EDP.

Illustration by Wiley, Composition Services Graphics

✔ **Establishing professional development goals for the upcoming year:**
This should be one or two SMART development goals to enhance performance in the employee's current role. Specific actions to be taken to achieve these goals should be included.

✔ **Identifying longer-term career goals:** The idea here is to identify one or two SMART development goals that will help the employee make progress toward longer-term career interests. This section of the EDP may comment on next possible jobs or include stretch assignments to help the employee grow. If the employee wants to remain in his current position, this section of the EDP should identify ways to enhance job satisfaction.

✔ **Succession planning:** Part of any career conversation should include a discussion of the employee's potential. Is the employee a potential successor to her boss? If not, why not? If so, when? What does the employee need to do to enhance her succession potential?

Figure 16-2 contains a sample form you can use to fill out this portion of the EDP. Again, feel free to copy this as needed.

Research suggests that when managers and employees jointly set and agree to goals (instead of managers simply dictating goals to employees), employees are *five times* more likely to achieve them.

EDP

Employee Name _____   Review Period_____
Position Title _____   Office/Department _____
Salary Grade_____   Supervisor Name_____

Performance and Development Agreement

Performance Goals for Upcoming Year

List 6-8 high-impact goals to be achieved in the upcoming year, linking goals to one or more of the company's strategic priorities

Goals/Measures	Relevant Strategic Priority	Timeframe

Performance Goals for Upcoming Year

Choose 1-2 development goals to focus on this year to enhance performance in the current role

Goals/Measures	Learning and Development Actions (not any specific training, resources, or support needed)	Timeframe for completion

Career Development Goals for Longer Term (Within 3 Years)

Identify 1-2 development goals to help make progress toward longer-term career interests

Figure 16-2:
A sample road-map form for an EDP.

As you develop this road map, you may want to consider the "three circles" I mention in Chapter 4. The first circle represents what the employee likes to do, the second circle represents what the employee is good at, and the third circle represent what needs to get done. The more these circles overlap, the more engaged the employee will be. Try filling in a three-circles diagram (refer to Chapter 4) for your employees as you develop their EDP.

Using the employee development plan

So, how do you use an EDP? Here's a breakdown:

1. **The manager completes the EDP forms (refer to Figure 16-1 and Figure 16-2).**

   This step includes providing an assessment of the employee's past performance, as well as a road map for the future. (The manager can partner with his HR manager as needed for guidance writing effective goals, providing reinforcing and constructive feedback, and so on.) For best results, the employee should also complete the EDP form and submit it to the manager; this will aid in discussion during the EDP meeting (see Step 3).

2. **The manager shares the draft EDP with the second-level manager.**

   They meet to review the employee's performance and discuss her priority goals.

3. **The manager and the employee meet to discuss feedback and agree on goals for the upcoming year.**

   They discuss results and accomplishments against goals, and feedback about strengths and improvement areas. Both the manager and the employee clarify and agree on performance and development goals for the upcoming year. The idea is to spend as much time, if not more, discussing future goals as reflecting on past performance.

4. **The manager and the employee sign the EDP and submit it to the HR manager, retaining copies for their own files.**

In many organizations, this process occurs annually. However, as I discuss in Chapter 8, your Gen X and Gen Y staff may crave more frequent feedback. It may be wise to consider implementing semiannual, quarterly, or even monthly (yes, monthly) "checkups" to review performance and goals. Particularly for Gen X and Gen Y workers, doing so will boost engagement and drive discretionary effort.

Rating systems

Some organizations have begun experimenting with five-star rating systems for managers, similar to those used by many universities for students to rate professors. As crazy as this approach sounds, it does make some sense. After all, Generation Y will soon be the dominant generation in the workforce (if they're not already), and they've long been accustomed to rating everything from restaurants to razor blades using online services such as Yelp, TripAdvisor, and Amazon.

Conducting 360 assessments

Earlier, I mention that an EDP should include a summary of the employee's 360-degree assessment. So, what's that?

I'll answer that question by taking a cue from Socrates's playbook and asking another:

What is one key drawback of the traditional one-on-one review?

Easy. The manager serves as the sole judge and jury of an employee's performance. That means the manager is limited to telling each direct report how she measures up to the job *as the manager understands it.* It's taken for granted that the reviewer and the reviewed share the same perception of the employee's job requirements and of what is meant by "good" or "poor" performance; often, however, this is not the case.

A 360-degree assessment solves this problem by combining self-review by the employee with anonymous feedback from those surrounding the individual, including peers, supervisors, direct reports, and even clients. The result? A review that provides a fuller picture of how the person's skills and demeanor are viewed by others. This review often reveals important aspects of performance — think collaboration with colleagues from different departments — that a traditional review would miss. Instead of simply distinguishing between the excellent, the mediocre, and the deficient, the 360-degree assessment captures valuable feedback about an employee's behaviors and traits (remember those?), past performance, developmental needs, and strengths.

360-degree assessments are particularly important for first-line managers. Why? Because in addition to learning how they're assessed by colleagues and superiors, they also find out how they're leading, directly from those who are being led. Enabling junior staff to comment on their managers' performance bolsters the credibility of the review process. Not only that, but it fosters engagement by demonstrating to junior staff that their experiences matter and their opinions are important. This practice can also help reveal to higher leadership whether there is alignment between the company's overall goals and those of an individual department.

Performing a 360-degree assessment

Performing a 360-degree assessment involves asking the following questions:

- ✔ **What are the employee's strengths? In what areas does the employee need to improve?** Be as specific as possible.

- ✔ **How would you rate the employee in the following behaviors, skills, and competencies?** Choices include "Excellent," "Strong to Very Strong," "Good," "Some Skill, Not a Strength," "Minimal," and "Not Observed or N/A."

    • **Customer satisfaction:** The employee performs with (internal or external) client satisfaction in mind as an important goal while not compromising the integrity of the work. The employee identifies client needs and manages the relationship to the benefit of the client.

    • **Technical competence and knowledge:** The employee is competent and keeps abreast of new developments in the field. The employee is respected and sought out as a resource, and enhances other people's professional or technical skills.

    • **Quality:** The employee is committed to quality. He incorporates quality standards into existing operations. The employee ensures that work delivered to clients meets all requirements and standards.

    • **Productivity:** The employee completes the expected volume of work in the time allotted while meeting quality standards. She willingly works on multiple and additional assignments as required and uses time wisely.

    • **Initiative:** The employee is self-motivated and resourceful. He searches for new ideas and demonstrates a sense of urgency about next steps. The employee takes responsibility for technical and behavioral growth by learning new skills, cross-training, taking coursework, and so on. He also explores new ways to apply existing resources.

    • **Communication:** The employee has the necessary written and oral skills to effectively perform her job responsibilities. The employee clearly expresses thoughts, ideas, and concepts. She effectively communicates with subordinates, peers, supervisors, and clients, and listens effectively.

- **Planning and organization:** The employee budgets and uses time effectively. He follows through on work in a timely and cost-effective manner. The employee also effectively schedules people and resources to meet goals, making wise use of other people's time.

- **Dependability:** The employee's work requires minimal follow-up. She follows through on commitments. She completes assignments by the scheduled deadline.

- **Teamwork:** The employee works effectively as team member, applying tact and courtesy in dealing with others. The employee exhibits persuasive skills for team effectiveness and promotes cooperation. He works effectively with other departments, client service centers, and regions, and contributes to strategic initiatives within the framework of his own job and ability.

Note: If the employee is a manager, additional behaviors, skills, and competencies will apply, including leadership, goal setting, mentoring/employee development, motivation, and quality and risk management.

Getting the best results

The 360-degree assessment not only provides a more balanced view of an individual's performance, but also can build trust and strengthen lines of communication between management and staff. As a result, engagement will likely be enhanced as well.

That being said, companies implementing this tool for the first time will likely contend with an apprehensive staff at best, or outright distrust at worst. The fact is, inviting feedback from one's staff can be intimidating all the way around — which is why companies soliciting this feedback must ensure complete anonymity.

If your company already has trust issues, it may be worth outsourcing the 360-degree review process to a third party or at least considering partnering with a third-party technology provider. This often assuages employees' fears about confidentiality.

I also strongly suggest that you filter and composite all feedback before passing it on to the person being reviewed. Otherwise, any nasty comments — even if there's only one — will haunt the poor reviewee for weeks to come, even if said nastiness was buried in praise. Not that the review shouldn't include negative comments — it should. It's just that a supervisor, from an impersonal distance, can put them in their proper context, presenting them as a statistic to be reviewed as a subset of total comments.

The goal is to provide a clear and constructive portrait of any given individual in the organization, not to provide a platform for complaint or derision.

For best results, consider starting with a pilot program. That way, you can gain early acceptance among a select few while also tweaking the process. Then roll the program out companywide — first to managers, and then to your rank-and-file workers. In my experience, after people undergo their first 360-degree review, their fears subside, and communication and trust often improve.

Collecting "more of, same as, less of" feedback

Yet another effective performance assessment tool is what I call "more of, same as, less of" feedback. This tool essentially turns the tables on the typical performance assessment, enabling employees to provide feedback about managers.

To gather this feedback, a facilitator — someone other than the employees' manager — calls together the manager's direct reports. The facilitator then gives the employees the opportunity to discuss what the manager should do more of, what the manager should do less of, and what the manager should keep the same. (Note that a similar approach could be taken not just to gather feedback on a manager, but also on any given program, process, department, or individual.)

If you're the facilitator of a "more of, same as, less of" feedback session, here's what to do:

1. **Start by explaining your role in the session — that of neutral facilitator.**

   You're there to guide the process, and you'll neither contribute feedback on the manager nor comment on the feedback provided except to help guide the discussion. Remind participants that this is a supportive session, not a call to burn the manager in effigy.

2. **Explain that the group is to create three lists — "More Of," "Same As," and "Less Of."**

   These lists will be compiled on three separate flip charts.

3. **Cover the ground rules.**

   There are two:

   - **The group will only document traits by consensus.** If one person suggests an item for the list, but no one else agrees with it, it doesn't get added.

- **What happens in Vegas stays in Vegas.** Nothing that gets said in the session should be repeated outside it (except those items that are ultimately communicated to the manager in question, of course).

4. **Assign duties.**

   Pick three volunteers to serve as scribes (one for each list). Also, select three volunteers to serve as coaches. (More on coaches in Step 8.)

5. **Start with the "Same As" list to help get the discussion flowing.**

   As participants discuss the items for this list, ideas will naturally spill over into the other two lists. Be aware that you may have to help facilitate this process at first, helping participants recognize on which list their idea should be recorded. As ideas are presented and agreed upon by the group, the scribes should record them on the appropriate list.

   Although you may need to jump in here and there, particularly at the beginning of the session, try to take a back seat during the discussion. Intervene only when the group gets hung up on semantics, can't reach a consensus, or needs help expressing a thought.

6. **Move on to the other lists.**

   Take care to ensure that the lists are balanced. You don't want 84 entries in the "Less Of" list but only 11 entries in the "More Of" list.

   Years ago, I facilitated a "more of, same as, less of" meeting for a rather unpopular manager. As we filled out "More Of" and "Less Of" lists, the manager's "Same As" list was glaringly empty. I pleaded with the group to come up with some "Same As" traits. One participant finally remarked, "Well, he is clean . . .." "Seriously?" I said. "That's it?" But from "clean," we were able to populate the "Same As" list with such traits as "organized," "structured," and "orderly."

   Also, make sure that double-edged comments show up on both the "More Of" and "Less Of" lists. For instance, "tendency to micromanage" might show up on the "Less Of" list, while "willingness to let others make decisions" might show up on the "More Of" list. Or "fewer e-mails on weekends" might appear on the "Less Of" list, while "respect for work-life balance" might appear on the "More Of" list.

   Finally, encourage members of the group to express themselves with humor or metaphors. For example, instead of putting "hyperactivity" under "Less Of," you might write "coffee." This will help lessen the sting when the manager sees the list.

7. **As the sharing of ideas winds down, check to make sure no one is withholding comments.**

Often, body language will help you determine this. Look for people subtly catching each other's eyes, smirking, frowning when something is said, nodding in agreement, shaking their heads in disagreement, or simply raising their eyebrows.

8. **When the lists are complete, talk to the coaches you selected back in Step 4.**

   These volunteers will present the information in the lists to the manager. Urge them to provide as much detail about each list item as possible so the manager can fully grasp their meaning. Remind the coaches that they're speaking for the group — in other words, they should use phrases such as "We felt . . .," "We thought . . .," and "The group agreed . . .." Also, remind the non-coaches in the session that they should feel free to pipe up often and lend support.

9. **After checking the group's anxiety levels (and reassuring them if necessary), contact the manager and ask her to join you in the session.**

   This call shouldn't come as a surprise; the manager should already be aware the session is taking place. While the manager is in transit, take down the "More Of" and "Less Of" lists, but leave the "Same As" list on display. Human nature being what it is, if all three lists are exposed, the subject of the review will inevitably focus on the "Less Of" list. The easiest feedback to digest will be the "Same As" feedback, and it serves as a good icebreaker for the feedback to come.

10. **When the manager arrives, restate the ground rules.**

    Encourage her to ask questions during the session to ensure she completely understands the points being made. Reassure the manager that no defense is required. Also, inform the manager that she'll be provided with a copy of each list, so no note taking is required. (Don't forget to follow through on this last bit after the session.)

11. **Ask the coaches to present each list, starting with the "Same As" list, moving on to the "More Of" list, and finishing with the "Less Of" list.**

    To ensure you end on a positive, however, the facilitator should wrap up with some of the more positive comments from the "Same As" list.

    As the facilitator, take a back seat during the discussion. Try to keep silent and let the group do the work.

12. **At the session's conclusion, thank the participants for their candor and remind them that it's their job going forward to support their manager in her efforts to improve.**

    The idea is for them to serve as cheerleaders as time goes on. They're all in this together!

The Secret of Your Succession: Building Succession into Performance Appraisal

We all know we're going to die. We just don't *think* we're going to die. This is the challenge with succession planning. We tend not to spend lots of time thinking about our demise — or, with respect to succession planning, our need to develop someone to take over in the event that we get hit by a bus or, preferably, promoted.

If your firm does a lousy job succession planning, don't worry. You're in great company. It's the rare firm indeed that focuses on this important topic. Why? Here are just a few of the reasons given to me over the years by managers and clients:

- ✔ **"No one else can do what I do."** False. Everyone is replaceable — something I found out early in my career. Back in those days, I believed *I* was irreplaceable. For one thing, I was a known high-potential employee. For another, I was the youngest employee in the company to be granted company stock. In fact, I thought I was so valuable, I had to give four weeks' notice when I decided to move on, and even worked until 7 p.m. on my last day. A month later, I followed up to see if they'd found someone to replace me. As it turned out, they didn't need to. They just shifted my responsibilities around. Talk about humbling!

- ✔ **"If I develop my successor, that person will take my job."** In defense of those managers who are reluctant to develop their successors, their concern has some merit. Since the mid-1980s, corporate America has become a tough place to work, what with the seemingly constant reductions in force (RIFs), reorganizations, mergers, and cost cutting. Heck, we've built whole company cultures around job insecurity! It's no wonder we don't develop successors. The way I see it, job insecurity is the greatest obstacle to successful succession planning. Not surprisingly, organizations who have cultivated the trust of their employees have less of a problem with this. The same goes for firms with a history of promoting from within.

- ✔ **"There is simply no time to develop my successor."** Another truism. Many organizations don't budget the time or the training to make succession planning stick. To ensure successful succession planning, it's not enough to have trust — you also need time.

To aid in succession planning, tie it into your performance appraisal process. It's a natural extension of the EDP. Succession planning also plays a part in engagement. When companies have a strong succession plan in place, particularly if it involves frequently hiring from within, employees naturally feel more confident and engaged.

Identifying successors

The fact of the matter is, retirement en masse of a generation renowned for its workaholism — that is, the Baby Boomers — is only a few years away. Who is going to fill those seats?

Often, managers have a good sense of which employees have what it takes to move up. If so, managers must take steps to ensure the right people get promoted. That means formalizing their choices by putting pen to paper, so to speak. That is, managers should keep a file of who should serve as their successors. Managers should also note who should succeed any employees they oversee.

With respect to the latter, managers should, as part of the performance review process, ask each of their direct reports to identify at least one successor. For example, if the direct report is a project manager, that project manager should identify at least one employee who could take over her job if necessary. Ideally, said project manager could identify employees who are ready now, who will likely be ready in six months, and who could be ready in one year or more. Then, together with her manager, the project manager could set an action plan to ensure those employees get the training and preparation they need to step up. Figure 16-3 contains a template for use in this effort.

Successor	Readiness (Check One)	Action Plan
	□ Ready now □ Ready in 6 months □ Ready in 1 year or more	
	□ Ready now □ Ready in 6 months □ Ready in 1 year or more	
	□ Ready now □ Ready in 6 months □ Ready in 1 year or more	

Figure 16-3: Use this template in succession planning.

Illustration by Wiley, Composition Services Graphics

The great disconnect

Sometimes, we identify someone with great leadership potential — someone who could serve as a successor — without mapping that person's potential against how critical his position is to the success of the company. Or worse, we leave someone with marginal talent in a position that is critical to the business. Figure 16-4 contains a simple matrix to help managers match their employees' leadership potential with the criticalness of their position. Using this matrix, you can determine whether potential leaders (and successors) are in the right job, given their potential.

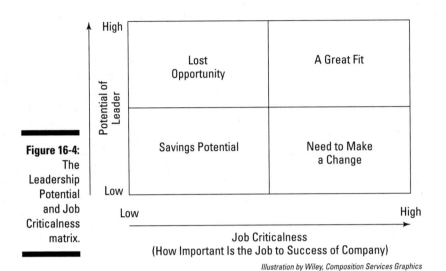

Figure 16-4:
The
Leadership
Potential
and Job
Criticalness
matrix.

Leadership development

A big part of succession planning is leadership development. But what's the best way to do that? Funny you should ask. Early in my career, my employer asked me to lead a project to identify the very best leadership development practice. To my surprise, I discovered that there is no one-size-fits-all best practice. In fact, the only "best practice" I could identify was simply for firms to find the leadership development practice that worked best for them.

Terrific leadership development options include the following:

✓ **Cross-training:** If you want to boost engagement while developing leaders, introduce cross-training as a leadership development staple. No, I don't mean that employees should go for a run one day and a swim the next (not that that's a bad thing); I mean they should be rotated into different jobs and different departments. This will encourage them to develop new skills. The best leaders are those who have training in diverse areas. They're generalists, not specialists. They haven't spent their whole professional lives on a single career ladder. (***Remember:*** Think "career lattice," not "career ladder.")

✓ **Stretch assignments:** The most popular leadership development tool is the stretch assignment — that is, asking an employee to take on more than she has been asked to do previously (or perhaps more than the employee thinks she is capable of doing). Although there is risk (such as the risk of spectacular failure), the upsides of stretch assignments are many. And even if the employee fails, the experience can be enormously beneficial (as long as the employee is permitted to return to her original position — something trusting organizations allow).

✔ **Internal leadership development:** General Electric, known for its extensive in-house leadership training, has proven that you can have a best-in-class corporate university focused on leadership development. Sure, not all firms have the resources of GE, but they can do many things to build their own leadership development programs. Programs can include formal leadership training facilitated by outside consultants or inside experts; high-potential programs, in which high-potential employees take part in solving a company challenge; attendance at a senior management team meeting or offsite; inclusion in a cross-sectional task team with members; and so on.

✔ **External leadership development:** There are numerous outstanding external leadership programs. These range from the one-day Dale Carnegie–type training workshops to three-month-long executive education offerings at elite universities. Offer external leadership development programs to key succession-planning candidates and/or high-potential employees.

According to researchers at Dale Carnegie, leaders indicate two additional elements that best supported their development: strong mentoring within the organization, and access to good networks both inside and outside the organization. Such networks could be informal (such as friends, family, clergy, and colleagues in other industries) or formal (such as networks with associates in professional organizations).

Chapter 17

You Win! Rewards and Recognition

....

....

*I*f you have a child — or, for that matter, a dog — you know that positive reinforcement is key. It's not enough to simply tell said child (or dog) how you want him to behave; you must also recognize his good behavior with a kind word and perhaps even reward him with, say, a treat. (Snausages, anyone?)

The same is true in business. It's not enough to simply communicate your business goals to your staff and measure their progress against them. You must also recognize and perhaps even reward them for achieving those goals.

This chapter discusses both rewards (which usually have a cost associated with them) and recognition (which is typically free or of minimal cost) as essential components of an effective engagement strategy.

The Rewards of Rewarding: Understanding Rewards

What do rewards have to do with engagement? In and of themselves, rewards don't foster engagement, but they do help foster achievement, which drives engagement.

So, what constitutes a reward? Try closing your eyes and thinking of the word *reward*. What comes to mind? If you're like me, you thought of a cartoon bag with dollar signs on it, Scrooge McDuck style. Or maybe you envisioned a "Wanted, Dead or Alive" poster with the word *REWARD* emblazoned across the bottom. Either way, what came to mind was cold, hard cash.

It's no different in business. The vast majority of employers reinforce our perception that rewards are analogous to money, cash, coin, dough, bread, Benjamins, or whatever other term comes to mind when you think of bonuses, raises, and promotions.

What an opportunity lost! Rewards can be about so much more than giving cash. The fact is, you have any number of tools available to you when it comes to rewarding employees, with money being just one. In this section, I fill you in on your options.

Designing a total rewards strategy

Instead of limiting rewards to moolah, I urge you to adopt a total rewards strategy. That means expanding your definition of rewards beyond cash. A total rewards strategy may include the following:

- **Base salary:** Yes, this refers to money. (I didn't say you shouldn't reward employees with cash; I just said you shouldn't reward employees *only* with cash.) Obviously, your employees need to earn a living. Generally speaking, to maintain engagement, you should compensate employees at, slightly above, or slightly below the industry-standard midpoint. If you go too high, you risk your competitive position in the marketplace. Plus, you may tumble farther than others in an economic downturn because base salaries are not variable. If you go too low, however, you face retention and recruitment issues. And although I'm on record saying that money is not an engagement driver with most employees, it can be a *disengagement* driver if employees in your company become aware that those in similar firms earn more than they do. As for employee benefits, offering the industry standard or slightly better is a good idea.

- **Incentive compensation:** Although I'm a proponent of market-rate base salaries, I'm a fan of above–market rate incentive compensation such as bonuses and/or profit sharing. Why? Because offering employees a more significant share of the company's overall gains fosters engagement by reinforcing the company's and employee's mutual commitment. Not only does it say, "When we win, we win together," but it also proves it. In addition, research shows that firms that cautiously manage their fixed payroll costs (that is, base salaries) while allowing for greater frequency and variability in bonuses and profit sharing can better survive a down year and typically require fewer layoffs. (Believe me: Over time, layoffs *will* erode employee engagement, no matter who you are!)

- **Promotions:** Companies with engaged cultures promote from within. Rewarding achievement with stretch assignments and promotions is critical to building a high-performing and engaged workforce. Note, however, that successful companies generally balance internal promotions with external hires, thereby ensuring that the firm brings in new thinking and approaches.

✔ **Training and development:** Sending deserving employees to offsite training programs, executive education programs, conferences, or seminars should be part of your total rewards strategy. Training represents a trust-building reciprocal commitment: How can we, as a company, help you, the employee? And how can you, the employee, help us? Training and development opportunities are one of the surest paths to a mutually satisfying outcome. This is especially true as the Baby Boomers retire and Gen X ascends. Although members of Gen X often suffer from "middle-child syndrome" — they feel caught between two significantly bigger generations (Boomers and Gen Y) — the fact remains that the leaders of tomorrow will emerge from this generation. How your organization deals with their development will surely influence its standing in the decades to come. The bottom line? Up-and-coming stars need mentorship and training, and they must be challenged with stretch assignments that push above and beyond their job descriptions in order to gauge their succession potential.

Employment development should be disproportionately slanted toward those who are deserving of training. It should be viewed as a reward for their being held in high esteem. Avoid the temptation to commit to or advertise offering, say, "40 (or some set number) hours of training for each employee." Although born of good intentions, this approach turns training and development into an entitlement or satisfaction program. Let's face it: Your high potentials and top performers deserve greater company investment to reinforce the mutual commitment of engagement, but not everyone does!

I used to work with an executive who was selected to attend a week-long program at Harvard University's Executive Education and Management Training Program. He often told me it was a highlight of his career. But between you and me, it was mutually beneficial. The year he attended the program, we had failed to meet our plan, so we didn't give out bonuses. However, he was a star employee, and we wanted to reward him with *something* — hence, his selection for the trip to Harvard. Interestingly, although I worked with this executive for a decade, he never once mentioned to me any cash bonuses he received from the company. Funny what people remember!

✔ **Task team or committee involvement:** Many organizations populate task teams or committees by selecting volunteers or on an "it's your turn" basis. Employers with an engaged culture, however, populate these teams with their top performers, creating a sort of golden aura over these groups. The result? Employees view their involvement in these groups as a reward for their performance.

✔ **Time off:** More and more often, employers are offering employees time off in lieu of a paid bonus as a reward for their accomplishments. As work-life balance continues to be a growing theme in the workplace, you'll find that both Generation X and Generation Y often favor time off instead of cash bonuses. This reward is often a win-win: The employee is glad to have a choice, and the company saves cash. Plus, offering time off is a relatively inexpensive reward, because the vast majority of employees feel a certain obligation to make up the work via discretionary effort. (There's that term again!)

✔ **Flextime:** Rewarding top performers with increased flexibility is wise. They've earned the right for the added freedom. Besides, more often than not, they'll respond to this increase in flexibility with higher work output and engagement! Many employers resist offering flextime for fear that they won't be able to offer it to all employees. But flextime is not an entitlement; it's a reward. If an employee has attendance and/or performance issues, then no, that employee has not earned the right to enjoy flextime. In addition, some positions simply don't allow for flextime. For example, the office receptionist has to be in the office during set hours — there's just no room for flexibility there.

Consider issuing benefit and reward statements at the end of each year to remind employees how much the organization invested in them. The statement could reflect salary and bonus numbers, health-insurance premiums, time off, tuition reimbursement, and Social Security contributions. Reminding employees of the various benefits and rewards they've received helps reinforce both your mutual commitment and the employer value proposition (see Chapter 10).

Developing your compensation strategy

You should diversify your approach to rewards, but compensation is still a key part of the equation. Unfortunately, some managers use what I call the "peanut-butter approach" to paying their employees. That is, they simply use "number of employees" as the denominator in their salary or bonus pool and spread everything around evenly, like peanut butter on a piece of bread.

No doubt this practice is born of good intentions: Managers don't want any particular employee to be disappointed or feel slighted. Managers may even think this approach will satisfy all their employees equally, or use the "We're a team!" excuse to justify their distribution strategy. But the sad fact is, this approach is about as effective as a paper parasol in a typhoon. It simply doesn't work. Why? Because employees are not created equal, nor do they achieve equal results. In other words, business is not T-ball — not everyone deserves a trophy.

If your goal is employee engagement — and it is — then rewards, including pay, must be tied to performance and achievement. If you don't reward your high performers more than your average and below-average employees, you do not incentivize your high performers to continue with their high-performing ways or your average and below-average employees to improve.

Over time, this will result in a culture of mediocrity. (Not to pick on unions or public-sector compensation structures, but collective bargaining of pay increases, where everyone gets the same percentage raise, do not create a high-performing culture. Instead, it can erode employee engagement, as high-performing employees perceive that their achievements aren't being recognized.)

To reinforce the importance of high performance, successful firms pay their "stars" — those high-performing people who routinely achieve results, as well as embracing the firm's values — a disproportionately high amount. Indeed, I often tell clients that they should pay their top performers so much that the competition could never afford them. It's money well spent!

Early in my career, merit-increase pools were often in the double digits. (Yep, those were the good old days!) But these days, and for as long as most people can remember, merit budgets have been in the 3 percent to 4 percent neighborhood. This has created a challenge for managers: How do you allot such a pool to adequately reward your top performers and maximize engagement?

I'll tell you how *not* to allot it: by using the peanut-butter approach. Take great care in determining who gets what. For guidance, look to the compensation matrix in Figure 17-1. You can use this matrix to help you divide up a merit pool or even a bonus pool. Although other factors — such as an employee's position in her salary grade, the employee's tenure in the position, market conditions, and so on — may be at play, this tool offers managers a great place to start.

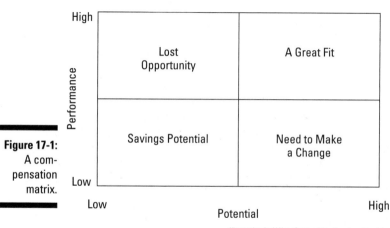

Figure 17-1: A compensation matrix.

Illustration by Wiley, Composition Services Graphics

Looking at Figure 17-1, if X is the average reward, then

✔ *Transition employees* **(the 10 percent to 20 percent of employees who aren't quite making the grade) should receive no merit increase.** Not to be harsh, but they shouldn't be rewarded for failing to perform. If you're inclined to give them something, just remember: Your top performers will, in effect, subsidize it. As any toddler can tell you, that's no fair!

✔ *Investment employees* **(the 10 percent to 20 percent of employees who really matter — who function above and beyond the norm and define the standard for exceptional performance) should earn double the average merit increase or bonus.** They should be rewarded extra for their excellence.

✔ *Performers* **(the 30 percent to 35 percent of employees who are strong and steady workers, but who don't yet display their full potential) deserve your average bonus.**

✔ *Potentials* **(the 30 percent to 35 percent of your talent pool who haven't yet reached their potential because they haven't yet had time to develop) deserve your average bonus.**

If you want to boost the merit increases and/or bonuses of your performers and potentials a bit, give the edge to potentials. They're likely to be new or junior staff for whom the slight boost will be more closely tied to specific, recent achievements.

Turn to Chapter 12 for help identifying transition employees, investment employees, performers, and potentials.

As you assess your employees' performance, decide which metrics carry the most weight. Some metrics will likely be more important than others, and they should be rewarded for accordingly. For instance, suppose you're a software firm, and your competitors have recently passed you in new products launched. In that case, you may decide that in the coming year, special performance metrics will reward new product development. It's also important to build in both quantitative and qualitative metrics (see Chapter 16 for specific examples).

Here are a few other tips that pertain to developing your compensation strategy:

✔ **Communication about rewards must be frequent and transparent.** The distribution of rewards for high performance should not be kept secret. For example, if John is being given a plum assignment to reward him for his high performance, others should be told why John received the assignment. Ditto if Mary is being promoted to head up the chain's largest store. After all, you want people to strive to achieve, and to recognize that those who *do* achieve are rewarded. That said, I'm not a fan of organizations that share specific dollar amounts. That is, if Mary also earns a cash bonus for her efforts, the dollar amount of that bonus should be kept private.

✔ **Consider tenure and staff level.** The more junior a person is, the less his compensation should depend on overall company performance. Instead, it should relate more to achievements within a team or department or business unit. For senior employees — think executives and managers — the link to overall company performance should be much more explicit.

✔ **Correlate compensation and bonuses with the employee's potential to grow and learn.** A satisfied employee doing a decent job who shows no interest in advancement or training should eventually "max out" her salary. In other words, it may not be in the company's best interests to continue investing in that person. In these instances, bonus or variable pay is the more appropriate incentive to maintain that "C" level of engagement.

✔ **Avoid greasing the squeaky wheel.** You know the type. The loud Little League parent who always manages to get his marginally talented kid on the all-star team. The whiny diner in the booth behind you who gets her meal for free. Sadly, these squeaky-wheel types are all too familiar — and are all too common in business. As a manager, avoid giving in to the employee who is always complaining about something, even if giving in feels like the easier thing to do.

Your other employees are watching! The last thing you want is to train your entire staff to be a pain in your behind by consistently rewarding that one squeaky wheel!

✔ **Do not overpay.** I know what you're thinking: "But you just said to overpay your stars." Yes, you're right. In some situations, like when it comes to your superstars, paying above market rate is a good thing. But for the other 90 percent of your employees, you should target your base pay at the market rate (although you can vary pay to some extent to reflect differentiations in performance). On a related note: If you're looking to really annoy (read: disengage) your employees, then go right on ahead and pay a new hire who has the same skills and tenure as your incumbents more than your existing staff. Nothing will irritate employees more than finding out the "new kid" earns more than they do! That type of unfairness will quickly extinguish your employees' engagement.

✔ **Hot markets and sectors should be rewarded with variable pay whenever possible.** I once worked for a large engineering firm that landed a new solid-waste project. We couldn't find enough qualified mechanical engineers with solid-waste experience and had to overpay those we had just to be able to successfully hire the additions to the project.

Fast-forward three years. The project was finished, and we were left with a surplus of talented but overpaid solid-waste engineers. They were so above their peer group elsewhere in the company that we couldn't get other managers in different departments to take on their bloated salaries. Why? It wouldn't be fair to their employees. See, these managers understood disengagement years before the term became common nomenclature. We ultimately had to lay off these high-priced but talented engineers. A better approach would've been to offer the in-demand engineers a "project premium" amount for the duration of the project. This way, their base compensation would've been equitable with other divisional staff when the project ended. They also wouldn't have felt as entitled to this premium, compared to what showed up as part of their base salary. No market stays hot forever.

✔ **Don't confuse rewards and recognition.** Rewards should be reserved for something significant: a promotion, a year-end bonus, the quarterly bonus for new orders, and so on. In contrast, recognition should be reserved to highlight an event, an episode, or something above and beyond. You risk disengaging a deserving employee if you reward year-end performance with a $50 American Express gift certificate, which would be far more suitable to recognize an employee's above-and-beyond efforts in assembling a new committee. Think of it this way: Rewards should be somewhat substantial; recognition should be more symbolic. In other words, with recognition, the point is your acknowledgment of the employee's hard work, not the value (if any) of the award itself.

On a related note, don't confuse recognition with a simple thank-you. They're two different things. A thank-you is to show appreciation for the norm. Recognition should be reserved for when someone goes above and beyond. If you over-recognize the norm, you tend to cheapen the spirit of recognition.

✔ **Be fair (not to be confused with being equal).** Although money is not a primary engagement driver, it can certainly *disengage* staff if they feel they're being rewarded unfairly compared to others in their group (internally to the company or externally to the market).

One more thing: Some people in select industries may be highly motivated by money. Examples include the doorman in your hotel lobby, who enthusiastically helps you with your luggage, and the waitress at your favorite restaurant, who consistently delivers your meal with a smile. For these people, the behavior/reward cycle is almost immediate and, therefore, quite powerful. In my experience, however, these occupations are the exceptions. For the vast majority of people in the vast majority of occupations, a more critical driver is achievement.

To prove this point, I often ask senior executives, working in teams, to construct paper airplanes and then see whose team's can fly the farthest. During these contests, serious-minded, buttoned-down business types often excitedly cheer on their teams' planes. Indeed, shouts and high-fives are not at all uncommon. Afterward, I ask them, "Why were you behaving like that over a paper airplane contest, knowing that you weren't going to be paid any money or receive any prize if you won?" The answers I get — and the corresponding expressions on their faces — indicate that this amusing little team-building game has demonstrated a truth that many bottom line–oriented executives rarely think about: Achievement — not money or prizes — is its own engagement driver.

By the way, as a follow-up hypothetical to the paper-airplane exercise, I often ask these same executives two questions. First, I ask them, "If I gave each of you $5,000 tomorrow, in two or three weeks, would you be working any harder?" Most, if they're being honest with themselves, say no . . . although at least one person per session usually responds jokingly, "Give us the money, and we'll let you know!" Second, I ask them, "If I cut your salary by $5,000 tomorrow, in two or three weeks, would you be less engaged?" In this case, the group can clearly see that there would be erosion in engagement.

Avoiding reward pitfalls

Have you ever heard the phrase "No good deed goes unpunished"? It refers to the fact that beneficial actions often go unappreciated (or may even be met with outright hostility). And if the actions are appreciated, they often just lead to additional requests.

Unfortunately, this maxim holds true for rewards, too. For example, many employees begin to see rewards as *entitlements* — something they expect to receive. This is exacerbated by the peanut-butter approach I mention earlier, because marginal employees expect to be rewarded for their, well, marginal efforts. ***Remember:*** Rewards must be *earned*.

Another common pitfall with rewards is the "it's my turn" response. This often happens with employee-of-the-month or employee-of-the-year awards. With these, people may assume they should be up for the award simply because they've been around for a while. But again, the reward must be earned.

Perhaps the most egregious pitfall is one that often results from long-term incentives and other "handcuffs" designed to entice people to stay on — even if they're long past their "best by" date. Case in point: A few years ago, I ran into a former colleague of mine from 100 years ago, back when I taught public school. "How's it going?" I asked. "Are you still teaching?" He answered, "Well, I can't stand the kids anymore, but I have to hang in there for eight more years so I can collect my pension." I've come to believe that any program in any organization, public or private, that encourages its least-engaged employees to stay is deeply flawed. Yes, it's good to reward longevity, but not in lieu of performance. Rewarding longevity in and of itself can lead to unintended consequences, such as encouraging your least-engaged employees to stay.

Rec Center: Recognizing Employees

A few years back, I visited one of my client's remote offices, a known high-performing site. While there, I noticed a palpable buzz in the air. The reception-ist welcomed me with an amazingly warm smile and everyone I encountered in the halls greeted me in a similar fashion. Navigating the rows of work stations, I noticed that most everyone appeared totally focused on their jobs, but that their focus was occasionally interrupted by laughter and healthy banter. Walking by conference rooms, I saw people standing up, scribbling on flip charts, obviously in the midst of brainstorming sessions. At the end of my visit, which went well beyond the usual 5 p.m. quitting time, I realized that hardly anyone had left — even though this was a typical 9-to-5 office setting.

While having dinner that night with some members of the office's manage-ment team, I mentioned what I'd seen and asked how they'd achieved it. One man explained that a few years back, a junior employee had observed to the office manager that no one in the office ever seemed to go out of their way to recognize anyone's contributions. Sure, the office wasn't performing at its current levels, but there certainly was enough positive activity to merit the occasional compliment! Yet, it wasn't happening. "What if," the junior employee said, "every employee was instructed to set aside a block of time to recognize others?" The employee went on to suggest that all employees be required to create a recurring Microsoft Outlook reminder for just this purpose. They could select any window that fit their schedule, but they had to commit to recognizing someone — a colleague, subordinate, boss, client, vendor, whoever — on a weekly basis. See, this young employee understood that if people get recognized, they tend to recognize others. Suddenly, employees were being recognized more than ever before . . . and the culture was transformed.

This story has reminded me over the years how critically important recog-nition is to culture, performance, and yes, engagement. There is simply no reason not to recognize your employees — although I've heard plenty of excuses. Here are just a few:

✔ "I know it's important, but I don't have time for that stuff."

✔ "I mean to do it, but I forget."

✔ "Their paycheck is their recognition."

✔ "No one recognized me when I was working my way up the ladder!"

✔ "We focus on what's broken around here, not what's working."

✔ "People get embarrassed when you recognize them publicly."

✔ "It'll just turn into a popularity contest."

✔ "If I start recognizing people, I know I'll accidentally leave someone out."

Do any of these sound familiar? Well, contrary to these statements, the vast majority of people want to be recognized. Who doesn't love a good pat on the back every now and again? Indeed, it feeds into our fundamental need as humans to feel appreciated or valued. Receiving recognition even stimulates a physiological response — namely, a little hit of dopamine, which is related to the brain's perception of pleasure (among other things).

Believe me, in all the years I've worked in business, I've never once heard an employee say "People recognize way too much around here!" In fact, in almost every company I've come across, employees are starving for recognition. This explains why most employers score quite low on recognition-related scores when they conduct employee engagement surveys. And the problem is only going to become bigger as more and more Gen Y workers mob the workplace. As mentioned in Chapter 8, experts say that members of Gen Y need — nay, expect — to be recognized eight times per day.

Building a recognition program

I've come to realize that the only way firms can boost recognition is by formally introducing a recognition program — one that is measurable and has meaning. A 2012 survey by the Society for Human Resource Management (SHRM) backs me up. It notes the following:

✔ When asked whether employees were satisfied with the level of recognition they receive for doing a good job, 34 percent of companies with formal recognition programs answered yes, compared to 18 percent of companies without such a program.

✔ When asked whether managers and supervisors effectively acknowledge and appreciate employees, 55 percent of companies with formal recognition programs answered yes, compared to 36 percent of companies without such a program.

✔ When asked whether employees were rewarded according to their job performance, 64 percent of companies with formal recognition programs answered yes, compared to 36 percent of companies without such a program.

When designing your own recognition program, you'll want to consider the following:

- ✔ **Be sure your recognition program is in alignment with your department's and your organization's goals.**

- ✔ **Be clear on your overall objectives.** That will help you determine what behaviors to recognize.

- ✔ **Decide what specific behaviors, events, and episodes you want to recognize.** Again, this will depend on your objectives.

- ✔ **Establish and communicate your recognition guidelines.** Your employees need to know what they need to do to be recognized. Make your guidelines fair and consistent, while launching a fun and exciting communication plan.

- ✔ **Establish a budget.** Remember how I said that engagement isn't free? Well, the same goes for recognition. Sure, some recognition techniques are gratis, but the best recognition programs are those that have been budgeted for. The recognition awards themselves can be nominal in nature (again, this is not a bonus program), but you do need a budget to give the program credibility. (For more on establishing a budget, see the next section.)

- ✔ **Define your recognition "currency."** Will you give cash? Gift cards? Points? Or maybe you'll go with merchandise — for example, mugs, T-shirts, or other goodies featuring your company's logo.

- ✔ **Establish the value of the reward.** What do you see as a typical reward value? If you're not sure, I suggest $100 or less. Anything higher will bump into traditional bonus/reward programs. *Remember:* The recognition is what matters, not the monetary value. You'll get more bang for your buck by recognizing two deserving employees with $50 gift cards than by recognizing one deserving employee with a $100 gift card.

- ✔ **Define and communicate your approval process.** The best programs are simple and non-bureaucratic, allowing for some level of peer-to-peer and team recognition along with the customary manager-to-employee kudos.

- ✔ **Add "recognition" as an agenda item to your weekly department meeting.** This should happen every week, effective immediately. Moreover, it should top the agenda. That way, you ensure that the topic is covered. This will also help to make recognition part of your cultural DNA. Plus, recognizing your top workers is much more likely to get people motivated than the usual moan and drone agenda items!

- ✔ **Measure and communicate your recognition results.** You get the behavior you measure. Successful programs, including recognition programs, measure both usage and the return on investment (ROI).

Setting a recognition budget

As part of your formal program, at the beginning of your fiscal year, establish a recognition budget. Set aside a nominal amount per employee — say, $50 to $100 — for managers to use to recognize their employees. Although your CFO may balk at the idea, this budget should be funded by headquarters rather than at the departmental level. If it's part of a manager's profit-and-loss (P&L) budget, he'll be more reluctant to spend it. Worse, if the department isn't doing well, it may not be able to afford the $50 per employee, even though it would go a long way toward boosting morale. (Believe it or not, token recognition items, such as those suggested in the next section, go a long way toward lifting the spirits of employees in an underperforming business!)

Finally, your program should measure recognition efforts. I have a client who posts year-to-date recognition budget and usage on a departmental level, enabling department managers to see in real-time where they stand in their recognition efforts.

Recognition ideas and best practices

Here are a few ideas and best practices to keep in mind as you build your recognition program:

- **Schedule reminders.** Having your employees schedule time to recognize colleagues is an easy and impactful way to encourage recognition.

- **Have swag on hand.** Invest in inexpensive company logo shirts, backpacks, jackets, and so on. These can be used to recognize employees for their accomplishments. To this day, I still wear a fleece pullover with my old company's logo, which I received as a thank-you for being part of a task team.

- **Keep gift cards handy.** Invest in some $50 American Express gift cards to distribute to employees who go above and beyond. You'll find your employees will appreciate them a lot! *Remember:* These aren't bonus checks — they're simply there to recognize high-performing employees.

- **Establish a formal award.** This might be an annual President's Award, given to the employee who submitted the most innovative idea, drove the best internal initiative, or won the best client. Don't overdo it, though. Although you could introduce countless team, office, store, and individual awards, employees may become cynical if they view them as a "flavor of the month" initiative. Also make sure that whatever award you do introduce will stand the test of time — good times and bad. You don't want to suddenly stop giving out the award! (Have you ever been to a place of business and seen a series of "Employee of the Month" plaques that mysteriously end in, say, March 2003? Haven't there been any good employees since?)

✔ **Catch someone doing something right.** Allow any employee in the company to recognize someone else for doing something right. This may even be something as simple as a cool postcard that one employee sends to another to tack on his or her cubicle wall.

✔ **Distribute handwritten notes from the boss.** In this era of communications technology overload, nothing beats an old-fashioned handwritten note acknowledging someone's accomplishments. Just ask Doug Conant, former CEO of Campbell's Soup. Conant made it a practice to write 10 to 20 notes a day — more than 30,000 in all during his tenure at Campbell's — to employees all over the world to recognize their achievements. As Conant notes in a YouTube video in which he discusses this practice, "It's something that people will treasure!" (To view the video, go to `http://youtu.be/CXiKm4fw9cM`.)

Providing positive feedback

It happens every time: After playing 17 holes of golf, not shanking a single ball, I inevitably step up to the tee for the 18th hole and envision my shot going haywire. I can't help it! And inevitably, I shank the ball 15 feet into the pond. Why does this happen?

Nine out of ten neuroscientists agree: When you paint a negative thought in your mind (or someone else's mind), you (or they) tend to replicate the negative image in reality. The same is true of positive images. Indeed, for years, athletes have known the power of positive thinking, and many top athletes work with specialized coaches to help them focus on the positive.

Well, the same thing happens in business. Bosses who focus on the negative tend to have negative employees and, ultimately, negative results. Bosses who reinforce the positive, however, often see positive results. It's like the old Mary Kay line, "If you think you can, you can!"

It actually works! Ask anyone who worked at Apple during the Steve Jobs era. They'll tell you that Jobs could get employees to do the impossible. How? Because he was so convinced the thing could be done, he was able to convince others. Apple employees called this trait "reality distortion." Essentially, Jobs's positive outlook distorted reality, making the impossible possible.

Building a celebratory culture

Healthy cultures understand the importance of positive thinking to help boost engagement, but they go one step further: They celebrate. What do they celebrate? Anything, really. Maybe a team recently won new business, thanks to their hard work on a proposal. Maybe a new hire has joined the group. Maybe the company exceeded its profit projections. Maybe an employee got a promotion. When you think about it, there are lots of things worth celebrating!

My brother is a well-known children's entertainer. He travels the country giving entertaining and motivating talks at schools, libraries, and civic events. One of his most beloved songs is "Party in the Park," a feel-good ditty, the theme of which is celebrating, partying, and spreading positive energy. I've often joked with my brother that our careers are quite similar. I just try to get organizations to "party in the office." At its core, my "song" is an attempt to convince leaders of the importance of engaging their workforces, including building a culture of celebration.

Where do you start if your company isn't accustomed to recognition, celebration, or focusing on the positive? Here are some tips to get you going:

- ✔ Uncover, link, and communicate your purpose, values, vision, and strategic plan, and build in milestones to celebrate. (For more on purpose, values, vision, and strategic plan, see Chapter 6.)

- ✔ Hire positive people. (See the BEST profile in Chapter 12.) **Remember:** You hire people for their strengths, and try to get them to evolve their weaknesses.

- ✔ Create bonding rituals or events that bring employees together. These might include cookouts, holiday parties, ethnicity food weeks, bowling, ski clubs, softball games, and so on.

- ✔ Base bonuses on both quantitative *and* qualitative rewards, including recognition and celebration.

- ✔ Establish and track a celebration budget. I hate to beat a dead horse, but you do get the behavior you measure, and that includes celebratory events.

- ✔ Accelerate promotions for Gen X and Gen Y staff. Let's face it: They're far more prone to "party in the park!"

- ✔ Communicate positive stuff. Build this into your communication protocol (see Chapter 5).

- ✔ Embrace corporate social responsibility, and get your employees involved.

Chapter 18

Help Me! Helping Struggling Employees

. . . .

In This Chapter

▶ Comparing aptitude- and attitude-based disengagement

▶ Helping underperforming employees

▶ Knowing when it's time to let an employee go

. . . .

*H*ave you ever heard someone say this: "Great news! I just received a job offer from Company ABC! I'm so excited! I can't wait to start work so I can fail miserably!"

Or what about this: "I'm so thrilled! I've finally found the perfect candidate. I can't wait for this person to join our team so he can fall flat on his face and get fired!"

Ridiculous, right? No one accepts a new job or assignment with aspirations of failure. And no manager would ever hire someone she thought would fail. Yet, it happens all the time.

The fact is, sometimes, employees struggle. This struggle typically manifests itself in poor performance. So, what can you do to help a struggling employee get back on track? First, identify the cause of the poor performance.

During the course of my career, I've dealt with employees with all manner of performance problems, ranging from delays in deliverables, to attendance issues, to lack of initiative and beyond. And in the vast majority of these cases, the root cause of the performance issue was — wait for it — a lack of engagement. If someone is not engaged in what he's doing, that person's dis-engagement will manifest itself in his performance. For example, you may see quality issues, a decline in customer service, attitude problems, absenteeism, even a decline in creativity.

After you identify the cause of the poor performance and figure out what's causing an employee to be disengaged, you can take steps to address the problem. For details, read on.

Copping an Attitude: Aptitude- Versus Attitude-Based Disengagement

You realize you have a performance issue with one of your employees. Now what? Effective managers are more like Columbo and less like Donald Trump. That is, they do some detective work to find out what's behind the performance issue instead of issuing a simple "You're fired!" to struggling employees. Too often, managers jump to the conclusion that an employee has to go, without doing the proper due diligence. What do I mean? Read on.

Determining whether the disengagement comes down to aptitude or attitude

There are any number of causes for disengagement. Arguably, these causes can be grouped into two categories: aptitude-related causes and attitude-related causes.

Aptitude-based disengagement: When an employee's skills are lacking

Generally speaking, if an employee is experiencing aptitude-based disengagement, it's because his job competencies don't meet the minimum requirements for the job. Usually, this occurs when an applicant overstates his qualifications and/or the hiring team doesn't effectively qualify a candidate. It can also occur when an employee is promoted sooner than his competencies allow — in other words, when people are promoted "above their pay grade."

Let me give you an example. When I was in high school, the track coach asked me to become the team's high jumper. I assume this was because I was on the boys' basketball team; Coach probably figured that meant I could jump or, as my kids would say, that I "had hops." Well, Coach was wrong — and I knew it. I simply didn't have the skill to compete. But, knowing there was no one else available to compete in that event, I gave it a go.

I tried my hardest. Twice a week, I headed over to the high-jump bar and Fosbury-flopped my heart out. Needless to say, I was not a success. I bent the bar. I got welts on my back. I could barely clear the minimum qualifying height. Soon, I became totally disengaged. I knew I didn't have the aptitude to succeed, and I started finding excuses to miss meets. My disengagement even oozed into my running, where I *did* have some skill. (I was no Usain Bolt, but I showed far more skill in running than in high jumping!) Eventually, I lost interest in being on the track team at all.

The same thing happens in business when we hire or promote someone beyond his competencies. If employees feel they can't "win" when they come to work in the morning, their engagement will eventually erode — even affecting areas where they *do* have some skill. This is something that "Best Place to Work" employers know — and why they almost always outspend their peers in training and development.

Don't let this discourage you from hiring or promoting people into stretch assignments. More often than not, talented people grow into their jobs and should be stretched beyond their current capabilities. There are times, however, when people just don't have the competencies to succeed, regardless of their admirable behaviors and traits.

Symptoms of aptitude-based disengagement include the following:

- ✔ **An increase in quality issues:** If you lack the skills to do a job, this *will* lead to quality issues.

- ✔ **A shift in focus to reactive (rather than proactive) tasks and duties:** An employee lacking skills will be more comfortable responding to ad hoc requests that will take him away from the job at hand.

- ✔ **An increase in task delegation:** Often, disengaged employees claim that others are more competent or better suited to handle a task, so they dump their work on others. They use delegation as their crutch instead of persevering to complete a difficult task.

- ✔ **Delays in deliverables:** If an employee lacking skill is struggling with a task, that person will need additional time to complete the assignment, resulting in delays.

- ✔ **Reluctance to embrace a new assignment:** If an employee is struggling in his job, he probably won't volunteer for or embrace a new assignment. Odds are, he'll feel too embarrassed to take on more.

There's another kind of aptitude-based disengagement: the kind that comes from being *overqualified.* There is a reason many experienced hiring managers avoid hiring people who appear to be overqualified. They've seen too many examples of overqualified employees quickly becoming disengaged in their jobs because their skills weren't being deployed or they were being asked to do things they did ten years ago. This challenge is exacerbated during a recessionary window like the one that occurred from 2008 to 2012, when jobs are scarce and workers become desperate and, therefore, willing to take lower-level jobs.

That said, there are times when you may want to hire or promote someone with more skills than the job requires. These examples include the following:

- ✔ When you're in a growth environment and you need someone with the skills to take you where you're going, not keep you where you are

- ✔ When someone will be playing a key mentoring role and his enhanced skills can be leveraged in a teaching capacity

- ✔ When you're hiring or promoting someone to a completely different discipline, industry, or focus area in which the newness of the surroundings will keep the employee engaged, even if the job itself is less than what he's qualified to do

- ✔ When someone is no longer looking to conquer the highest mountain (Often, people in the later stages of their careers fall into this category.)

Attitude-based disengagement: When an employee's behavior is the issue

Although disengagement and performance problems can certainly stem from a lack of aptitude, the vast majority of performance issues that arise in the workplace have their roots in the employee's attitude, or in a behavior or trait that isn't productive. (Remember the importance of the B and T, or behaviors and traits, from my discussion of the BEST profile in Chapter 12.)

The warning signs for attitude-based disengagement include the following:

- ✔ **Attendance issues:** Attendance issues come in the form of increased sick days, sudden absences, tardiness, and/or early departures. You've probably noticed that new employees always seem to show up on time. It's the rare bird, indeed, who shows up late to a new-hire orientation or calls in sick during the first month of employment. But over time, if employees become disengaged at work, they lose the bounce in their step and no longer jump out of bed with the same vigor. With a disengaged employee, a runny nose becomes a sick day. Employees who go above and beyond (read: engaged employees) tend to come to work early and often!

- ✔ **Lack of energy or excitement about the job:** I always told my kids that they should find a career doing something that engages them. "But how will we know if we're engaged at work?" they asked. My answer? If you look at your watch (or, more likely, your iPhone) and say, "OMG, is it 5 o'clock already! Where did the day go?," chances are, you're engaged. But if you're checking your watch (or iPhone) all the time and counting down the minutes until you can leave, chances are, you're bored in your job. If you're yawning every day at work, you may need more sleep — or you may not be engaged.

✔ **Loss of camaraderie:** This may include the employee distancing herself from company social events.

✔ **Quality issues:** I have two sons — one who loves taking care of the yard and one who doesn't. Unfortunately for the lawn, the one who loves mowing has moved into his own apartment, leaving the lawn duties to his younger brother. The younger brother, who does many other things well, is simply not a lawn guy. He's all about getting the lawn done as quickly as possible. Getting it done right is not a priority. Unlike his older brother — who, for whatever reason, took great delight in tending to the yard — my younger son is not engaged in this task, so he doesn't invest the necessary time to do a high-quality job. This simple example demonstrates what happens in the workplace when someone is engaged . . . and when someone isn't. Disengagement and quality issues go hand and hand; quality issues should serve as an early-warning system to help you gauge the engagement level of your workforce.

✔ **Customer-service issues:** A disengaged employee will lead to unhappy customers. Managers should continually monitor customer service results, complaints, and surveys, and perform informal "eyeball tests" to catch early indicators of employee engagement (or lack thereof).

✔ **Unwillingness to work additional hours or go "above and beyond":** This is the opposite of discretionary effort. Employees who don't show initiative are simply showing up, doing the minimum they're being paid to do.

✔ **Lack of new ideas or approaches:** One sign that an employee is disengaged is that she stops making suggestions. When I lead employee engagement surveys for clients, I carefully review the narrative comments — both the quantity and the quality — looking for new ideas and suggestions. Engaged employees try to make their workplace better. *Remember:* Engaged employees are there to *give* (including ideas); disengaged employees are there to *get*.

Most performance issues stem from attitude rather than aptitude. For this reason, managers must always be on the lookout for changes in an employee's attitude, mood, and/or behavior.

Looking at the reasons for aptitude- and attitude-based disengagement

It's all well and good to determine whether employees with performance problems have an aptitude problem or an attitude problem. But the more critical issue is *why*. To get to the bottom of this, ask yourself these questions:

✔ **Is the employee new to the company or position?** Maybe he simply needs more time to adapt. It's kind of like buyer's remorse — a similar psychology exists with new employees. After the excitement of landing a new job settles in, the new employee is faced with the reality of said job, not to mention the loss of friends and close colleagues at his old job. This is why it's so important for department managers to assign a "buddy" for a new hire to help see that person through his first three to six months.

✔ **Has the pace of change left the employee with outdated skills?** I once worked with a board member who was a big believer in what he called "the Law of Getting Stupider and Stupider." That is, as companies grow, employees need to grow in kind. If they don't, they risk getting stupider and stupider. This is another reason that engaged employers outspend their peers in training and development, and usually offer tuition reimbursement benefits! Remember, though, that engagement is all about building a mutual commitment. In other words, employees have a responsibility to the company to continue to invest in their own skills.

✔ **Are there barriers that prevent the employee from doing her job effectively and efficiently?** If so, is there anything that you, the manager, could do to help remove those barriers? One of my pet peeves is outdated company policies. Although they were originally put in place with good intentions, they often become outdated and ultimately wind up being major obstacles to getting work done efficiently and effectively. Ask yourself, "Are our department policies obstacles to getting things done, or do they serve as useful guidelines as a way to foster new ideas or approaches?"

✔ **Is the employee dealing with personal issues that are affecting his ability to do his job?** Chapter 4 talks about the need for managers to truly get to know their employees — to understand what drives them, to discover their intrinsic motivational drivers, and to show concern about their well-being. If you do this well, you'll be able to tell when there is a sudden change in an employee's personality or when something is troubling him outside of work. The empathetic manager has a far greater chance of engaging employees than the manager who shows little concern for the well-being of her staff. Simply asking your employees "How was your weekend?" (and truly being interested in the response) can reveal quite a bit about how happy or unhappy they may be outside of work.

✔ **Are there chemistry issues with the employee and her co-workers?** Accept one given: Not all your employees will like each other or always play nice in the sandbox. That's okay. What is *not* okay is when the chemistry between two people is explosive. In this situation, you may be able to resolve a performance issue simply by transferring one individual to a different department.

✔ **Do you, the manager, understand the employee's intrinsic motivations?** We all have different motivational drivers. Often, a performance issue is simply a disconnect between how a manager is leading and an employee's motivational drivers. (See Chapter 4 for more on what motivates employees.)

✔ **Is there a disconnect between the employee and the job or company expectations?** It's amazing how many performance issues you can resolve simply by reviewing the job description and/or job expectations. This is yet another reason the traditional, once-a-year performance review process simply doesn't work. By the time the manager and employee finally meet, the gulf between expectations and reality turns what should be a mere communication disconnect into a performance problem.

✔ **Does the employee feel that his skills are not maximized in the job?** Again, if you're regularly meeting with your employees, you'll learn about these frustrations before they grow into a performance problem. Using the "three circles" (see Chapter 4) is a great way to help align a manager and an employee.

Plotting employees using the aptitude/attitude matrix

Need help evaluating the cause of an employee's performance issues? You're in luck. The aptitude/attitude matrix (see Figure 18-1) is designed to do just that. Simply plot your employees in one of the four quadrants (see the descriptions that follow for guidance).

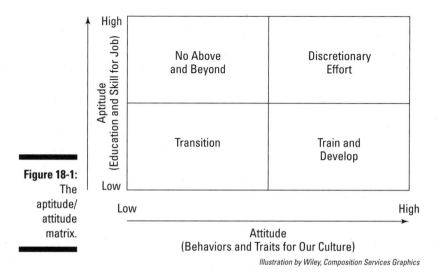

Figure 18-1: The aptitude/attitude matrix.

Illustration by Wiley, Composition Services Graphics

When managers plot their employees in this way, it not only allows for a sensible distribution of bonus dollars or salary increases (see Chapter 17), but also provides managers with a clear picture of who is engaged and who is not. Plus, it introduces an element of transparency in discussions about performance. After all, if an employee is underperforming, shouldn't he be told? If a manager sees a sudden change in an employee's behavior or attitude, shouldn't that manager address it?

The Transition quadrant

The Transition quadrant is for those employees with issues pertaining to both aptitude (the skills to do the job) and attitude (the behaviors necessary to succeed).

Why the name "Transition"? Because both the manager and the employee should understand that this is a temporary state. An employee in this quadrant must move — either to one of the other quadrants or out the door. This label enables managers to frankly assess their resources . . . and to deal with the sometimes-difficult conversation that follows an employee being placed in this box. It allows the manager to ask, "How can we work together to move you out of this box?" Hopefully, up . . . but if not, then out.

Of course, dealing with an employee in the Transition quadrant can be unpleasant. It's no fun telling people they're not making the grade — and it's even less fun to fire them (although that should be a last resort). But tolerating these employees' poor performance has ramifications beyond their own shortcomings — most notably that those employees who *do* perform will become increasingly disengaged due to the perceived unfairness.

As an aside, this helps to explain why, when there is a companywide layoff, assuming these "Transition" employees are the first to go, you'll generally see a spike rather than a dip in overall engagement. The first wave of layoffs often serves to cleanse the ranks of non-performers. Subsequent waves, however, tend to erode engagement, because performers are often caught in the tide.

The No Above and Beyond quadrant

This quadrant is for employees who still perform somewhat, but whose attitude indicates that their heads just aren't in the game. In other words, they're not engaged. Often, managers find that they have several employees who fit in this box.

If you have No Above and Beyond employees on your team, it's time to talk with them to find out why they're disengaged. Maybe they're in the wrong job. Maybe they're dealing with personal issues that are making it hard to stay focused. Perhaps they've reached a point where they've stopped learning and are just going through the motions.

Bad apple: Dealing with an organizational jerk

Every organization has at least one jerk. You know who she is. She doesn't share work or resources. She never helps out. She says nasty things about others. She's a know-it-all. She's arrogant. She doesn't live the company's values, and she never follows company policies or procedures. In other words, she's as toxic as Chernobyl.

So, why does this jerk remain employed? She may be related to the boss, or maybe she has dirt on a higher-up, but odds are, it's simply because she has mad job skills. In fact, she's probably a top producer for your firm.

One of the biggest challenges facing leaders in just about every firm, regardless of industry or nation, is dealing with someone who is a top producer but who rubs everyone the wrong way. On the one hand, leaders don't want to sacrifice the gains made by this employee. But on the other hand, this employee's bad behavior is causing other employees to disengage.

First, recognize that, often, a firm's most talented and brilliant employees will also be the most difficult to swallow. In many instances, they've earned the right to be treated a little bit differently. But there is a line. And when that line is crossed, leadership must take action. Otherwise, leaders risk losing credibility and eroding engagement. Leadership must define its "non-negotiables" — in other words, it must pinpoint and communicate that line. If an organizational

jerk crosses it, then it's up to leadership to show that person the door.

Remember: There was a reason Steve Jobs was fired from Apple his first time around. Even with his brilliance and talent — not to mention the fact that he founded the company — there came a point when Apple's board of directors simply got fed up with Jobs's arrogance and famously difficult personality!

Most organizational jerks can be reeled in with a simple talking-to. Firmly saying that their behavior will no longer be tolerated is the first step. A great tool to help frame this discussion is the what/how matrix, shown below. Essentially, you let the jerk know that you appreciate her performance (that is, the "what"), but that her behavior (the "how") will not be tolerated.

Of course, leaders will worry that such a discussion will prompt said jerk to quit. In fact, they may be so worried about this that they'll avoid having the conversation altogether. But the fact is, organizational jerks rarely quit — and if they

The What / How Matrix

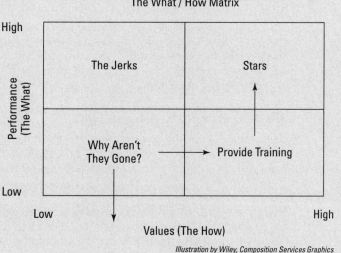

Illustration by Wiley, Composition Services Graphics

(continued)

(continued)

do, you'll usually recover from their lost production by way of a gain in co-workers' engagement levels. The bigger issue is what happens when the organizational jerk *stays*. This is where leadership comes in.

Effective leaders understand that the loss in production is a cost of doing business, but allowing said behaviors to go unchecked risks derailing a healthy culture and polluting the organizational waters. ***Remember:*** Your

employees are watching. Although top performers may have earned the right to a bit of special treatment, having different rules for different people is a major disengagement driver! Perhaps the chief people officer at a *Fortune* "Best Place to Work" company put it best: When asked the secret behind his company's success in always making the top 100 list, he answered, "We simply don't let our rock stars trash the hotel room!"

The real danger with these employees is that they may slip even further, into the Transition category, reducing the likelihood of salvation. To prevent this from happening, managers must identify these employees early.

The Train and Develop quadrant

In the lower-right quadrant are your Train and Develop employees. These employees may be junior, or perhaps they've recently been promoted to a new level of responsibility. They exhibit the behaviors and traits that are right for your culture and are excited to take on "above and beyond" duties but, because they lack tenure, maturity, skill, or knowledge, they aren't yet performing at optimum levels.

These employees are precisely the ones you should be targeting for training and/or mentoring. They're also the employees who need to be challenged with new tasks and asked to shoulder extra work during busy times. Why? Because employees in the Train and Develop quadrant are eager to help, gain much-needed experience, and prevent managers from burning out the organization's top performers — those residing in the Discretionary Effort quadrant (see the next section).

The Discretionary Effort quadrant

The employees in this quadrant are your stars! They're the ones who are competent and who exhibit "above and beyond" effort. They embody the behaviors and traits of your organization, and should be treated — and paid (see Chapter 17) — like rock stars.

Even though these employees are the ones you can least afford to lose, managers often take this group for granted. For example, managers may pile more and more work on employees in this quadrant. After all, they're dependable. Worse, managers may limit their career progression. ("I don't want to nominate Mary for a promotion because I don't want to lose her.")

Throw Me a Line! Helping Underperforming Employees

You know you have an underperforming employee. You have some idea why he's underperforming. So, to quote the infamous Dennis Hopper in what is clearly the best movie about public transportation ever produced, *Speed*, "What do you do? What. Do. You. *Do?*"

Here are several tips for helping an underperforming employee:

- ✔ **Demonstrate that you care about the employee's well-being as an employee *and* as a person.** Showing an underperforming employee that you care about her as an individual will go a long way toward determining whether that employee will improve. If your employees believe you're looking to document their performance issues as part of your plan to get them out of your department, you've lost them . . . *and* failed as a manager. Effective managers want their employees to succeed — and that includes underperforming employees. Learning why an employee is underperforming is key to the turnaround, as is showing the employee that you care about her well-being. If there is a turnaround, it's a win-win. If, by some chance, you determine that a turnaround isn't possible — because of a disconnect between the job and the skill set needed or between the individual and the firm's culture — then you should *still* show you care about the employee's well-being. That means trying to find a position in the company that will be a better fit.

- ✔ **Establish SMART goals and objectives for the employee, including several short-term goals.** The sooner you meet with an underperforming employee to determine the reason(s) for the underperformance, the sooner you can outline a game plan to minimize further slippage and get the employee back on course. Part of your plan should be to increase your face time with the underperforming employee and map out a series of SMART goals, including several easy-to-accomplish milestones, to give him some positive momentum upon which to build.

- ✔ **Provide resources for the employee to achieve said SMART goals and objectives.** It's not enough to just set goals for the struggling employee. You have to give that person the necessary resources to achieve the goals you set. These resources may include technology, products, and/or human resources. Does the employee have the proper tools to do her job? Is there a respected peer who can mentor or shadow the employee for a defined period of time?

- ✔ **Keep communication open and ongoing — in both directions.** This is so important. Indeed, in Chapter 5, I describe communication as the cornerstone of engagement. Unfortunately, many managers *reduce* communication with underperforming employees. It's human nature: We all tend to avoid conflict and unpleasant situations. But your underperforming employees need *more* communication, not less. Convincing underperforming employees that you have an open-door policy, and that they should come to you for additional guidance, is a must. Schedule a series of one-on-one meetings over the next three months in which you'll review the employee's SMART goals, as well as coach and assist him.

✔ **Ask the employee if she's happy with the company and her job.** Try taking the underperforming employee to lunch and asking, in a non-threatening way, if she's happy. Does she feel like she's a fit with the company? How does she view her level of performance? It's amazing how forthright employees become when they're asked how they're doing in a non-threatening manner.

✔ **Identify resources or go-to people.** The best onboarding programs provide new recruits with a list of resources, including key go-to people, to assist them as they navigate their new surroundings. Consider borrowing a play from this onboarding strategy for struggling employees. Give them a list of key people to seek out for assistance.

✔ **Identify and address training needs.** If you determine that an employee's underperformance is due to aptitude, focus your performance plan on development, via either mentoring or specific training.

✔ **Identify the employee's strengths and interests and build on them.** Everyone has strengths . . . even underperforming employees! Reiterating the employee's strengths to him should be part of your action plan. This not only bolsters the employee's self-esteem but also provides him with positive momentum on which to build.

✔ **Provide counsel (career and personal) to help the employee navigate through transition with dignity and self-esteem.** I once received a case of fine wine as a thank-you gift from a former employee I helped counsel out of the company. Why? Well, he claimed I treated him with respect, put his needs on par with those of the firm, and helped steer him in a new direction. What I did was actually quite simple: I treated him as if he were my mom and was underperforming. Yup, you heard me right. Next time you're dealing with a performance issue, think about how differently you would treat the person if she were your mom. Don't laugh . . . it works!

You're Fired! A Word on Firing

In spite of assertions to the contrary by Donald Trump, effective managers rarely fire their employees. Usually, it's only bad bosses, or bosses who make poor hiring decisions, who routinely give employees the ax. Good bosses — bosses who are engaged — have an ongoing performance-related dialogue with their employees, giving their staff the chance to improve long before their performance becomes cause for firing.

Firing an employee should *always* be a last resort. Engaged managers are eager to meet with employees at the earliest signs of trouble and to pursue an altruistic (rather than punishing) path to resolve the performance issue. In other words, these managers live by the age-old adage, "Treat people the way you would want to be treated." Treating underperforming employees with empathy is simply the right thing to do.

It's also the smart thing to do. Tri-branding links together your employment brand with your product or service brand, as well as third parties, including employees (see Chapter 10). If you fire an underperforming employee without giving him the chance to improve, you'll make that person very unhappy indeed. And with the proliferation of social media — including sites like Glassdoor (www.glassdoor.com), where people dish on their current and former employers — that fired employee will have many platforms on which to express his discontent. If that person is a "connector," then his negative message about your company may well be received by a wide audience, which may diminish your brand. Just as a restaurateur must contend with diners who broadcast their unpleasant experiences on sites like Yelp, employers must deal with employees who might damage their brands online.

That said, every now and then, there are legitimate reasons for terminating an employee. These include the following:

- ✔ Possession of drugs or alcohol at work
- ✔ Falsifying company records
- ✔ Falsifying one's academic or work history
- ✔ Insubordination
- ✔ Gross misconduct
- ✔ Stealing
- ✔ Damaging company property

Depending on the situation, you may even have to terminate an employee on the spot. Even then, try to maintain the employee's dignity and self-esteem. Walking the employee out the front door accompanied by security is *so* yesterday. Over time, such practices will do more harm than good to you as a manager and to your firm as an engaged employer. ***Remember:*** Other employees are watching how you treat their colleagues!

Part V
The Part of Tens

For ten tips for boosting engagement through recognition, head to www.dummies.com/extras/employeeengagementengagement.

In this part...

- ✔ Engage new hires to increase productivity and engagement.

- ✔ Find more books to learn more about employee engagement.

- ✔ Locate additional online resources to boost your understanding of employee engagement.

- ✔ Discover how engaged employees boost your bottom line.

Chapter 19

Ten Ways to Engage New Hires

In This Chapter

▶ Engaging new employees from the minute you say, "You're hired!"

▶ Keeping new hires engaged in the first days, weeks, and months

*Y*ou've been waiting since, like, forever to get this position filled. Finally — the newbie starts next week. Awesome! But will it be awesome for him? In other words, have you thoughtfully planned out how you'll engage this new hire? Normal emotions for a new employee include being anxious, feeling nervous, and suffering from a lack of confidence. (That'll happen to anyone who feels like he has to ask 10,000 questions in a single day!) Here are ten practical, low-cost ways to engage new employees and put their minds at ease. *Remember:* You don't have to be all old school about it — c'mon, have some fun!

Start Before the First Day

You can bet your new employee will be planning out her first day. This will include *everything* — the clothes she wears (Is it clean? Is it ironed?), the route she takes to work, where she parks, and so on. Likewise, as a manager, you should be making some plans of your own — plans that go beyond simply meeting this new employee at the door on her first day.

Specifically, call the new employee two days before she starts in her new role. Ask her if she has any questions about her first day, such as what time she should arrive and where she should go when she enters the building. You should also outline the expectations for the new hire's first few days, whatever they may be for your organization.

A lot of new-hire nerves occur because the incoming employee doesn't yet have all the facts. The more you can prepare her for that first day, the more at ease she'll be — and the more engaged you'll appear as a manager.

Make the New Hire Feel Welcome on Day One

Have you ever committed to a time-share presentation in exchange for a free dinner or complimentary theme park tickets? If you weren't able to escape before the salesperson handcuffed you to the table until you "invested" in a time-share unit, you may have experienced a few staples of time-share sales-manship, including how spectacular the model unit looks. I once attended a presentation where a women who I swear was Aunt Bee from the old *Andy Griffith Show,* was baking and handing out homemade chocolate-chip cookies. The décor, the cookies, the smell, and the niceness of Aunt Bee almost got the best of me. If my wife hadn't dragged me away, I may have got myself a time-share week (or two!).

So, what's the takeaway for new hires? Before they arrive on day one, make sure their workstations are "decorated" in a way that's inviting. Business cards have been ordered, the computer is set up, supplies are filled, and so on. Put flowers on the person's desk or work area, along with a welcome gift certificate. Change the screensaver on the person's computer screen to a message like, "Welcome, Mary Smith!" You can even put a welcome message for the new hire on the cafeteria menu board.

Load 'Em Up with Swag

Have you ever walked the aisles of a trade show, stuffing your conference bag with swag — cheap pens, balls, bobble-head dolls, yo-yos, and so on — all sporting some company's logo?

The fact is, everybody loves swag, including new hires. Giving all new hires a pullover with the company logo, a coffee cup, a baseball cap, a computer backpack, or what have you isn't prohibitively expensive. This symbolic gesture not only serves as a great engagement driver, but also helps in your company's branding — or, more specifically, it's tri-branding — efforts. (For more on tri-branding, turn to Chapter 10.)

If you can, be creative! Present the swag as a "Welcome New Hire Kit" or as "New Employee Survival Gear." You don't have to be Martha Stewart — just try to do something more than tossing a T-shirt (which may or may not fit) on the new hire's desk.

Give the New Hire a Welcome Tour

Odds are, your new hire has put plenty of pressure on herself to adapt quickly to her new job environment. To help ease this pressure, plan a "Welcome Aboard" tour.

The key word here? "Plan." Don't play this by ear, corralling some random, unsuspecting employee to give the tour. Instead, work with team members to ensure that the tour is given by someone who is capable of showing the new employee around and answering any questions that arise, and who will enjoy doing so.

You don't have to roll out the red carpet. But do be thoughtful, mindful, and prepared. A tour guide will help the new employee feel welcome, respected, and more at ease.

Stop Making Snoozer Introductions

The first few days at a new job usually involve a major brain dump. They're informative but probably not much fun.

How can you share important information with newbies about the company and other employees in a *fun* way? Easy . . . if you're dealing with a group of new employees. Simply gather them together, hand out index cards, and ask each new hire to write down one "amazing" thing about himself that others would find interesting. Then collect the cards, read them aloud, and have your new employees guess which person achieved which amazing thing. For example, you might ask, "Can you guess which one of you rides a Harley? Was born in Peru? Had an article published in a well-known national newspaper? Has gone sky-diving?"

This activity is a great and stress-free way to help forge friendships among your new hires!

Recognize That Cliques Exist — Even in the Business World

Although we would like to think we left cliques behind in high school, the sad truth is, we haven't.

Once, on my first day at a new job, I was invited to join the team for lunch. But on day two, the "team" walked right by me on their way to the cafeteria. Maybe they were waiting for me to join them . . . but of course, I was waiting for them to ask. It became obvious to me that they had been assigned to take me to lunch that first day, and now that they'd completed that assignment, they felt free to go about their merry way — without me! Soon, I managed to break into the group, but I'll always remember the feeling of isolation I experienced on that second day.

There will always be cliques at the workplace, but you don't want new employees to feel like they won't ever fit in. New workers don't have to be BFFs with their co-workers by the end of their first week, but they do need to be made to feel welcome.

To lower a new hire's angst about being the new kid, be sure to invite him to lunch . . . after his first day. If members of your department eat at a company cafeteria — or just tend to gather at a certain lunchtime spot — make sure the newbie is invited. Don't allow new hires to feel excluded, especially at the beginning of their tenure, when they're already ill at ease. Be aware and be proactive to help them join in some social circles. ***Remember:*** You were on the outside once, too.

Introduce New Hires to the C Levels

If at all possible, include a member of the C-suite (ideally, the president or CEO if the company is small enough) or the head of the business unit in the orientation process. This person could serve as part of the "Welcome Committee" and/or provide an overview of the company's culture.

Of course, this is more efficiently done if you're dealing with a group of new hires. If you're hiring only a single person, try to schedule a time that he can meet with a member of the leadership team. This can be as simple as a brief introduction in which the executive is informed of the new hire's presence and role and given the opportunity to shake hands.

The point is to create a culture in which the leadership is viewed as approachable. You don't want newbies to feel like they can't even say good morning to top executives on the elevator! New hires will feel more at ease if they're introduced to leaders, even if only briefly. After all, we all put our pants on one leg at a time.

Take the Mystery Out of It (and Stay More Productive Yourself)

New employees have a lot of questions — and that's a good thing. Their curiosity shows that they're engaged. Even if you have a new hire training program, realize that they're drinking from a fire hose. Some things simply won't sink in until the new hire is faced with a situation in which the information becomes relevant.

To help employees through those confusing early weeks of their employment, provide them with a list of people to contact when they have questions. For example:

- ✔ When you have a legal question about contracts, contact Claire. If she's out, try Jerry.

- ✔ When you need budget approval over $100, ask Allan. If it's under $100, don't ask. It's our policy.

- ✔ If you have a question about your benefits, call Brendan in HR. If he's out, ask for Ed.

- ✔ If you need to order software, contact Bruce in IT. For hardware questions, you'll need to contact Lynn.

Make their lives easier by including the names, titles, and extensions of these key individuals. Don't forget to tell new hires that if they have any questions about any processes, ask a team member, or feel free to ask you!

Have New Hires Meet with Key People in the First Month

Enter the time machine and think back to your elementary school years. Remember the excitement you felt when a new student entered your class? It always seemed like everyone wanted to be the new student's best friend (validating, yet again, the fact that humans are an extremely social breed). The same thing happens in the workplace. Smart organizations leverage this by immediately connecting their new recruits with key members of the firm, often on day one of orientation.

During the onboarding process, provide a list of key individuals to each new hire and suggest that they connect during the first 30 days. To ensure these meetings go beyond a simple "I'm Marissa Smith from Operations, and I just started, so I wanted to drop by and say hi," consider creating a one-page meeting questionnaire and checklist. This may include questions such as the following:

✔ What is your job at the company?

✔ How many years have you worked here?

✔ What is one thing that you've learned that will really help me be successful?

✔ How can I help you?

This is a great way to demonstrate your mutual commitment with the employee. In other words, it's not just the company helping the employee navigate orientation, but also getting the employee to actively "orient."

Another great idea — one that a client of mine adopted — is to have all new hires, during their first year on the job, include a tagline on their e-mail signatures that says, "Newly hired on _____." This tagline becomes a conversation piece and encourages others to reach out to the new hire. It also buys the new hire a bit of forgiveness if he struggles during his early days on the job.

Set Goals for New Hires

New employees can easily feel totally overwhelmed in their first few weeks, or even months, in a new job. There's so much to learn, and they want to achieve and perform their best. Even seasoned professionals with 20+ years of experience can feel like this when they switch jobs and change companies!

To help them, provide goals for a new hire's first week, her second week, and then for her 30-, 60-, and 90-day marks. This will help her to prioritize and focus, and will calm her anxiety. ("There is so much to learn! Where do I begin?") New hires don't want to feel needy, and they're anxious to achieve. Help them become more independent and confident.

Of course, this will require some cooperation with your HR department or among departments. But if your new employee was part of a group of new hires on day one, schedule some time on day 30 and day 60 for that group to share their reflections on being a new hire. You never know . . . you may even learn something!

Chapter 20

Ten (Or So) Additional Employee Engagement Resources

*R*eally? After all that, you want *more?* A little greedy, don't you think? Well, greedy or not, you've come to the right place. In this chapter, you find ten (or so) additional resources, including books, videos, reports, and websites, presented in no particular order, to help you understand engagement and drive it in your organization. You'll probably recognize several of the titles and authors, but a few may be unfamiliar to you. That doesn't mean they're any less important, just less famous.

Drive: The Surprising Truth About What Motivates Us, by Daniel H. Pink

In this work, Ryan Gosling plays a Hollywood stunt driver for movies by day and moonlights as a wheelman for criminals by night. Er, wait . . . that's the description for *Drive*, the movie. In the book *Drive* (Riverhead Books), author Daniel H. Pink asserts that the secret to high performance and satisfaction is people's ability to direct their own lives, to learn and create new things, and to do better by themselves and their world. Pink breaks down the belief that the best way to motivate people is through rewards (think: "carrot and stick"). Through extensive scientific research, Pink establishes that there are, in fact, three elements of motivation: autonomy, mastery, and purpose. Strapped for time or just sick of reading? Watch Pink's "Drive" YouTube video, spectacularly animated by RSA Animate, at `http://youtu.be/u6XAPnuFjJc`.

Investing in People: Financial Impact of Human Resource Initiatives, by Wayne Cascio and John Boudreau

Hmm . . . a book about risk, return, and economies of scale. You may be wondering, "Do I really want to read this?" If you're in human resources and you're passionate about employee engagement, the answer is an emphatic "Yes!" More than ever before, HR practitioners must empirically demonstrate a clear link between their practices and firm performance. In, *Investing in People: Financial Impact of Human Resource Initiatives* (FT Press), Wayne Cascio and John Boudreau show exactly how to choose, implement, and use metrics to improve decision making, optimize organizational effectiveness, and maximize the value of HR investments. Cascio and Boudreau reveal powerful techniques for looking inside the HR "black box," implementing human capital metrics that track the effectiveness of talent policies and practices, demonstrating the logical connections to financial and line-of-business goals. Using their powerful LAMP methodology (short for Logic, Analytics, Measures, and Process), the authors demonstrate how to measure and analyze the value of every area of HR that affects strategic value. Also included are powerful ways to integrate HR with enterprise strategy and budgeting and for gaining commitment from business leaders outside HR.

Gallup's State of the American Workplace Report

Gallup is a recognized leader in surveys and workplace engagement, and this report, which you can download free from www.gallup.com/strategic consulting/163007/state-american-workplace.aspx, shows why. It reveals the results of a study of U.S. workplaces between 2010 and 2012 (itself a continuation of a study from 2008 to 2010). Gallup's CEO, Jim Clifton, opens the report with a bold statement that sets the tone for the entire document: "The single biggest decision you make in your job — bigger than all the rest — is who you name manager." The report goes on to reveal the engagement level of American workers and how the people who manage these workers, more than any other factor, affect their level of engagement. It shows how "managers from hell" disengage their employees, costing American businesses at least $450 billion (yes, that's *billion,* with a *b*) each year. How much of that total is coming from your company's bottom line?

The Employee Engagement Group

Shameless plug: At www.employeeengagement.com, The Employee Engagement Group, a company headed up by yours truly, provides extensive free (yes, *free*) resources on the topic. You'll find articles, white papers, case studies, research, and videos from an extensive list of experts like Gallup, Towers Watson, and the *Harvard Business Review*. No membership is required!

1501 Ways to Reward Employees, by Bob Nelson

I thought Bob Nelson was an overachiever way back in 1994, when he came up with 1,001 ways to reward employees (and published them in a book of the same name). Since then, he has somehow found an additional 500 ways to nurture talent and retain employees.

A key component of engagement is recognizing and rewarding employees who exhibit the "right" behaviors, but it's often difficult to come up with innovative ways to do so — especially on a budget. *1501 Ways to Reward Employees* (Workman Publishing Company) is not just a list of reward ideas, however. It's much, much more. In this book, Nelson educates the reader on the fundamentals that make providing rewards and recognition effective. He explains the difference between rewards and recognition, why money is not enough (does that sound familiar?), and the benefits of appropriate rewards. Additionally, he outlines recognition strategies, and emphasizes the importance of recognition in attracting and retaining top talent. A well-used copy of *1501 Ways to Reward Employees* should be on the desk of anyone who manages people!

How to Win Friends & Influence People, by Dale Carnegie

An oldie and a goodie, Dale Carnegie's *How to Win Friends and Influence People* (Simon & Schuster) has long been a staple in the people-skills genre. First published in 1937, it has since sold more than 15 million copies. Based on an understanding of human nature that will never become outdated, Carnegie hit the nail on the head with his insights into how people work together. Carnegie believed that success is 15 percent professional knowledge and 85 percent "the ability to express ideas, to assume leadership, and to arouse enthusiasm among people." An early pioneer in engagement, Carnegie asserted that you can make someone want to do what you want them to by seeing the situation from his or her point of view and "arousing in the other person an eager want." Employee engagement is not about things, it's about people, and although this book is not marketed as an engagement book per se, the concepts in the book reflect the keys to an engaged culture.

Shackleton's Way: Leadership Lessons from the Great Antarctic Explorer, by Margot Morrell and Stephanie Capparell

Ernest Shackleton was the first engaged leader. Instead of using coercive leadership techniques, which at the time and in his industry (exploration) were common, Shackleton pioneered ways to lead people, resulting in mutual commitment and high performance through an increase in discretionary effort. If you haven't read Shackleton's story, don't walk but run to the nearest bookstore and pick up *Shackleton's Way: Leadership Lessons from the Great Antarctic Explorer,* by Margot Morrell and Stephanie Capparell (Penguin Books). I also recommend *Endurance: Shackleton's Incredible Voyage,* by Alfred Lansing (Basic Books), and the A&E movie *Shackleton,* starring Kenneth Branagh.

As a quick overview, Shackleton and his 27 men became stranded in Antarctica for almost two years. Under his leadership, all 27 men survived extraordinarily harsh conditions and often insurmountable challenges. *Shackleton's Way* takes the leadership skills of Ernest Shackleton and describes them through anecdotes and actions that can be practiced on the job immediately. It addresses many of the key factors covered in *this* book: the importance of hiring the right people; getting the best from each individual by relying on strengths and challenging weaknesses; crisis management (stranded on a chunk of ice qualifies as a crisis); developing teams and sub-teams for the really tough jobs; overcoming insurmountable obstacles; and much more. It's a definite must read for anyone looking for an extraordinary tale and practical guidance to becoming a leader who is able to create an engaged culture.

Who's Sinking Your Boat, by The Employee Engagement Group

This video, found on YouTube at http://youtu.be/y4nwoZ02AJM, illustrates the key concepts of employee engagement, exploring the topic in a light and entertaining fashion, using the analogy of a crew team rowing in a race.

Three team members are rowing like crazy, five are giving some effort, and two are actively trying to sink the boat. The statistics, culled in 2013, tell a story all their own. The message is clear: Engagement is essential for success . . . so why don't more companies do something about it? This video can serve as part of a presentation, an introduction to engagement for managers and employees, and/or a promotional video to kick off a new engagement initiative.

The University of Windsor Employee Engagement & Development Website

There's a Trivial Pursuit question that goes something like this: "If you wanted to get to Canada from Detroit, what direction would you travel?" Most people would naturally answer, "North." (Isn't all of Canada north of the United States?) But in fact, you travel *east* from Detroit, crossing the Detroit River into Windsor, the southernmost city in Ontario. Why am I telling you this? Because it seemed like a great way to introduce Windsor, home to the University of Windsor, which is itself home to one of the best internal employee websites to engage employees, with a focus on employee development, wellness, communication, and recognition — all keys to an engaged workforce. Developed and hosted by the Department of Human Resources, the site, found at www.uwindsor.ca/engagementanddevelopment, is easy to access, provides quick links to all resources, and offers an extensive collection of training and development opportunities. If you want a model on which to base your own internal engagement site, this one is a good place to start. (If not, at least you'll no longer live with the mistaken belief that you would drive north out of Detroit to visit Canada. You're welcome.)

Love 'Em or Lose 'Em: Getting Good People to Stay, by Beverly Kaye and Sharon Jordan-Evans

With replacement costs high and startup time critical, employee retention is more important than ever. That means hiring the right person the *first* time, even if it takes a little longer, and then retaining that person for as long as possible. *Love 'Em or Lose 'Em* (Berrett-Koehler Publishers) provides 26 strategies to keep talented employees productive and fully engaged. Citing research and experience with dozens of organizations, the authors present many examples of how today's companies have applied their retention strategies and increased their retention rates. The chapters are arranged alphabetically, from "Ask" to "Zenith." Each chapter includes a series of to-do lists, company examples, and an "alas" story drawn from the authors' personal experiences. The latest edition features new tips and to-do lists, stories, and additional research from the media and from the authors' own extensive knowledge.

Business Gamification For Dummies by Kris Duggan and Kate Shoup

For an in-depth look at gamification (introduced in Chapter 11), check out *Business Gamification For Dummies,* by Kris Duggan and Kate Shoup (Wiley). It goes beyond the discussion of using gamification to boost employee engagement to cover the use of gamification to entice and retain customers. With gamification, you pinpoint your business objectives and identify what behaviors will help you meet those objectives. Then you use game mechanics, combined with knowledge of what motivates your users (be they employees or customers), to drive those behaviors. *Business Gamification For Dummies* shows you the ins and outs of building your own gamification program to do just that.

Chapter 21

Ten Ways Engaged Employees Help Your Bottom Line

In This Chapter

▶ Recognizing the many advantages of engaged employees

▶ Backing up those advantages with numbers

Some people believe that employee engagement is just a soft science, all about "making employees happy" and other touchy-feely stuff like that. But the fact is, employee engagement has a real impact on an organization's bottom line. In fact, employee engagement can be so effective, even the numberiest of numbers people can appreciate its importance! This chapter outlines ten key effects of an engaged workforce on a company's profitability.

It's All About the Effort, Baby!

Someone once said, "Hard work is the yeast that raises the dough." (Get it? Dough, like money?) Hard work is also synonymous with "above and beyond" effort or *discretionary effort* — a term you may see in this book one or two (or 800) times.

When you engage your employees, you capture their heads *and* their hearts. As a result, they put forth a tad more effort than they would otherwise, and most likely, a tad more effort than your competitors' employees. The aggregate effect of all your employees giving a tad more effort, or of their discretionary effort, is exponential.

When you capture the discretionary effort of your employees, you win. If you don't, you risk losing. It's that simple. I've devoted my career to helping managers engage their workforce because I've seen it work!

Voluntary Turnover Is Expensive

There's no doubt about it: Turnover is expensive. Indeed, according to some studies, the true cost of replacing a departing employee — factoring in recruiting costs, training and development, loss of production, and so on — is, on average, 100 percent of that person's salary — or more, depending on the person's role in the company.

Worse, voluntary turnover often leads to something I call the "Pied Piper effect." You see this at parties all the time: Toward the end of the evening, a few people will stand up and say, "Well, it's getting late . . . we'd better get going." What usually happens? Everyone else starts asking for their coats. This happens at work, too. When someone quits, it often prompts others to consider alternative employment options. I've seen it time and time again.

Not surprisingly, however, voluntary turnover among engaged employees is significantly less than among employees who have "checked out," so to speak. Indeed, a 2013 *Gallup Business Journal* article asserts that firms with a highly engaged workforce enjoy 65 percent less voluntary turnover than firms with a disengaged staff! Obviously, given the cost of replacing an employee, this has a favorable effect on your bottom line.

I'm Really Not That Sick!

The aforementioned Gallup report included another interesting tidbit: Employers with a disengaged staff see a whopping 37 percent greater absenteeism than their engaged counterparts. This reinforces observations from my own personal experience: Engaged employees come to work, while disengaged ones are quick to stay home. (Not surprisingly, that same Gallup survey reported that employers with an engaged workforce enjoy 22 percent higher profitability than companies with a disengaged staff. Coincidence? I think not.)

The Bottom Line Is the Bottom Line

Have you ever worked with someone who did something wasteful — maybe he tossed a whole ream of printer paper in the recycling bin after spilling soda on the top few sheets, or poured half a pot of coffee into the drain to brew a fresh batch — only to defend himself by saying, "They have plenty of money around here!" or "Have you seen the cars those guys in the C-suite drive?"

An engaged employee would never do this. Engaged employees treat the company's resources as if they have a personal stake in the company. They're invested — with their heads and with their hearts — in the business, and they don't waste resources. They walk around like they own the place . . . but in a good way.

Of course, to prevent wasteful behavior, leaders must demonstrate that they're walking the walk themselves. Obviously, that means they must not be wasteful. In addition, they must prove their mutual commitment to their employees. If a company's leaders eat in their own dining room, park in an executive parking lot away from the "peons," or enjoy other "us versus them"–style perks, then odds are they won't find their employees eager to protect each paper clip!

A Happy Customer Is a Returning Customer

By now, hopefully you get the cycle: Engaged employees lead to satisfied customers, which leads to business success. As the iconic Harvard Business School instructor Ben Shapiro, who has written countless case studies on customer satisfaction, says, "You take care of your employees first and foremost, then they will take care of your customers, and then you can just put the cup under the dispenser and watch the nickels fall in."

Don't believe me (or Ben)? Try flying on Southwest Airlines, shopping at an Apple or Nordstrom store, or staying at the Four Seasons. You'll see firsthand the connection between employee engagement and customer satisfaction! And not surprisingly, these are all examples of companies with healthy bottom lines.

Innovate or Perish

Polaroid. Wang. Blockbuster. Eastern Airlines. American Motors. What do these organizations have in common? These companies were once dominant in their industries. They were great places to work. They built their cultures on employee satisfaction, offering their employees lots of "stuff." These cultures, however, did not place a strong enough emphasis on sustainable innovation. As a result, when faced with a changing market, these organizations, and countless others, lost their competitive advantage — and in most cases, filed for Chapter 11 protection or shut down altogether.

Employers who seek to engage their employees invite diversity of thought by being inclusive, seeking input from junior staff — rather than simply from those employees who are responsible for the status quo — to help create the future. For their part, engaged employees are curious, are committed, and give above and beyond.

Engaged employees also suggest new ideas and process improvements. Indeed, when I lead employee engagement surveys for clients, employers who score well overall also tend to receive responses from employees who are rich in ideas for process improvements and other suggestions. Commentary from employees of low-scoring organizations inevitably include critiques and complaints.

Could an engaged workforce have saved Polaroid, Wang, Blockbuster, Eastern Airlines, and American Motors? I can't say for sure. But it would've given them a fighting chance!

Hey, Want to Work for My Company?

When you eat a great meal at a new restaurant, or stay at a charming bed-and-breakfast, or fall in love with your new car, what do you tend to do? Simple: You tell people!

For years, marketing and branding experts have identified the importance of word of mouth in advertisement. If someone you know recommends a restaurant, hotel, or product, odds are you'll be more likely to try it than you would a competitor's. The same is true with employers. If someone you know recommends her employer, the next time you're in the hunt for a new job (assuming you're in the same industry), you'll be more likely to apply there.

Engaged employees are more apt to recommend their employers than employees who are disengaged. If your employees are engaged, this can save you big money in recruiting costs. More important, studies show that recruits who are referred to you by existing employees are more likely to be engaged, have longer tenure, and be high-performing employees themselves! That's a win-win-win.

"I'll Volunteer"

Engaged employees are quick to volunteer to help out, even when not asked. They're the first to jump onboard companywide task teams and committees. They're even willing to help out another group for the good of the company.

Because engaged employees are so willing to go above and beyond, they see bridges between departments and business units where their disengaged counterparts see walls.

You won't hear an engaged employee respond, "Not my department!" when someone seeks his aid. And when employees help each other, everybody wins!

Doing Well by Doing Good

As I mention in Chapter 6, research indicates that firms that clearly articulate their purpose outperform their peer group by a factor of six. Six! Moreover, purpose-driven employers create cultures of employees with a deep purpose. However, you don't get purpose-oriented employees solely by capturing their heads. Purpose-driven organizations capture both the heads *and* the hearts of their employees. Therefore, these employees are more emotionally committed to their employer. Purpose-driven employers also see spikes in the number of employees participating in corporate social responsibility efforts, volunteerism, giving-back initiatives, and so on — all of which ultimately show positive business results.

Can You Expand Your Margins?

For my left-brain readers, here are the facts, Jack: In a 2012 study of 32,000 employees at 50 companies across 30 countries conducted by Towers Watson, companies with low engagement scores had an average operating margin of just under 10 percent. Those with average engagement scores fared slightly better, with average operating margins of 14 percent. But those with the highest engagement scores had an average one-year operating margin of — wait for it — 27 percent. Boom!

Index

About the Author

Bob Kelleher is an award-winning author, thought leader, keynote speaker, and consultant. He travels the globe sharing his insights on employee engagement, leadership, and workforce trends. Bob is the author of Amazon's top-selling employee engagement book for 2011, *Louder Than Words: 10 Practical Employee Engagement Steps That Drive Results* (BLKB Publishing), and the critically acclaimed 2012 book *Creativeship: A Novel for Evolving Leaders* (BLKB Publishing).

Bob is the founder of The Employee Engagement Group, a global consulting firm that works with leadership teams to implement best-in-class leadership and employee engagement programs, workshops, and surveys. He has recently introduced the world's first virtual, cloud-based employee engagement resource center, the Engage On-Demand Resource Library. Bob's website, www.employeeengagement.com, is one of the world's most visited employee engagement websites, and is a terrific source for articles, best practices, tools, and resources on the topic.

Bob can be seen or heard on national media (most recently on CNBC, CBS Radio, and NBC News, as well as in *Bloomberg Businessweek, Forbes, Fortune, Training,* and Yahoo!), and is a frequent guest writer and contributing editor for many national publications.

Bob has spoken with audiences around the world, has presented to the leadership teams of many of the world's top companies, and is a frequent conference presenter, including at those hosted by Aberdeen, the Conference Board, the Human Capital Institute, Linkage, Melcrum, and the Society for Human Resource Management (SHRM).

Before becoming a speaker, author, and entrepreneur, Bob spearheaded award-winning employee engagement programs and initiatives during his years as chief human resources officer, executive vice president of organizational development, and chief operating officer working for firms ranging in size from 800 employees to 47,000 employees.

Bob holds a BS in education and an MBA. He lives in the Boston area with his wife, Candy, and their three children, Marissa, Brendan, and Connor.

Dedication

To my past: Mom and Dad, as you watch down from heaven, just know that you did good. Real good. I miss you every day.

To my present: My wife, Candy, you are my soul mate, best buddy, inspiration, and the greatest mom to our kids I could have ever hoped for. I so love you! And Ed, you continue to be such a precious bridge, linking our past to the grandkids' future.

To my future: Marissa (and new mate, Drew), Brendan, and Connor, you guys continue to make Mom and me proud of who you are, what you've become, and where you're going! I love you guys!

Author's Acknowledgments

Special thanks start with you, Stacy Kennedy, first, for finding me and helping to convince me to take on this project, and second, for your graceful style and demeanor in handling the business side of partnering with Wiley. Additional thanks go to editor Elizabeth Kuball, whose diligence in keeping the project on track was at times demanding but often necessary. Without your ongoing attention to our timeline, we might have been stressed to meet our various milestones. Most important among the Wiley team, thank you, Kate Shoup. Partnering with you enhanced the project. Your calming demeanor, hilarious e-mails, and brilliant writing made this project so much more enjoyable.

I would be remiss in not thanking all whose research helped add credibility to this book. Dale Carnegie, Gallup, SilkRoad, and others, you are great at what you do, bringing the science to support my practical experiences, tools, and intuition regarding all things engagement. You collectively have made a terrific business case that employee engagement drives business results.

Technical editor Kevin Sensenig, thank you for agreeing to take on this project and providing such great technical oversight. This book is richer because of your involvement.

Dr. Wayne Cascio, thank you for agreeing to pen the foreword to this book. There is no one out there whose work I admire more. Not only are you brilliant, but you are an amazing man.

Work colleagues Steph Mello, John Konselman, and Allan Benowitz, thanks for your ongoing support making our firm a success and your tolerance of my schedule. You guys are the best.

Marissa, Brendan, and Connor, thanks for being the world's best kids, and for implicitly contributing to this book by allowing me to observe how your generation communicates, works, and thinks. Firms *must* figure out how to engage your generation if they're going to win in the future, and your willingness to allow me to peek into your thinking will help the readers of this book.

Lastly, thank you, Candy, the world's greatest wife and mom, for pushing me to take on this project even though you knew it would cost me many weekends.

Publisher's Acknowledgments

Acquisitions Editor: Stacy Kennedy

Project Editor: Elizabeth Kuball

Copy Editor: Elizabeth Kuball

Technical Editor: Kevin J. Sensenig, PhD

Project Coordinator: Patrick Redmond

Special Help: Kate Shoup

Cover Image: © iStockphoto.com/kristian sekulic